Method and Theory in American Archaeology

Method and Theory

BY GORDON R. WILLEY

AND PHILIP PHILLIPS

in American Archaeology

THE UNIVERSITY OF CHICAGO PRESS

CHICAGO & LONDON

Standard Book Number: 226-89888-1

Library of Congress Catalog Card Number: 57-11215

THE UNIVERSITY OF CHICAGO PRESS, CHICAGO 60637
The University of Chicago Press, Ltd., London

To JAMES ALFRED FORD

Preface

In the summer of 1952, as a result of numerous discussions, we decided to set down our thoughts on certain methodological and theoretical questions in American archaeology. The original plan was an article in two parts: the first, a statement of what we believed to be the minimal aims of archaeology and the basic operations directed toward the achievement of these aims, and the second, some theoretical formulations about New World prehistory. The first part was subsequently published under the title "Method and Theory in American Archaeology: An Operational Basis for Culture-Historical Integration."[1] The second part followed a year and a half later as "Method and Theory in American Archaeology II: Historical-Developmental Interpretation."[2] The comments and criticism which these papers drew from colleagues and students have kept us interested in the subject, and, as a result, we have rewritten both original papers and combined them, along with an introduction, originally published as a brief journal article,[3] in the present volume.

A good many of the revisions and additions we have made to the original papers are the result of second thoughts, which we trust are better than the first ones. Others, by no means the least substantial, are the direct result of critical comments and suggestions on the part of colleagues in archaeology and anthropology. To list them all would provide a roster of impressive proportions. We would, however, like to single out Albert C. Spaulding and Irving Rouse for the time, interest, and advice they have expended in our behalf.

1. Phillips and Willey, 1953.
2. Willey and Phillips, 1955.
3. Phillips, 1955.

Finally, a word about the restrictive connotation of the qualifying term "American" as used in our title and throughout the book. Obviously, the methods, theories, and ideas in general which are propounded and discussed in this work are not limited to the Americas any more than archaeology is so limited. Many, or most, of them have originated in the Old World with Americanists as late borrowers. We have used the qualification inasmuch as our own experience is in the American field and all the examples and subject matter are so confined. There is another reason for using the term. In no other large part of the world does archaeology stand so completely on its own feet as in the New World. The historic continuities and documentation binding past to present are infinitely weaker here than in the European, Middle Eastern, and Asiatic areas where archaeology has been carried forward. American archaeology complements, but is in no sense an adjunct of, history; hence its methodology stands in somewhat sharper relief than the methodology in many parts of the Old World. This is not a denial of the vital importance of historical and ethnological data in interpreting the American past, but such considerations lie outside the scope of this book.

GORDON R. WILLEY
PHILIP PHILLIPS

Contents

ix

Introduction

American Archaeology and General Anthropological Theory

It has been said that archaeology, while providing data and generalizations in such fields as history and general anthropology, lacks a systematic body of concepts and premises constituting *archaeological theory*. According to this view, the archaeologist must borrow his theoretical underpinning from the field of study his work happens to serve, or do without. Whether the latter alternative be an admissible one does not seem to be an arguable point. Acceptable field work can perhaps be done in a theoretical vacuum, but integration and interpretation without theory are inconceivable.

The above remarks apply to archaeology in general, but the sole concern of this study is American archaeology. It seems to us that American archaeology stands in a particularly close and, so far as theory is concerned, dependent relationship to anthropology. Its service to history in the narrower sense, i.e., as the record of events in the past with the interest centered on those events, is extremely limited, because for pre-Columbian America there is in effect no such history. The use of traditions derived from native informants and other documentary sources of the contact period as starting points for pushing back into the unrecorded past—the "direct historical approach"—is not archaeology serving history, but the reverse. As a technique of investigation, American archaeology, like archaeology generally, provides useful data for geology, paleontology, climatology, etc., and it recovers valuable material for art museums and the study of aesthetics, but it is not involved theoretically with any of these subjects. To paraphrase Maitland's famous dictum: American archaeology is anthropology or it is nothing. The American archaeologist, unless he thinks he can dispense with theory altogether, is therefore obliged to take a stand on some of the basic questions of general anthropological theory. This we shall do briefly in the following pages.

The methods outlined in this study, and our arguments in their behalf, are predicated on two general theoretical assumptions: (1) that anthropology is more science than history, and (2) that the subject matter of anthropology is both society and culture. The first part of this statement appears to settle out of hand the position of anthropology in respect to the dichotomy science-history, a question that has vexed philosophers ever since the emergence of anthropology as a field of study. It seems to us that the force of this antithesis is largely spent. There is now considerable agreement among theorists that the world of anthropology is a mixture of recurrent and unique events acting and reacting upon each other in a tremendously complex fashion. The only serious disagreements are in respect to the role and importance of the two components of the mixture. Our view is that the part played by recurrent events, though it may be the smaller, is the more significant; and that this is just as true for an archaeology devoted to the service of anthropology as it is for anthropology itself. Archaeology, in the service of anthropology, concerns itself necessarily with the nature and position of unique events in space and time but has for its ultimate purpose the discovery of regularities that are in a sense spaceless and timeless.[1] And, since it appears that a comparative method will be most likely to disclose such regularities, it follows that the archaeologist is faced with the responsibility of finding, in the seemingly endless flow of cultural and social events, forms and

1. This we hope will not be taken to mean that the events referred to take place outside space and time. In this and all subsequent references to space and time in this study, it is of course geographical space and chronological time that are denoted.

systems of forms that are not only comparable to each other but also comparable to, or at least compatible with, the forms and systems of forms of cultural or social anthropology.[2] We shall return to this point later.

The second article of belief referred to above is that the subject matter of anthropology is both society and culture, another polarity that is not standing up under analysis. The interpenetration of social and cultural facts now seems to be taken as axiomatic. Following Kroeber and others, we have chosen to regard them here as *aspects* of the same basic reality. Definition of this basic reality is fortunately outside the scope of the present inquiry. It is sufficient for our purposes to characterize it loosely as patterned human behavior. Archaeology, of necessity, deals very largely with patterned human behavior in its cultural aspect. In American archaeology especially, we have tended to suppress the social aspect altogether. Some Americanists have been drawn into the extreme position that sees in culture an independent order of phenomena, intelligible in terms of itself alone—the "cultural superorganic." Most of us, without subscribing to the superorganic view of culture, have nevertheless operated "as if" it were a fact. In our opinion even this moderate position, though operationally expedient and to a certain extent inevitable, is ultimately detrimental to the main task of archaeology, which is to organize its data in terms of a real world, a world in which cultural and social phenomena (to name only these) are inextricably mingled.

The reader will have noted by this time that we are driving toward an accommodation between the seemingly opposed methods and outlook of archaeology and cultural anthropology. Compari-

2. "Social anthropology" in England, "cultural anthropology" in the United States—these are not precise equivalents but are closer, it seems to us, than practitioners in the two countries appear to believe. From the detached point of view of the archaeologist, at any rate, they are practically synonymous terms. In this study we follow the American usage but without any convictions regarding the predominance of the cultural over the social aspect of our subject matter.

son may be facilitated by considering the operations of the two disciplines on three levels of organization that are generally applicable to all scientific analysis: *observation, description,* and *explanation.* The accompanying diagram is a crude attempt to show how the operations of archaeology and cultural anthropology can be considered as converging toward a synthesis from one level to the next.

Explanation	Processual interpretation	Ethnology
Description	Culture-historical integration	Ethnography
Observation	Field work	Field work
	ARCHAEOLOGY	CULTURAL ANTHROPOLOGY

On the observational level, archaeological and cultural anthropological field work are placed far apart on the diagram because of wide differences in the phenomena observed. These differences, however, can be too easily overemphasized. Cultural anthropology observes group behavior and the products of group behavior in their twofold aspects, social and cultural. Its primary concern is with the social aspect, but certain categories of behavior, notably those which are symbolized in language, art, myth, etc., may be studied very largely in their cultural aspect. Archaeology observes primarily the materialized products of group behavior but has considerable opportunity to observe symbolized behavior in the forms of art, iconography, and (rarely) written language, and occasionally touches social behavior through inferences, as in the interpretation of burial practices, house plans, settlement patterns, roads, irrigation systems, and the like. Thus it appears that the raw materials of the two disciplines are not so different after all; what is different is that archaeology is obliged to view its material almost entirely in the cultural aspect. It has sometimes attempted to turn this limitation into an asset by embracing the cultural superorganic, as already noted.

The term "culture-historical integration," as used here, covers almost everything the archaeologist does in the way of organizing his primary data: typology, taxonomy, formulation of archaeological "units," investigation of their relationships in the contexts of function and natural environment, and determination of their internal dimensions and external relationships in space and time. However high-sounding these terms, it appears that the activities represented by them remain essentially on the descriptive level. Explanatory concepts, such as acculturation, diffusion, and stimulus diffusion, are utilized, but the aim is primarily to describe what happened to specific cultural units at specific times and places; no attempt is made (on this level) to draw generalizations from these observations and descriptions. Culture-historical integration is thus comparable to ethnography with the time dimension added, but we dare not push this analogy too far, because the archaeologist's descriptive formulations, like his observations, lie mainly in the cultural aspect of his subject matter. Later in this book we make a plea for unit concepts that are intelligible in the social aspect as well, but we are under no illusion that any except the very smallest of them can be precisely equated with correspondent units of social structure. Nevertheless, we have placed culture-historical integration and ethnography closer together on the diagram than their respective field operations, in the belief that archaeological unit concepts can and should make more sense in terms of the social aspect than is generally supposed.

So little work has been done in American archaeology on the explanatory level that it is difficult to find a name for it. It might have been left blank on the diagram to emphasize this lack. The term "functional interpretation," which has gained a certain amount of currency in American studies, was used in the original version of this diagram but is not entirely satisfactory, since it implies that the functional is the only explanatory principle involved. We have substituted here the broader "processual interpretation," which might conceivably cover any explanatory principle that might be invoked. In the context of archaeology, processual interpretation is the study of the nature of what is vaguely referred to as the culture-historical process. Practically speaking, it implies an attempt to discover regularities in the relationships given by the methods of culture-historical integration. Whatever we choose to call it, the important consideration is that, on this explanatory level of organization where we are no longer asking merely what but also how and even why, our formulations must be viewed in both their cultural and their social aspects.[3] It is not possible to go about investigating culture-historical processes and causality without reference to the efficient causes of cultural change, which are people or groups of people, and therefore lie in the social aspect of reality. Perhaps it is fair to say that there has been a lack of progress in processual interpretation in American archaeology to date precisely because unit formulations have been put together with so little reference to their social aspect. In the same vein of optimism already displayed, we have put processual interpretation and ethnology (which includes among its many meanings the operations of cultural anthropology on the explanatory level) side by side on the diagram to suggest a further convergence of aims, if not of practice. At this point, the archaeologist is in effect a cultural anthropologist,[4] but it is well to remember that his activities on this level are conditioned by his formulations on the descriptive level and that

3. To name only two of the important factors in a complex equation. Geographical and ecological factors, already present on the descriptive level, carry over with increased importance onto the explanatory level. These have been deliberately ignored in our diagram, which is focused on the special relationships between the cultural and social aspects of anthropology. The same neglect of physiological and psychological factors should be noted.

4. This point has been very well put by Walter Taylor, who also rationalizes the operations of archaeology on a series of levels that differ in detail from ours but can be reconciled with them, as in the following passage: "When the archaeologist collects his data [observational level], constructs his cultural contexts [descriptive level] and on the basis of these contexts proceeds to make a comparative study of the nature and workings of culture in its formal, functional, and/or developmental aspects [explanatory level], then he is 'doing' cultural anthropology and can be considered an anthropologist who works in archaeological materials" (1948, p. 43).

these in turn have special characteristics which it is our purpose to describe.

Diagrams and models have the happy faculty of proving whatever they are designed to prove, and ours is no exception. Nevertheless, we think that this model, in spite of the crude simplification inherent in any system of "levels," represents a pattern that is not wholly fictitious. As archaeology, in the service of anthropology, moves from one operational level to the next, it is compelled to pay more attention to the social aspect of its subject matter, until there takes place on the explanatory level an actual convergence with cultural anthropology and the possibility of an eventual synthesis in a common search for sociocultural causality and law.

Part I

An Operational Basis for Culture-Historical Integration

Chapter 1

Archaeological Unit Concepts

"Culture-historical integration" is the term we have chosen to designate what we regard as the primary task of archaeology on the descriptive level of organization. The procedural objectives of culture-historical integration have tended to be divided, in theoretical writings on American archaeology, between the reconstruction of spatial-temporal relationships, on the one hand, and what may be called contextual relationships, on the other.[1] Operationally, neither is attainable without the other. The reconstruction of meaningful human history needs both structure and content.

Cultural forms may be plotted to demonstrate geographical continuity and contemporaneity, but, when we move to establish historical relationships between them, we immediately invoke processes like diffusion, trade, conquest, or migration and in so doing shift the problem from the bare frame of space and time into the realm of context and function. Conversely, the processes named have no historical applicability without control of the spatial and temporal media in which they operate. Taylor was undoubtedly correct in stating that American archaeologists have placed heavy

1. Taylor, in the work already cited (1948), puts these procedures on two distinct levels of interpretation, which he calls "chronicle" and "historiography." See also Willey's (1953a) use of the terms "historical" and "processual." The latter term was used by Willey in reference to the description of the way in which specific cultures function in specific times and places, not as we are using it in the present study in reference to the attempt to draw generalizations from culture-historical data. All four terms, "chronicle," "historiography," "historical," and "processual," in the writings cited, refer to operations on the descriptive level of organization as defined in the present study.

emphasis on the skeletal chronicle at the expense of the recovery of what he calls "cultural context," but a review of the recent literature indicates a strong trend in the contrary direction. We submit that this is now an area of agreement for American archaeology: *culture-historical integration is both the spatial and temporal scales and the content and relationships which they measure.* The essence of this study's departure, if it may be called a departure, is that these objectives are not regarded as being on different and unequally significant levels of interpretation or as even being capable of effective separation operationally. It seems to us that the apprehension and formulation of archaeological unit concepts involve the simultaneous investigation of contextual and spatial-temporal relationships.

A method basic to archaeology on the descriptive level is taxonomy. Under this general heading, the archaeologist deals with two sorts of concepts: types, and cultures or, as we prefer to say, archaeological units.[2] The former usually pertain to artifacts or other products of technology but may be used in connection with other categories of cultural behavior such as burial types. Some archaeologists also apply the type concept to full archaeological assemblages, or units as we would call them, using the designation "culture type." While this usage has the apparent virtue of economy through elimination of the conceptual difference between type and unit, we prefer to keep them distinct, because we think that unit concepts have certain characteristics not shared by artifact types and that these in turn have important methodological bearings. Our interest here is centered on unit concepts, but a few re-

2. There is a good deal to be said for and against the prevailing use of "culture" to denote every conceivable kind of archaeological unit. It is very convenient in many cases where we do not really know what kind of unit we are dealing with, but it is conducive to sloppy thinking. We shall be trying here to confine its use to units of a certain magnitude, maximum units in fact, but are not enthusiastic about the cumbersome "archaeological unit" as an alternative. When the context is clearly archaeological, perhaps the term "unit" will suffice.

marks on the concept of type as applied to artifacts will serve to get us into the subject.[3]

There is, happily, a general working agreement among American archaeologists about what constitutes an artifact type, though there is still some dispute about what it signifies in terms of the basic reality that we have postulated as the subject matter of archaeology. The principal difference of opinion may be crudely stated as opposition between those who believe that types are arbitrarily "designed" by the classifier and those who think that types exist in nature and that the classifier "discovers" them. According to the first view, types are simply analytical tools that are to be judged solely on the basis of their usefulness; the second maintains that they have, or should have, behavioral reality in the sense that they would be recognized as norms, the "right way," in the societies that produced the objects being typed. Our attitude is that these opposing views are not completely antagonistic. We maintain that all types are likely to possess some degree of correspondence to this kind of reality and that increase of such correspondence must be the constant aim of typology.[4] The actual procedure of segregating types is therefore a more complex operation than is suggested simply by such words as "design" or "discovery," and is in effect a painstaking combination of both.

No less laborious than artifact typology are the procedures involved in the formation of archaeological units, in which we have to consider not only the relationship of forms as such but their spatial and temporal relationships as well. Disregarding the latter for the moment, we may begin our consideration of the nature of

3. Another valid objection to the use of "culture type" as a synonym for "archaeological unit" is that we need such a generalizing term when we want to talk about a type of culture without reference to any specific time or place. A "theocratic irrigation state" (Steward *et al.*, 1955, p. 65), for example, is a culture type that may in theory occur wherever the necessary cultural and natural preconditions are present.

4. Cf. Phillips, Ford, and Griffin, 1951, pp. 63–64, for a discussion of the problem of the "empirical" versus the "cultural" type as applied to ceramics. Those inclined to take sides on this question are advised to see Evans, 1954; Ford, 1954*a*, 1954*b*, 1954*c*; and Spaulding, 1953*a*, 1953*b*, 1954*a*, 1954*b*.

unit concepts by examining their strictly formal characteristics. We are seeking a broad definition that will cover all sorts of units, from those whose content may consist of a very small number of highly specialized forms to units represented by the fullest compendium of cultural data that can be recovered by the most refined techniques of investigation and the most imaginative interpretation. It is plain, therefore, that the size or comprehensiveness of the assemblage is no criterion. What is required rather is that the constituent forms be *physiognomic*, *recurrent*, and *internally consistent*. To borrow a phrase from V. Gordon Childe, they must relate to one another in a way that permits us to assume them to be "the concrete expressions of the common social traditions that bind together a people."[5]

So much for the formal content of an archaeological unit of whatever magnitude. Now the particular interests of archaeology also require that this content be placed in the contexts of geographical space and time. It is often maintained that this is something the archaeologist does after the unit has been defined. However sensible in theory this may appear, in practice it does not work that way. The working procedure, as every archaeologist knows, is initial formulation, investigation of spatial and temporal dimensions, reformulation, reinvestigation of spatial and temporal dimensions, and so on indefinitely. The operation is immensely complicated by the fact that the fixing of these *internal* dimensions is, more often than not, dependent on *external* relationships. We have only to recall certain essential conditions of our unit's existence. In the same place, but before or after it in time, were similar units whose contents intergrade with its content in so-called transitional periods that are almost impossible to establish with precision; beside it in space were other contemporaneous units with similar intergrading at frontiers equally difficult to draw. Yet we maintain that the fixing of these spatial and temporal boundaries, however difficult, is an essential part of the definition of the unit. Small wonder that the unavoidably arbitrary nature of such operations

5. Childe, 1950, p. 2.

has led many archaeologists to believe that an archaeological unit is nothing more than a fragment excised from a spatial-temporal continuum, a fragment that could not be said to have existed as a unit before it was named and defined.

The same problem confronts us here that we have already discussed in connection with artifact typology. An archaeological unit, as described above, may appear to be a rational construct in terms of the observed facts of cultural continuity and cultural relationships, but what are the chances that it corresponds in any real sense to an intelligible unit of culture-history? In our original paper we took the position that such correspondences may eventually be possible but that "the archaeologist is on firmer footing at present with the conception of an archaeological culture as an arbitrarily defined segment of the total continuum." In a long and exceedingly astringent letter to the authors, Albert C. Spaulding attacked this position with such force that we have obtained his permission to quote a portion of it here.

It is true that any assemblage represents a segment of a continuous stream of cultural tradition extending back into time, but once you grant the purpose of a scientific exposition of culture history, the process of classifying the time stream with respect to its cultural characteristics is anything but arbitrary. It should be classified in terms of events which are themselves associated with a cluster of other new events so as to yield a succession of distinct culture types. A possible exception to this generalization would be a segment of a continuum in which culture change did not occur, or in which change occurred at a uniform rate so that it could be represented as a straight line on a graph. In the hypothetical case of no change, classificatory subdivision would serve no useful purpose that I can think of and would be arbitrary; in the case of a slanting straight line, subdivision would in a sense also be arbitrary, since a complete description would require no more than a statement of the point of origin, slope, and point of termination (if any) of the line. In fact, the two cases are basically the same case. However, widely accepted cultural theory indicates that the normal pattern is one of relative stability, then rapid growth through the introduction of a critical new element followed very quickly by a number of other new elements, then a period of relative stability, and so on. Plotted on a time against culture change graph, this results in an ogival growth curve, and the recognition of the sharp curves is a scientific obligation of the archaeologist. The segments so recognized are certainly not the result of arbitrary classification; the changes in slope of the line are just as characteristic of it as is its continuous nature. So time itself is continuous and proceeds at an unvarying rate, but culture change in relation to time probably never proceeds at an unvarying rate, and useful archaeological classifications of chronology are those which have sharp rate changes as their limiting points. A good chronological classification yields a number of periods, each of which is characterized by a distinctive "culture" ("culture type" in my terminology), and the proper job is to pinpoint the critical element so that the time of its invention can be made to serve as the starting point of the new period.

To consider a second implication of "space-time-cultural" continuum, space itself is a continuum, but culture is not uniformly distributed in that continuum. To get off a lofty crusher first, there are no archaeological sites in the middle of the Atlantic Ocean, either on the surface or on the bottom. On a more sensible plane, archaeological materials characteristically occur in discrete clusters [we call them "sites"] in space, and the task of describing them includes discovery of their boundaries—there isn't any arbitrary slicing up of a uniform continuum involved in the problem. To turn now to what I think you actually have in mind, it is quite conceivable that the cultural characteristics of components might vary uniformly or continuously (i.e. in infinitely small steps, or at a uniform slope, so that the spatial position against cultural content graph, time controlled, shows a curve or straight line instead of a noticeably jagged line), but I am uncertain as to how important this is in fact. I think that ethnographic evidence strongly indicates that if any considerable number of components over any substantial area were considered, a classification of culture type with respect to space would reveal fairly neat clustering, not simple polarity or radiation. Certainly you would concede this if sharp ecological boundaries were involved. Discovery of clustering at the multicomponent level would eliminate the claims of arbitrariness effectively. In summary, then, your vague and sweeping talk about arbitrary slicing up of a continuum results in the confounding of several important cultural problems and leads to methodological obfuscation, not clarification.

Without yielding entirely before Spaulding's assault, we are prepared to admit that the assumption of a more or less unvarying rate of cultural change in a spatial-temporal continuum has been overdone, by us as well as by others. We now prefer to say that the archaeologist is on a firmer footing with the concept of an archaeological unit as a provisionally defined segment of the total continuum, whose ultimate validation will depend on the degree to which its internal spatial and temporal dimensions can be shown to coincide with significant variations in the nature and rate of cultural change in that continuum. In simpler terms, it is the archaeologist's job to be aware of the arbitrary nature of his unit concepts and, at the same time, alert to the possibility of making them less arbitrary.

Absorbing as this question of cultural continuity and change must be to all archaeologists, it is really not an issue in the present discussion. Our object here is to show that a fundamental, unvarying characteristic of all archaeological unit formulations of whatever magnitude is that they are arrived at by combining three sorts of data: formal content, distribution in geographical space, and duration in time. These three ingredients are present, though not always explicit, in all unit concepts but may differ significantly in the part they play in the formulation. Variations in content, generally but not always a function of the limits of available information and the archaeologist's ability to draw inferences therefrom, need not concern us here. Our interest centers rather on variations in spatial and temporal dimensions and particularly on the fact that there is no regular (or constant) relationship between variations in these two dimensions. Probably a large share of our classificatory difficulties and the ensuing arguments could be avoided by the general recognition of this fact. It becomes essential, therefore, in the definition and use of archaeological unit concepts of whatever nature to understand precisely what quantities of space and time are involved in the formulation.

In the search for practicable units of study, American archaeologists have invented a large number of unit concepts and designated them by an even larger number of names. Our initial requirement, therefore, is a comprehensive nomenclature by means of which existing schemes and their working parts can be roughly equated. We have committed ourselves to the proposition that all unit concepts, whatever the outlook and intentions of their originators, have implicit spatial and temporal dimensions. Therefore, they can be differentiated by reference to the amounts of space and time they are thought to involve. If these premises be granted, it seems a reasonable approach to bring one of these two variables under control before considering it in combination with the other. The spatial factor is easier to deal with; so we may begin by setting forth a series of geographical categories that we have found useful in this connection.

SPATIAL DIVISIONS

A *site* is the smallest unit of space dealt with by the archaeologist and the most difficult to define. Its physical limits, which may vary from a few square yards to as many square miles, are often impossible to fix. About the only requirement ordinarily demanded of the site is that it be fairly continuously covered by remains of former occupation, and the general idea is that these pertain to a single unit of settlement, which may be anything from a small camp to a large city. Upon excavation, of course, it rarely turns out to be that simple. The site is the basic unit for stratigraphic studies; it is an almost certain assumption that cultural changes here can only be the result of the passage of time. It is in effect the minimum operational unit of geographical space.

A *locality* is a slightly larger spatial unit, varying in size from a single site to a district of uncertain dimensions; it is generally not larger than the space that might be occupied by a single community or local group. It is hardly necessary to add that such limits as are implied in this qualification have the variability found in the size and settlement patterns of local groups from one sort of society to another. In strictly archaeological terms, the locality is a geographical space small enough to permit the working assumption of complete cultural homogeneity at any given time. This is not to say that two or more discrete archaeological units might not, under special conditions, simultaneously occupy the same locality, or even the same site. For example, it has long been thought that people carrying an intrusive Salado culture occupied certain sites of the Gila-Salt region of south-central Arizona and coexisted peacefully with the indigenous Hohokam populations.[6] If this is the correct interpretation of the archaeology of the sites in question, it reflects a rather uncommon situation.

Examples of localities well known in the literature of American archaeology are given below in connection with the discussion of local sequences.

A *region* is a considerably larger unit of geographical space usually determined by the vagaries of archaeological history. Quite often it is simply the result of concentrated research by an individual or group. Rightly or wrongly, such a region comes to be thought of as having problems of its own that set it apart from other regions. Regional terms are those most often found in the titles of archaeological papers of wider scope than site reports. Through constant reiteration they become fixed in the literature and achieve a kind of independent existence. Regions are not altogether without reference to the facts of geography, however. In stressing the accidental factor in their formation, we must not overlook the tendency for environmental considerations to assert themselves. In portions of the New World where physical conditions of sharp diversity prevail, archaeological regions are likely to coincide with minor physiographic subdivisions. An excellent example is furnished by the Glades region comprising the southernmost portion of the Florida peninsula. Here the relationship between culture and a highly characterized environment has been particularly close throughout the entire span of the archaeological record.[7] Many other similar examples could be cited, and the effect would be to show that, of the various spatial units considered here, the region offers the most favorable field for the detailed study of the relationships between culture and environment.

In terms of the social aspect of culture—and here we must tread warily—the region is roughly equivalent to the space that might be occupied by a social unit larger than the community, a unit to which we may with extreme trepidation apply the term "tribe" or

6. Gladwin *et al.*, 1937, p. 13.
7. Goggin, 1949, pp. 28–32.

"society." This rough equation is based on what we know of American tribal distributions in early historic times and must be accorded the same flexibility that we see in the size of those distributions. The same caution is required in attempting to characterize the region in terms of the cultural aspect. Generally speaking, it is a geographical space in which, at a given time, a high degree of cultural homogeneity may be expected but not counted on. As we shall see later, it is quite possible for more than one archaeological phase to occupy a region at the same time.

An *area* is a geographical unit very considerably larger than a region; it corresponds roughly to the culture area of the ethnographer. Archaeological areas, like regions, have come into existence by common consent, but the element of historical accident is reduced somewhat by the fact that many individuals and institutions are likely to have been involved in their investigation. They tend to coincide with major physiographic divisions. That the North American Southwest, for example, has maintained its identity as an archaeological area through more than a half-century of intensive investigation is certainly due in large part to culture-environment correlations of a positive nature. It is hardly necessary to add that, although the area as defined here may have general physiographic integrity, its limits are not so easy to draw on a map as those of the smaller region. The southeastern United States is a case in point; it has to be defined afresh every time anyone writes about it. The problem is a familiar one in culture-area studies.

It often happens that there are territories of geographical extent intermediate between the region and the area which possess qualities and degrees of cultural unity that give them a definite usefulness in archaeological or ethnographical studies. We refer to such spatial units as *subareas*. A case in point might be taken with reference to Middle America (or Mesoamerica), which has been defined quite specifically as a culture area.[8] Embracing southern Mexico and upper Central America, Mesoamerica has a distinctive culture content and patterning; yet within this sphere of common cultural

8. Kirchhoff, 1943.

likenesses there are differences of traditionally recognized significance. As but one example, the cultures of the lowland Maya country stand in sharp contrast to those that are adjacent to them. Their art, architecture, ceramics, calendrics, and writing bind the Maya lowland territory into an obvious unit of history. At the same time, these Maya lowlands are too complex and diversified to be organized as a region, as that cultural-geographical term is defined here. Workable Maya regions might be the Petén, the Usumacinta, the Motagua-Chamelecón, or the several divisions of Yucatán, etc. In consequence, the useful term "Maya lowlands" signifies a subarea.

BASIC ARCHAEOLOGICAL UNITS

The concepts about to be discussed under this heading were referred to in our original paper as "formal or content units" to express the fact that the element of content is more important in their formulation than the spatial and temporal dimensions. Use of such a term, however, suggests that they are different in kind from what we later describe as "integrative" and "maximum" units, which is not strictly true. It seems preferable, therefore, to call them simply "basic units," which indeed they are.

The *component*, a useful term which has achieved nearly universal currency in eastern North American archaeology, has been defined by W. C. McKern as the manifestation of a given archaeological "focus" at a specific site.[9] Strictly speaking, in the McKern system, the component is not a taxonomic unit. In theory the basic unit of classification is the focus, comprising a number of components, and the same may be said of what we designate as a "phase." It is a working assumption that no phase worthy of the

9. "The manifestation of any given focus at a specific site is termed a *component* of that focus. This is in no sense an additional type of culture manifestation, one of the five class types; rather, it is the focus as represented at a site, and serves to distinguish between a site, which may bear evidence of several cultural occupations, each foreign to the other, and a single specified manifestation at a site. In many instances several components, each at cultural variance with the other, may be found to occur at a single site" (McKern, 1939, p. 308).

name will fail to manifest itself in more than one component. In practice, of course, it often happens that a phase is initially defined on the strength of a single component, i.e., a site or a level within a site, but the expectation is implicit that other components will be found and the original definition modified accordingly. It will be noted later, however, in the discussion of the social implications of the phase, that it is theoretically and actually possible for a phase to consist of a single component.

The *phase* is, in our opinion, the practicable and intelligible unit of archaeological study. Choice of the term accords with prevailing usage in a preponderance of New World areas, including the Southwest, most of South America, and all of Middle America. Kidder has defined the phase in the following terms: "A cultural complex possessing traits sufficiently characteristic to distinguish it for purposes of preliminary archaeological classification, from earlier and later manifestations of the cultural development of which it formed a part, and from other contemporaneous complexes."[10]

Like Kidder, we prefer "phase" to the approximately equivalent "focus" because of its stronger temporal implication. The emphasis cannot be placed entirely on time, however. Modifying Kidder's definition slightly, we would prefer to describe the concept as *an archaeological unit possessing traits sufficiently characteristic to distinguish it from all other units similarly conceived, whether of the same or other cultures or civilizations, spatially limited to the order of magnitude of a locality or region and chronologically limited to a relatively brief interval of time.* It must be acknowledged that this definition gives a specious impression of uniformity. It would be fine if phases could be standardized as to the amount of space and time they occupy. Unfortunately, there are so many variable conditions entering into the formulation that it is neither possible nor desirable to define the scope except within rather broad limits. A phase may be anything from a thin level in a site reflecting no more than a brief encampment to a prolonged occupation of a large number of sites distributed over a region of very elastic proportions.

10. Kidder, Jennings, and Shook, 1946, p. 9.

It will be noted that Kidder's definition of phase lays more emphasis on cultural continuity than ours, since it implies necessary relations to what goes before and what comes after. We have freed it of this requirement to provide for the many instances in which we simply do not know what goes before or comes after, or for those less frequent occasions when a new phase appears as an intrusion without apparent relationship to any precedent continuity. In any case, whether as an instance of continuity or of discontinuity, the phase most often appears as one member of a series that will be referred to hereinafter as a "local" or "regional sequence." These terms will be defined presently, but let us first examine a little more closely the spatial and temporal implications of this basic archaeological unit.

We have already alluded briefly to the impossibility of close delimitation of the phase in respect to the dimensions of time and space. It may help to clarify the problem to consider it in relation to various levels of cultural development. In Part II of this book we will describe a developmental scheme for New World archaeology with five hypothetical stages: Lithic, Archaic, Formative, Classic, and Postclassic. It is not necessary to anticipate the definitions of these stages to point out here that the spatial and temporal dimensions of phases are not likely to be the same on all stages. For example, in the Lithic stage, in which a migratory, hunting-gathering economy is postulated, phases can be expected to occupy more geographical space than in the sedentary Formative stage. There is no regular reduction from stage to stage, however; in the Classic and Postclassic stages the spatial dimensions of phases may also be larger than in the Formative but for a different reason: the sociopolitical groups are larger. Temporal dimensions, on the other hand, may actually exhibit a regular diminution from stage to stage, if the commonly held assumption is correct that the rate of cultural change accelerates with increased advancement and complexity. Without elaborating this point or further refining the definition, we wish simply to emphasize that the concept of phase has no appropriate scale independent of the cultural situation in which it is applied. This is not so great a deficiency as might appear. Looked at internally, so to speak, phases may have very considerable and highly variable spatial and temporal dimensions; looked at from the total range of New World culture-history, they are very small quantities indeed, and it is from this point of view that they assume a sort of rough equivalence, enabling us to use the concept of phase as an operational tool regardless of the developmental stage involved.

As typological and stratigraphic analyses become more refined, it often becomes desirable to subdivide phases into smaller (primarily temporal) units, and it seems best to regard these as *subphases* and to give them numbers instead of names. It also sometimes happens that two or more phases in the same locality or region, originally set up as independent units, subsequently appear to be more intelligible as subphases of a single unit, though they continue to be operationally useful in sequences and area correlations. It is clearly impossible to lay down any precise rules governing the formation of subphases. In general, their use seems appropriate in cases where differences apply only to a few specific items of content or where such differences are expressible only in variations in frequency. In other words, if it is impossible to present a sensible account of the culture of a unit except in terms of what went before or came after, it is probably better regarded as a subphase. It is hardly necessary to add that subphases and components are entirely different kinds of subdivisions of the phase.

TEMPORAL SERIES

A *local sequence* in its purest form is a series of components found in vertical stratigraphic succession in a single site. It may also, however, be a composite series made by combining shorter stratigraphic "runs" from various portions of a site or from several sites within a locality, or it may be derived from seriating components by various means without benefit of stratigraphy at all. However obtained, the local sequence has this important feature: it is local. The spatial dimension, by definition, is small enough to permit the working assumption that differences between components reflect differences in time.

We have already referred to the fact that members of a local sequence, though technically regarded as components, are often referred to as phases on the ground that they are local manifestations of the larger units and, also, that it is theoretically possible for a phase to be represented by a single component. The local sequence may, therefore, be defined as *a chronological series of components, phases, or subphases, within the geographical limits of a locality as defined in this study.*

Local sequences, which are the very stuff of archaeology, abound. A famous example of the kind of sequence based upon a single site is at the ceremonial Maya center of Uaxactún, in the Guatemalan Petén. The Uaxactún sequence was determined by combinations of "dirt" and architectural stratigraphy revealed in long and intensive excavations.[11] The sequence runs the gamut of the Middle American Formative and Classic stages and probably represents some two thousand years of more or less continuous human occupation. Continuity throughout all phases of the sequence is provided by ceramics which, in spite of several marked innovations, show a recognizable local evolution. The earliest Formative stage phases are the Mamom and Chicanel, in that order, and these are followed by Matzanel, generally considered Proto-Classic. The Classic phases, well represented in temple and palace construction, are the Tzakol and Tepeu. R. E. Smith, who defined and named these phases, has recently subdivided the latter two into subphases: Tzakol 1, 2, 3, and Tepeu 1, 2, 3.[12] A comparable, but slightly more complex, local sequence is the one at Kaminaljuyu in the Guatemalan highlands, near Guatemala City. This is an extensive ceremonial and dwelling center, and a long Formative-through-Classic sequence of Maya occupation and building was worked out

11. Ricketson and Ricketson, 1937; A. L. Smith, 1950.

12. R. E. Smith, 1955, pp. 21–25.

here by the cross-matching of numerous mound, tomb, and refuse excavations over a very large site zone.[13]

Kroeber's pioneer seriation of seventeen Zuñi ruins by means of surface pottery alone was limited to sites that could be reached in an hour's walk from the modern pueblo. This classic study thus affords a striking illustration of the local sequence and the advantages of keeping it local. "Particularly does the necessity of concentration apply geographically. A promising site here and another a hundred miles away may show striking differences in innumerable respects. But in the present chaos of knowledge who can say which of these differences are due to age and which to locality and environment?"[14]

We have spoken of local sequences built up by comparing stratigraphies and seriations from a number of sites within a relatively small, circumscribed territory. The Virú Valley, on the north coast of Peru, is an example.[15] The valley is about fifteen miles long and three miles wide at its widest point. In prehistoric times it was densely occupied. Although the valley is not a single site, or site zone, there are no contemporaneous cultural differences from one part of Virú to another. Its ceramic and architectural series are, indeed, local. Quite likely, when more sequential information is available from neighboring north coast valleys, it will be seen that Virú joins conveniently with several others to form a regional sequence. Such a regional sequence is suggested by the frequent references to the "North Coast" on Peruvian culture sequence charts,[16] though it must be pointed out that the regional integrity of the Peruvian "North Coast" is still to be demonstrated.

A *regional sequence* is not merely a local sequence with larger spatial dimensions. The difference can best be approached from the

13. Kidder, Jennings, and Shook, 1946; Shook, 1951; Shook and Kidder, 1952.

14. Kroeber, 1916, p. 21.

15. Ford and Willey, 1949; W. C. Bennett, 1950; Strong and Evans, 1952; Willey, 1953c; Collier, 1955.

16. Bennett and Bird, 1949, p. 112.

operational standpoint. In the normal extension of archaeological information, components, subphases, phases, and local sequences multiply, and questions of wider relationships come to the fore. Ideally, the archaeologists of a region come together in a harmonious session where a careful matching of local sequences produces a new sequence of larger scope. Actually this happy event occurs but rarely. What more often happens is that phases and local sequences gain in scope by a sort of osmosis. They flow outward, so to speak, often propelled by their originators, uniting to themselves their weaker correlates over a widening circle. The process is necessarily accompanied by a progressive generalization of definition until much of their original usefulness to research is impaired.

Nevertheless, we will assume for the sake of argument that local sequences remain local and that regional sequences are the result of correlating them—not combining them, be it noted, because in the process the original formulations are retailored to fit the wider spatial and (sometimes) deeper temporal dimensions. The phase now appears in its widest practicable extension and at its farthest remove from the primary data; at any rate, it is our contention that the concept of phase cannot safely be extended beyond the limits here described. With these operational conditions in mind, we may define the regional sequence as *a chronological series of phases or subphases within the geographical limits of a region as defined in this study.*

One of the firmest sequences in North American archaeology is that established by James A. Ford and his associates in the southern portion of the Mississippi alluvial valley, centering approximately about the mouth of the Red River in Louisiana.[17] This is an instructive example in which stratigraphy in a small number of closely related sites at the center (Marksville locality) and seriation of a large number of sites extending out from the center have been skilfully combined in a regional sequence of great strength but sufficient flexibility to permit the incorporation of new formulations from time to time. The unusual vigor of the "Lower Valley"

17. Ford, 1936; Ford and Willey, 1940, 1941; Ford and Quimby, 1945; Quimby, 1942, 1951; Ford, 1951, 1952.

sequence is manifested by a tendency to dominate in correlations with other sequences in neighboring regions, but it is important to point out that its strength derives from the hard core of stratigraphy at the center. If there is any valid criticism of this sequence, it is that it tends to take in too much territory. Workers in the delta of the Mississippi and adjacent coastal regions, for example, have tried to fit their data into it, not without considerable strain, which is scarcely to be wondered at, considering the sharp environmental differences involved in such an extension.[18] This is a case of the "osmotic" tendency noted above. It also exemplifies another source of difficulty, to wit, the confusion that inheres in practically all archaeological sequence formulations between culture and chronology. As soon as we begin to rank cultural phases in order of time, they tend to become "periods." As periods, of course, they are theoretically not spatially limited; they may be extended indefinitely. If the Marksville phase of the Lower Valley sequence is merely the interval between points E and F on a continuous time band (as in Ford's recent writings), then anything that can be established as lying within that interval, in the delta, or anywhere else for that matter, can also be called Marksville. The catch is that Marksville is and will remain more than a mere chronological period. The interval marked off by points E and F is determined by cultural criteria in the first instance; the identification of other material as belonging to that interval (in the absence of independent calendrical dating) is determined by those same cultural criteria. When the latter are not sufficiently in conformity with the cultural criteria for comfortable identification, it is a sure sign that the limits of the particular phase in question, either spatial or temporal or both, have been exceeded. We shall have considerably more to say about this ever present problem in the sections devoted to area syntheses.

Another strong regional sequence, though expressed largely in ceramics, is exemplified by the Petén region of the central part of the lowland Maya subarea. The key local sequence is that at

18. McIntire, 1954.

Uaxactún, already referred to, but stratigraphies at Benque Viejo and San José can be correlated with ease.[19] There are also indications from other sites in the same general vicinity, in both Guatemala and British Honduras, that ceramic types and their sequences are in close harmony. In sum, an archaeological region of at least fifty miles in diameter, and probably considerably larger, can be established around Uaxactún, and the local sequence at that center can be expanded into an equally valid sequence for the region.

Before we leave the subject, it may be well to emphasize the artificiality of the relationship between phase and region in a regional sequence. We have said that the maximum practicable spatial dimension of the phase is comparable to that of the region, but no actual geographical coextension is implied. Such a one-to-one relationship may occur fortuitously, because it often happens that a region comes into existence on the heels of a phase, so to speak; but there is no reason to expect that earlier or later phases will also coincide with that region. In fact, the chances are that they will not do so. As an example, there is a neat coincidence of region and phase on the Florida Gulf Coast at the time of the Weeden Island phase. The latter is relatively uniform in its entire extent from the vicinity of Pensacola (if not farther west) south and east to Charlotte Harbor below Tampa Bay.[20] This correlation breaks down, however, if we move either backward or forward in time. On an earlier level, the Santa Rosa–Swift Creek phase seems much more restricted in its distribution, and at a later time the old Weeden Island region is divided between the Fort Walton phase in the north and the Safety Harbor phase in the south.

INTEGRATIVE UNITS

In our first paper we designated the large-scale unit concepts *horizon* and *tradition* as "integrative devices," but we now prefer to call them "units" in tardy realization of the fact that they are not radically different in kind from other unit concepts described in

19. Thompson, 1939, 1940.
20. Willey, 1949, chap. vi.

this study but, rather, different in the uses to which they are put. We call them "integrative" because, in our opinion, they constitute the most practicable means for effecting culture-historical integration on a geographical scale larger than that of the region. They are not the only means, however, and, before we describe them further, it will be necessary to consider the problem of large-scale integration in more general terms.

One good result of our first presentation of the nomenclature advocated here was a paper by Irving Rouse[21] in which, and in subsequent correspondence with the writers, he looks with favor on our basic units (component and phase) and their use in local and regional sequences but expresses some misgivings in regard to these larger integrative units (horizon and tradition) and the way we proposed to use them. Rouse maintains that it is necessary to distinguish three "levels of interpretation" and three corresponding methods of correlating phases in large-scale area comparisons: "descriptive," "distributional," and "genetic." The first has to do with formal comparisons of the sort employed in the McKern taxonomic system and does not apply to the problem of culture-historical integration as we understand it. His "distributional correlation" is a strictly spatial-temporal ordering of phases in which the unifying criteria are theoretically independent and extracultural—nothing more or less than position in geographical space and time—in contrast to his "genetic correlation," which does not scruple to use culturally determined criteria. We agree that our integrative units operate mainly, if not entirely, on Rouse's genetic level of interpretation. He defines "genetic" very broadly, applying it, if we understand him correctly, to any relationship between discrete units resulting from some form of historical contact. We prefer "integrative," which we have been using in practically the same sense, because it carries no implications of phylogeny. This is a minor verbal difference, but, when it comes to a general evaluation of the role of genetic or integrative concepts in archaeology,

21. Rouse, 1955.

we find ourselves in disagreement. Rouse takes what seems to us an overcautious view:

> For these reasons, I would suggest that the genetic approach is not in itself an efficient method of ordering the phases, i.e. of making broad-scale syntheses of cultural relationships, although it may be useful as a check upon syntheses established by other means. It would seem prudent to make one's basic synthesis by means of descriptive or distributional correlation and then to point out the genetic relationships only in the instances where sufficient data are available and they indicate that this type of relationship has occurred.[22]

In our view, the only synthesis worthy of the name is a culture-historical synthesis. We have Rouse's own word for it that descriptive and distributional correlations tell us nothing about cultural or historical relationships; the first tells us whether cultures are like or unlike, the second places them in space and time. How are we to achieve by either or both of these means a "broad-scale synthesis of cultural relationships"? It would seem axiomatic that cultural relationships can be revealed and expressed only by means of integrative concepts that are culturally determined. This may be unfortunate and is certainly productive of circular reasoning, as Rouse points out, but we do not see how it can be helped. The culturally determined integrative units that we are about to consider are admittedly inefficient and hard to handle, but they constitute, in our opinion, the principal means for the realization of what we have repeatedly defined as archaeology's primary task—culture-historical integration.

Failure in our original paper to distinguish between the terms *horizon* and *horizon style*, which we used interchangeably, drew some well-merited criticism, thanks to which we here make that distinction and offer what we hope is a more sensible discussion of the whole subject.

The horizon-style concept, introduced into Andean archaeology by Max Uhle[23] and later formalized by A. L. Kroeber,[24] has amply

22. Rouse, 1955, pp. 719–20.

23. Uhle, 1913.   24. Kroeber, 1944, pp. 108–11.

proved its utility in that area. It differs from other unit concepts described in this study in that the content is of a limited and specialized nature and the spatial and temporal dimensions are combined in very unequal proportions. In theory, a horizon style, as the name implies, occupies a great deal of space but very little time. It may be roughly defined as a specialized cultural continuum represented by the wide distribution of a recognizable art style. On the assumption of historical uniqueness of stylistic pattern, coupled with the further assumption that styles normally change with considerable rapidity, the temporal dimension is theoretically reduced to a point where the horizon style becomes useful in equating phases or larger units of culture in time that are widely separated in space. As one of the present authors has already observed: "The horizon styles are the horizontal stringers by which the upright columns of specialized regional development are tied together in the time chart."[25]

Thus the horizon style is one culturally determined means of establishing a horizon, but the latter must be defined in broader terms. This is the step we neglected to take in our first paper. The horizon-style concept has a limited application, since it presupposes a level of aesthetic development that many archaeological cultures in the New World failed to reach. It is conceivable, however, that other kinds of cultural data might serve equally well to mark horizons, although this is a proposition that has not been sufficiently investigated. We have in mind such items as highly specialized artifact types, widely traded objects, new technologies, unusual modes of burial, or peculiar ritual assemblages—in other words, any kind of archaeological evidence that indicates a rapid spread of new ideas over a wide geographic space.

Rouse recommends a stricter definition of the horizon. In a letter to the authors, written subsequently to his paper from which we have just quoted, he makes it clear that his conception of the horizon is on his distributional level and operates ideally with independent extracultural dating criteria, whereas ours, he points out,

25. Willey, 1945a, p. 55.

is on the genetic level and is therefore unsuitable for use in distributional correlations and should be called by another name. If we could be convinced that it is possible at all times to maintain a clear cut distinction between distributional and genetic methods of correlation, we would be inclined to accept this suggestion. However, it seems to us that certain horizon styles—or horizons, to use the more inclusive term—can be looked upon as both distributional and genetic in Rouse's terminology. For example, the presence of Southern Cult horizon-style elements in various far-flung cultures of the southeastern United States links those cultures genetically, in the very broad sense that they reflect some kind of contact, but the cultures so linked are quite different from one another and, so far as we can see, have very different genetic relationships in all other respects. Though the genetic implications cannot be ignored, the primary concern of the archaeologist with the Southern Cult style is often purely distributional: he thinks of it as a horizon marker whose appearance in various regional sequences is useful in cross-dating. However, we are prepared to waive this point and agree that it is best to use only independent, extracultural dating in distributional correlations or, as we call them here, area chronologies. We adhere, therefore, to our original notion of the horizon, not quite agreeing that it cannot be used for purely temporal correlations, but freely admitting its kinship with the concept of tradition on the genetic level of interpretation.[26] The horizon, then, may be defined as *a primarily spatial continuity represented by cultural traits and assemblages whose nature and mode of occurrence permit the assumption of a broad and rapid spread.* The archaeological units linked by a horizon are thus assumed to be *approximately* contemporaneous. The word is italicized because it is recognized that horizons based on cultural criteria unsupported by independent dating may have considerable temporal depth and that the assumed

26. We trust that the reference to Rouse's "levels of interpretation" is not producing confusion in respect to our "levels of organization" as described in the introductory section of this study. All his levels fall within the definition of our descriptive level.

correlatio.1 is not necessarily horizontal but may, and probably does, have a "slope" depending on the amount of time required for the spread of the elements used as horizon markers. Notwithstanding these limitations, the horizon is an invaluable integrative unit for the investigation and expression of external relationships over wide geographical areas. If we have agreed that it is of dubious value in establishing purely temporal equations, it is merely to avoid blurring the useful distinction between Rouse's distributional and genetic methods of correlation in the formation of area chronologies, a point we shall return to later.

Tradition is another integrative concept that seems to have originated in South American archaeology. A familiar, not to say indispensable, word in any historical context, "tradition" has of late acquired a special meaning in archaeology, or rather a number of meanings, for it is still in an early stage of formulation and does not mean the same thing to all who use it. Owing to the fact that the concept is designated by a term that has long been used in archaeological writings, it is difficult to say just when it began to be a methodological tool. In the Andean area it came into use as a counterpoise to the horizon style and was at first applied only to pottery. Once it became apparent that the utility of the horizon style depended upon the combination of broad spatial and short temporal dimensions, it was clear that some other formulation was needed to express a different kind of ceramic unity in which these proportions were reversed. This gave rise to the term "pottery tradition," certainly not a verbal innovation, but perhaps the first use of the term "tradition" with a definite methodological sense.

The relationship of the two concepts, horizon style and pottery tradition, proved to be so important in Peruvian archaeology that one of us may be permitted to repeat himself, as follows:

These speculations concerning the relationships of the later White-on-red styles to the earlier component styles of the White-on-red horizon lead us to wonder if there are not other widely inclusive historical units of an order different from that of the horizon style. It appears certain that the Peruvian Andes and coast were a unified culture area in that the important culture developments were essentially local and basically inter-related for at least a thousand years. This fundamental cultural unity justifies seeing ceramic developments in terms of long-time traditions as well as coeval phenomena. The concept of a pottery tradition, as used here, includes broad descriptive categories of ceramic decoration which undoubtedly have value in expressing historical relationships when the relationships are confined to the geographical boundaries of Peruvian-Andean cultures. The pottery tradition lacks the specific quality of the localized pottery style, and it differs from the horizon style in that it is not an integration of artistic elements which has been widely diffused at a given time period. A pottery tradition comprises a line, or a number of lines, of pottery development through time within the confines of a certain technique or decorative constant. In successive time periods through which the history of ceramic development can be traced, certain styles arose within the tradition. Transmission of some of these styles during particular periods resulted in the formation of a horizon style, other styles in the continuum of the tradition remained strictly localized. The distinction between a horizon style and a pottery tradition should be kept in mind as the two are opposable concepts in archaeological reconstruction.[27]

Shortly after this idea of tradition had first been injected into Peruvian studies, Wendell Bennett enlarged the concept very considerably under the name "area co-tradition." This formulation he defined as "the over-all unit of cultural history of an area within which the component cultures have been inter-related over a period of time."[28] The emphasis implied in the "co-" is on the linkage of whole cultures, each with its own history and persistent traditions, and on the area in which this linkage takes place. Thus the area co-tradition is a vast enlargement over the simple tradition in terms of content, since it is no longer confined to a single technological development but becomes a broad coalescent cultural continuum. At the same time, it introduces a restriction in that stable geographical boundaries are implied.

The subsequent history of the area co-tradition and the controversies that grew out of attempts to apply it in other areas[29] need

27. Willey, 1945a, p. 53.   28. W. C. Bennett, 1948, p. 1.

29. Martin and Rinaldo, 1951; Willey, 1953a, pp. 373–74; Rouse, 1954; Cotter, 1954.

not detain us, since we are not proposing to incorporate the concept in the nomenclature described here.

About the same time that the Peruvianists were beginning to talk about pottery traditions, McGregor introduced the term into the archaeology of the Southwest with somewhat different connotations. He defined tradition very broadly as "more or less deeply rooted human characteristics—persistent attitudes or ways of doing things—which are passed on from one generation to another,"[30] thus emphasizing the non-material and configurational aspects of traditions and the social and behavioral continuities reflected in their persistence. He maintained that characteristic attitudes can be inferred from material traits and that the determination of traditions (as defined by him) is not only possible but essential in making broad archaeological comparisons. McGregor's traditions are for the most part technologically oriented: house types, pottery, ground stone, etc.; he merely advocates that they be formulated in terms of the preferences and attitudes they reflect. There is nothing revolutionary in this, but it is a point of view that cannot be too often stated.

The first significant use of the tradition concept in eastern North American studies, so far as the authors are aware, was by John Goggin, whose definition follows:

My concept of Florida cultural traditions is similar in theory but more inclusive in content than a ceramic tradition. A cultural tradition is a distinctive way of life, reflected in various aspects of the culture; perhaps extending through some period of time and exhibiting normal internal cultural changes, but nevertheless throughout this period showing a basic consistent unity. In the whole history of a tradition certain persistent themes dominate the life of the people. These give distinctiveness to the configurations.[31]

Goggin recognizes ten cultural traditions in Florida archaeology, allowing to them a great deal of latitude in spatial and temporal dimensions. It seems to us that here he has discovered the outstand-

30. McGregor, 1950. (Paper submitted in 1946.)
31. Goggin, 1949, p. 17.

ing merit of the tradition as a methodological tool, namely, its flexibility. Goggin also, rather more than others who have used the concept, emphasizes the importance of environmental factors in the shaping and conserving of traditions. Here again he has put his finger on another virtue of the concept. It offers a most effective means for giving expression to culture-environment correlations.

From the examples just given, it may be seen that the concept of tradition has been expanded considerably since its first use in Peruvian archaeology. In our original paper we expressed satisfaction with this growth and gave a definition of our own that was as broad as, if not broader than, any previous ones. It may be asked, however, whether by such radical expansion the tradition is not deprived of some of its utility as an integrative unit. In the blunting that is inseparable from increased generalization it tends to lose its primary significance of long temporal continuity as a counterpoise to the broad spatial continuity represented by the horizon. Furthermore, since the publication of our first paper, we have come to realize that, for expressing the maximum segmentation of culture-history, the old standbys "culture" and "civilization" will not be easily supplanted by such cumbersome expressions as "full cultural tradition." We are therefore now proposing a return to something like the original meaning of tradition in Peruvian archaeology, with emphasis put back on single technologies or other unified systems of forms rather than on whole cultures. The tradition thereby takes its former place as a means to integration, with the culture or civilization standing as the product of integration. Our first definition is accordingly amended to read: *an archaeological tradition is a (primarily) temporal continuity represented by persistent configurations in single technologies or other systems of related forms.* The lack of specification in respect to the spatial dimension may be supplied by the use of qualifying terms, as in "regional tradition," "areal tradition," and so on.

This definition of tradition takes us not quite all the way back to the original pottery tradition of Peruvian archaeology. Some expansion is left, in that traditions may be based on more complex systems of forms than that represented by a single technology. We have in mind something like the functionally interrelated trait complexes of the ethnographer. About the same amount of expansion is involved in substituting the concept of horizon for the horizon style. The working relationship between horizon and tradition, therefore, remains the same as between horizon style and pottery tradition in the passage quoted above (pp. 34–35).

After making the decision to cut back the tradition, as outlined above, we received a manuscript copy of the report on the Society for American Archaeology's seminar on "Cultural Stability" held at Ann Arbor in August, 1955. At this meeting the concept of tradition was thoroughly anatomized. In defining it as "a socially transmitted form unit (or series of systematically related units) which persists in time," the conferees were careful to avoid any qualifications as to size, either in terms of content or in spatial and temporal dimensions, beyond the obvious implication of long duration in the clause "which persists in time." They were evidently prepared to think of "whole cultural traditions," but most of the discussion, and nearly all the examples, applied to traditions of less than whole cultural scope. Our impression is that such limitation made the tradition a more useful tool in their investigation of cultural stability. "Thus, although it is logically necessary to entertain the possibility of traditions ranging from the smallest to the largest, it is also important to recognize that the cultural and historical significance of a tradition diminishes toward either size extreme."[32]

The reference in the Ann Arbor definition to social transmittal serves to emphasize the fact that traditions operate on Rouse's genetic level of interpretation, perhaps even more surely than horizons. Thus, if we may express the reciprocating relationship between them without too flagrant a confusion of categories, the tradition gives depth, while the horizon gives breadth, to the genetic structure of culture-historical relationships on a broad geographic scale.

In seeking to polarize such essentially fluid concepts as horizon

32. Haury *et al.*, 1956, p. 39.

and tradition, we have unavoidably overstressed their salient features and produced an impression of profound difference between them that may be misleading. Looked at from the broader view of total archaeological method, horizon and tradition are not really very different. Both are unit concepts in the sense that their formulation involves the combination of cultural data and spatial-temporal dimensions. They differ considerably in the nature of the cultural data and, theoretically, in the quantities and proportions of the spatial and temporal dimensions; we have stated with tiresome repetition what those differences are supposed to be, but in practice such standards are difficult to apply. Our first apprehension of a major archaeological continuity, as of the proverbial elephant in the dark, is usually so tenuous that we do not know what it is or what to call it. The same continuity may be viewed by one investigator as a tradition, by another as a horizon. Even when the outlines are fairly clear, it may still be thought of either way, depending on the problem under consideration. For example, Hopewellian zoned rocker-stamped pottery, when looked at from the standpoint of its geographic extension in the eastern United States, may be quite legitimately thought of as a horizon phenomenon; on the other hand, when the interest is centered on the course of its development through successive phases in a particular region, it may equally well be regarded as a tradition. This is perhaps an extreme example of the fluidity we have praised in describing these integrative concepts.

There remains but to mention briefly the useful but largely neglected concept *climax*. In reference to the integrative units just described, the climax may be defined as *the type or types of maximum intensity and individuality of an archaeological horizon or tradition.* This is necessarily a value judgment, but only in relation to the horizon or tradition involved. In whole cultural terms the climax becomes *the phase or phases of maximum intensity and individuality of a culture or civilization.* So far as possible, in this wider context, the emphasis should be multilinear, not confined to exquisite developments in aesthetics. Such developments may conceivably take place in periods of low cultural intensity. Theoretically, there should be a climax in every horizon, tradition, culture, or civilization, on all stages of development. Our choice of the term "classic" —which means about the same thing—to denote the climactic stage of New World culture is by no means intended to preclude its use in more humble contexts. Any horizon or tradition may have its classic type, as any culture or civilization may have its classic phase. The word makes equal sense whether we are talking about the classic black stirrup-mouth jar of the Chavín horizon, the classic Folsom point of the fluted-point tradition, the classic Pueblo III phase of the San Juan Anasazi culture, or the classic stage of New World culture as a whole.

OPERATIONAL RELATIONSHIPS OF BASIC AND INTEGRATIVE UNITS

Before we go on to a consideration of large-scale area schemes and maximum archaeological units, it may be well to summarize briefly the working relationships between the unit concepts so far described, because these constitute, in our opinion, the most effective apparatus for the integration of the primary archaeological data. These relationships are crudely diagramed in Figure 1, which is designed to show the difference between the basic units, component and phase, and the integrative units, horizon and tradition, not in their nature as archaeological units but in the way they operate in large-scale integration. The relationships in the component-phase system are predominantly formal and static; those in the horizon-tradition system are fluid and historical or, as Rouse would say, genetic. In the first pair, the spatial and temporal dimensions that inhere in all archaeological unit concepts are, in this larger context, reduced to negligibility. This is what permits us to refer to the phase as the "manageable" unit of archaeological study. It can be manipulated in large-scale area schemes as though its internal dimensions were non-existent.

Up to this point most archaeologists would probably go along, though many, depending on the areas in which they have worked, would prefer to use other terms in place of "phase." Where our point of view differs is in the conviction that the phase, as defined in these pages, is the largest archaeological unit that can be so manipulated. Our later discussion of some of the characteristics of the maximum units, culture and civilization, we need anticipate

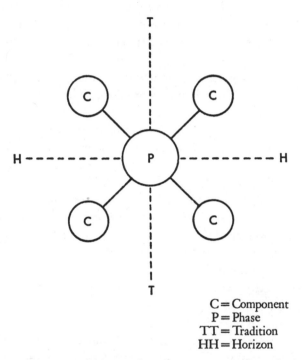

C = Component
P = Phase
TT = Tradition
HH = Horizon

FIG. 1.—Diagrammatic integration of components, phase, horizon, and tradition.

here only to the extent of pointing out that these are in a very real sense the ends, not the means, of culture-historical integration. Their vastly greater internal spatial and temporal dimensions, particularly the latter, render them completely unmanageable as units of study in both formal and spatial-temporal comparisons. Forms are fluid, changing constantly through space and time; with expansion of these dimensions, the changes in forms *within* the unit are such that the unit can only be described in progressively more general terms—the familiar phenomenon of shorter trait lists for larger taxonomic subdivisions. For example, at the Woodland Conference in 1941,[33] eastern North American archaeologists laid down a formal definition of the Woodland cultural pattern couched in such general terms that, as later discovered, but for the inclusion of pottery, it fitted the Archaic pattern just as well.[34] In a similar manner, temporal relationships between large units become impossible to describe through excess of internal time dimensions and the consequent possibilities of overlap. Failure to recognize this is responsible for many fictitious problems. The Adena-Hopewell problem, a long-standing subject of debate, might be cited as an example. The sequential arrangement of these two cultures in the Ohio Valley and their correlation with other units of comparable dimensions in eastern North America became faintly ridiculous when radiocarbon dates indicated a probable overlap of several centuries in their time spans. This is not to maintain that spatial and temporal relationships of cultures and civilizations are not legitimate problems for the archaeologist, but to point out simply that in this wider arena the variables of space and time are more difficult to control. Such questions certainly cannot be investigated and expressed by the crude diagrammatic methods ordinarily employed in large-scale area schemes.

To return to the cabalistic diagram in Figure 1: if it be granted that the component-phase system operates mainly with relationships of a formal nature, it will certainly be allowed that horizons and traditions belong to a different system—a system in which the element of formal content is reduced in importance, while the variables of space and time have the dominant roles. The real point, however, is not how like or unlike these two pairs of units may be, conceptually or operationally, but that there is no built-in taxonomic relationship between them. Components and phases enter into horizons and traditions; their external relationships are expressed

33. Woodland Conference, 1943.
34. Sears, 1948.

by these units, but they are not combined to form them. In fact, the opposite is more nearly the case. A single phase may conceivably enter into more than one horizon. For example, the Esperanza phase in the highland Maya sequence at Kaminaljuyu, Guatemala, participates in both the basal-flanged bowl horizon and the Teotihuacán tripod-jar horizon.[35] The basal-flanged bowl, of presumably lowland Maya inspiration, is a widespread horizon marker for the period of the Early Classic cultures in southern Middle America. The tripod cylinder jar, deriving from Teotihuacán about the same time, has an even more extensive distribution and imitation. As for traditions, there is certainly no question that a number of these may, and usually do, converge in a single phase. This is clearly seen, for example, in the Mochica phase of the north coast of Peru. Mochica red-and-white modeled pottery represents a convergence of the old Cupisnique, or north Peruvian Plastic and Incised, traditions, with the north Peruvian White-on-red tradition that first made its appearance in the Salinar phase.[36] In sum, the effectiveness of this apparatus, as we see it, depends on the free interplay of basic and integrative units without rigid limitations of a systematic nature.

35. Kidder, Jennings, and Shook, 1946, p. 250.
36. Willey, 1945a.

Chapter 2

Archaeological Integration

The integrative units described in the preceding section are well adapted to express the extraordinarily complex and fluid relationships of archaeological phases over wide geographical areas, but they cannot furnish the rigid spatial-temporal frames that archaeologists seem to find so reassuring. For these we generally turn to some system of matching phases from region to region, expressing the results by means of a diagram in which the regional sequences are arranged in parallel columns with their phases stacked up like boxes, scaled against a real or imaginary vertical time band at one side. Illustrations are available in current archaeological literature in great profusion and variety. The appearance of an archaeological report without such a diagram would in fact be something of a curiosity today. This is what Rouse, in the paper already cited, has called "distributional correlation of phases," and the resulting diagram, of which he presents an excellent model,[1] is often referred to as an "area chronology."

We have expressed agreement with Rouse that so far as possible such a scheme should be effected by means of independent, extracultural cross-dating, e.g., radiocarbon dating, dendrochronology, river-channel and river-terrace sequences, discrete geological and meteorological events (volcanic eruptions, droughts, etc.)—in short, any available techniques of dating that do not involve assumptions about culture. Unfortunately, in the present stage of

1. Rouse, 1955, Fig. 2, p. 716.

archaeological development in the Americas we rarely, if ever, have sufficient dates of this kind; consequently it is difficult to find in the literature examples conforming to Rouse's model. Even in the Southwest, where tree-ring dating has made such remarkable progress, it appears that dates are still insufficient for interregional correlation.[2] Therefore, present area chronologies in the New World do not scruple to employ any sort of correlation data that comes to hand—descriptive, distributional, or genetic. They are often dressed out to look like real chronologies by the addition of a few calendrical dates, usually guesses, marking off the "periods" on one side of the chart. These seldom date more than one of the phases that are correlated to form the "period," the correlation being really based on cultural similarity, horizon phenomena, trade objects, etc., and the well-worn assumption that these reflect contemporaneity. In other words, the correlations are not based on independent dating so much as the dating is based on the correlations. A casual glance through the literature of American archaeology of the past twenty-five years will reveal numerous examples of such charts. The Peru-Bolivian, or central Andean, area is especially well represented.[3] For Middle America it is also easy to cite similar chart presentations.[4]

Outstanding examples of area schemes that are virtually without benefit of dating are to be found in the southeastern United States. Here, owing to the failure of independent dating techniques to develop as rapidly as in some other areas, it has become a habit to equate widely separated archaeological units on strictly formal principles, and, whether as cause or effect, there prevails a sweeping assumption of synchrony of culture change throughout the area. Does culture *A* have plain fiber-tempered pottery? If so, it equates in time with culture *B*, which has plain fiber-tempered pot-

2. Wheat, 1954, p. 577.

3. Kroeber, 1944, p. 112; Willey, 1948a, p. 9; Bennett and Bird, 1949, p. 112. These are but a few samples.

4. Armillas, in Kroeber, 1948, p. 116; Kroeber, 1940, pp. 484–85; MacNeish, 1954b, p. 623; Wauchope, 1950; Sorenson, 1955, pp. 54–56.

tery. The possibility that the relationship may be genetic, and therefore not necessarily synchronous, is not entertained. We are so fond of this method of reasoning in the Southeast that we tend to ignore the few independent (radiocarbon) dates that we have. As a recent example, William H. Sears's excellent final report on excavations at the Kolomoki site in southwestern Georgia contains an elaborate correlation of southeastern sequences against a calendrical scale, but no radiocarbon dates appear on the chart, nor are they mentioned in the text.[5]

There is an unfortunate tendency in area chronologies of this culturally correlated variety for the periods to take on some of the characteristics of developmental stages. The larger the area, the more likely is this to happen. The best example in recent literature is the scheme for "Eastern United States" as set forth in the monumental Cole Anniversary Volume under the editorship of James B. Griffin.[6] The area, which takes in everything from the Plains to the Atlantic, is too large, in our opinion, for any practical archaeological purposes. Nevertheless, Griffin addresses himself to the heroic task of correlating hundreds of phases and cultures in this vast area into a succession of "culture periods," defined, as the term implies, both chronologically and culturally but necessarily in such broad terms as to be little more than general stages in the development of American culture. In some of the contributions to the volume, the terms "period," "culture," and "stage" are used interchangeably, depending on the exigencies of the moment. Deliverance from this kind of semantic ambiguity will come when current techniques of absolute dating have reached a point of such dependability that we can place a given unit within a temporal frame, on the one hand, and in a developmental sequence, on the other, without confusing the two operations.

We are forced to conclude that the pure area chronology based on distributional criteria alone is, in the New World at least, a

5. Sears, 1956, p. 80.
6. Griffin, 1952a.

presently unattainable ideal. But, with the rapid accumulation of radiocarbon and other types of independent dating now taking place, it is a certain possibility in the future. In the meantime we must be content with the sort of hybrid area schemes now in vogue. There is no harm in them so long as we are clear about how they are made and what they mean, but, when they lead us to think that we have discovered something about the way culture "works," it is time to be on guard. In any case, it will be entertaining to compare them with true area chronologies when these are available.

MAXIMUM UNITS: CULTURE

AND CIVILIZATION

We have tried to show that area chronologies express the spatial-temporal relationships between archaeological phases, while horizons and traditions express their culture-historical relationships. These are unquestionably their primary functions, but, on a more abstract level of interpretation, all these units and devices may be considered means by which the archaeologist gropes for the major segmentations of culture-history. There is clearly an irresistible urge to relate cultural forms to their largest possible contexts, expressed in the terms "culture" or "civilization" as used by students of culture-history when they are referring to events on a world-wide scale. We did not sufficiently take account of this urge in our first paper, which was conceived in terms of practicable archaeological methods and was not particularly concerned with ultimate ends. We found in the phase an operationally manageable unit, i.e., a unit small enough in spatial and temporal dimensions to be manipulated in area correlations and sequential schemes. Phases were to be related in larger culture-historical organizations by means of concepts such as the horizon and the tradition, but it was ruled that these were strictly integrative units and that the phases were not to lose their identity in these larger formulations. But the urge for totality was at work, with the result that the definition of one of these concepts, the tradition, was so broadly stated as to include the "full cultural tradition," which is, in effect, a self-sufficient archaeological unit more like the phase, with greatly amplified spatial and temporal dimensions, than like a mere device for expressing relationships, as advertised. In short, here was a serious contradiction, which we now find it necessary to remove.

The solution we have chosen has already been described: to cut back the concept of tradition to something like its original scope, taking from it the expanded connotation of "full cultural tradition" and returning that connotation to the unit concept of "culture" or "civilization," where it has always lodged. Thus, the phase remains the manageable unit; horizon and tradition remain the integrative units for expressing relationships between phases; culture and civilization, the maximum units reflecting the major segmentations of culture-history. In a strictly methodological context, and subject to the developmental relativism which applies to all unit concepts, culture and civilization can be treated as equivalents. As a somewhat arbitrary specification, however, applicable to the New World only, we suggest that "culture" be used to denote maximum units on all stages up to and including the Formative, reserving the term "civilization" for such units on the Classic and Postclassic stages.

THE SOCIAL ASPECTS OF ARCHAEOLOGICAL UNITS

We have described a number of archaeological unit concepts and discussed their working relationships, but we have allowed questions of their social meaning to accumulate in the belief that these can be more sensibly dealt with under a single heading. The task of finding social equivalents for archaeological units is beset by the most formidable difficulties, most of which stem from the fact that the kinds of data archaeology depends on are precisely those elements of culture that diffuse most readily across social and political boundaries. Consequently, we seldom experience the satisfaction of feeling that our units are coextensive, either spatially or temporally, with corresponding social units, even in the simplest and most explicit of archaeological situations. However, we must remind the reader that, according to our theoretical position, archaeological units are formulated on the descriptive level of organization with a view to their use on the explanatory level and, to qualify for the latter, must be intelligible in *both* the cultural and the social aspects of the behavior that is our subject matter. So we are obliged to keep in mind the possibility of social equivalents to our unit formulations, even when we cannot say with any degree of assurance what they are.

In the case of archaeological units of the smallest magnitude, however, we are on fairly solid ground. The social equivalent of the component is the "community," as defined by Murdock and others: "the maximal group of persons who normally reside together in a face-to-face association."[7] Murdock's three types of community— band, neighborhood, and village—manifest themselves archaeologically in the component, and it is even possible sometimes to tell which type is represented. So far, so good. The equivalent of phase, then, ought to be "society," and in a good many cases it probably is. The fact that, in practice, phases often consist of a single component need not disturb us; on the lower levels of cultural development the society likewise may consist of a single community. At the other end of the developmental scale, however, society becomes a larger concept, spatially at least, than phase. We shall return to this point presently in discussing the social aspect of our maximum units, culture and civilization. For the purposes of the immediate discussion, let us think of society in its minimal sense, as "a group of people acknowledging a single political authority, obedient to a single system of law, and in some degree organized to resist attack from other such societies."[8] How does this relate to the concept of phase? Logically the correspondence is reasonable. Such a society comprises a number of communities; the phase comprises a number of components; component equals community; therefore, phase equals society. Unfortunately, in practice it does not work. We have no means of knowing whether the com-

7. Murdock, 1949, p. 79.
8. M. A. Smith, 1955, p. 4.

ponents we group together into a phase are the same communities an ethnographer (supposing such a person happened to be on hand) would group into a society. We cannot be sure that the individual members of these communities would recognize themselves as belonging to the same "people." They might not even speak the same language. Ethnography offers abundant examples of different societies sharing a material culture that would be impossible to differentiate archaeologically. It would be only slightly more difficult to find examples in which the material culture of individual communities within a society diverged sufficiently to cause them to be classified archaeologically in separate phases. A frontier garrison community, organized specially for defense, might be a case in point.

More vexing, perhaps, are questions having to do with the stability of material and social culture through time, a dimension happily ignored by the ethnographer. We have laid down the rule that the temporal dimension of the phase must be kept within manageable limits, but this is admittedly in terms of the somewhat prodigal view of time held by the archaeologist. We are not forgetting that the life-span of our phases is ordinarily determined by the persistence of material traits which can be remarkably stable. Within such a span it is conceivable that social changes might be sufficient to enable our hypothetical ethnographer to speak of several societies. Conversely, under special conditions, even a primitive population may exhibit revolutionary changes in material culture without losing its identity as a society. We have abundant examples of this in recent colonial history.

In sum, it looks as though the present chances are against archaeological phases having much, if any, social reality, but this does not prevent us from maintaining that they can have and that in the meantime we may act as if they did have. We have already expressed a similar attitude in connection with artifact typology. Just as, with the inevitable refinement of archaeological techniques, it will become increasingly possible to define types in terms of social behavior, it will become likewise increasingly possible to define phases in terms of social structure. This possibility must be reckoned with, but it is not really the point of the present discussion. We do not maintain that every, or even any, specific phase is the archaeological expression of an extinct society. We simply call attention to the fact that there is a certain conceptual agreement between phase and society. Both are intelligible units of their respective fields of study. They have similar *roles* and similar *scales*, and in this crucial matter of scale both exhibit the same relativism with respect to the level of cultural development. This congruence, we contend, qualifies the phase as the intelligible unit of comparative study and, thus, offers the best hope of incorporating archaeology into general anthropological science.

The integrative units, horizon and tradition, because of their incomplete cultural content, cannot be regarded as self-sufficient in the cultural aspect; so there is an a priori case against their intelligibility in the social aspect. This is not equivalent to denying that they are socially transmitted. These units are the archaeological expressions of the processes of diffusion. They have come into existence in response to an awareness that particular forms and systems of forms—as distinct from whole, functioning, cultural units—flow through geographical space and time in a manner seemingly independent of the cultural matrices in which they are found. It is beside our purpose to investigate the mechanics of diffusion, or the question of how they may be detected in archaeology—a subject for a lengthy treatise in itself—but we suppose that in the main they operate through the agency of individuals or organized groups, such as trading companies, religious bodies, armies, and migrating populations, which, with the exception of the last, are not complete and self-sufficient social units. In general, therefore, horizons and traditions fail to meet the test of intelligibility in the social aspect, and no more need be said about them here.

When it comes to the social aspect of the maximum units, culture and civilization, we are on more difficult terrain. Here the problem of stage-relativism becomes acute. We have arbitrarily defined the culture as the maximum unit on all developmental stages up to and including the Formative. Even with this specification, there is still a tremendous variability in its connotations, both cultural and social. On the lowest stage, the Lithic, the term "culture" usually refers to single technologies or "assemblages" reflecting a similar economic adjustment shared by a large number of social groups. The content of such a "culture" is seldom sufficiently complete or physiognomic to suggest that a single homogeneous society is responsible. Put the other way around: on this level we are unable to infer the existence of social units large enough to be coextensive with these "cultures." It would perhaps be preferable to organize these incomplete data—all archaeological data are incomplete, but Lithic data are more so—in terms of phases and traditions, eschewing the term "culture" altogether. We do not really expect this wholesome suggestion to be followed, but, if we could at least eliminate "cultures" represented by a single type of projectile point, it would be progress in the right direction.

On the Archaic stages of development, the situation is a little different. Archaic phases are generally richer in cultural content; spatial and temporal dimensions tend to be smaller. It seems to be possible in some cases to organize the data into larger units than phases, for which the term culture stands without benefit of quotation marks. It is difficult to say, however, what the social equivalents of such cultures might have been. We have inferred elsewhere that social organization in the Archaic stage had not generally proceeded beyond the level of complexity represented by the tribe, but this is a gratuitous assumption that might not stand up under investigation. In short, it remains to be shown whether or not the unit, culture, is intelligible in the social aspect on the Archaic stage of development.

The Formative is by definition the stage of the appearance of new economic patterns, and these we assume to have been accompanied by the formation of societies of greater scale and complexity than existed theretofore. Ethnohistory furnishes examples in the numerous confederacies, and we have abundant evidence of the existence on this stage of religious and ceremonial organizations far exceeding in scope anything that could be represented by a phase in archaeology. This would seem to be the stage on which the unit, culture, becomes intelligible in the social aspect. However, it is difficult, even in an ethnohistoric context, to make satisfactory equations between archaeological and social units on this level of cultural development. In the case of the Iroquois Confederacy, for example, we can equate specific archaeological phases with the individual member tribes, but the unit "Iroquois culture" seems to have been shared by tribes that were not only outside the famous confederacy but in some cases not even affiliated linguistically. In a context that is largely prehistoric the difficulties are even greater. As a trial example we may consider the Coles Creek–Plaquemine culture, a Formative continuity in the lower Mississippi Valley lasting from about A.D. 900 to A.D. 1731 (date of the final dispersal of the Natchez tribe). We regard this as a unit because the elements of continuity from phase to phase seem to be stronger than the elements of change. Now what would be the social equivalent of such a continuity? Projecting back from ethnohistoric data, we know that there were several phases of this culture in the seventeenth century and that these phases pertain to discrete tribal groups, such as the Natchez, Taensa, Houma, Tunica, or Yazoo. There is no evidence that these tribes were united into a political federation. In fully prehistoric times it is possible that some sort of hegemony may have been imposed on these groups, but, if the pattern of opportunist warfare and ephemeral alliances that we see in historic times is any index to what happened earlier, it is inconceivable that any such hegemony could have embraced the full geographical range, or time span, of the Coles Creek–Plaquemine culture.

So far, in the discussion of possible equations between archaeological cultures and larger social units, our implicit definition of a social unit has been essentially a political one. We have also seen that it is extremely difficult to identify the correlates of political structure in an archaeological record. Leaving aside for the moment, then, the question of political forms, let us simply ask what kind of archaeological evidence might be indicative of larger social units. This, we feel, is the most fruitful starting point in the search for archaeological and social equations; and, in seeking evidence of this order, it is also our opinion that the Classic and Postclassic cultures of the New World offer more potentialities than the Formative.

One of the characteristics of Classic cultures in both Middle America and Peru is the possession of great art styles. These styles are symbolic systems. Their content and the contexts in which they are presented assure us that they permeated much of their cultural setting and that they were a part of the conscious awareness of the peoples of these cultures. For example, the recognition and appreciation of an art style like that of the lowland Maya imply a realization upon the part of the beholders that they are affiliated with other peoples who also recognize and believe in the symbolism of this same style. Such a sense of affiliation must necessarily have had social significance. It is difficult, perhaps impossible, to define the exact nature of the bonds giving coherence to such a social order or society in the large. They may, or may not, have been political. We have no definite knowledge about the ancient Maya political structure. Maya ceremonial centers from the Usumacinta to the Motagua may have been held together under a single authority, or each may have maintained a completely independent sovereignty. Religious ideology was undoubtedly one of the ties that held Maya society together. Not only does the art style suggest this, but widespread diffusion of uniform calendrical and hieroglyphic lore supports the interpretation. Yet the Maya bonds appear to have been more than the interchange of religious and astronomical ideas among a few priestly elite from the great centers or cities. Such may have been the mechanism of their original dissemination, but there are numerous signs that the ordinary Maya villagers who sustained the centers and the theocratic leadership also participated in, and had at least a peasant's understanding of, the ideas of the upper classes. These ideas, in so far as they were generally accepted, probably became much more than purely religious dogma. It is likely that they were assimilated into the values and beliefs of Maya peasant culture and that these values and beliefs were shared by Maya society in the same way that the art expressing these values was also shared by that society.

If we argue that stylistic unity may demonstrate social as well as cultural cohesion, for what other prehistoric American art styles can we build a case similar to that for the Maya? Teotihuacán? Zapotec (Monte Alban)? Mochica? Nazca? These four have the requisite qualities of greatness and pervasiveness. For each the imprint of the style is unmistakable, whether rendered in stone, pottery, wall painting, or textiles. Also, all four have the relatively tight territorial integrity which suggests a unity of a social kind. All four lack, however, those continuities into the ethnohistoric period that the Maya case possesses in some degree, and this makes it more difficult to be assured of common language, custom, and belief. What of the still older styles, Olmec and Chavín? For these the circumstances of remote antiquity and great geographic range lessen the possibility that the social dimension can ever be approximated. It may be, as has often been surmised, that Olmec and Chavín style occurrences, in their respective Middle American and Peruvian spheres, signify only religious, ideological, or cultist diffusions and that the ideas behind these styles never penetrated the receiving cultures to the extent that general values and beliefs were substantially modified. If so, there would be less reason to believe in the coherence and homogeneity of an Olmec or Chavín society. Perhaps these two styles represent an earlier stage in the civilizing process of social enlargement and homogenization that we have inferred for lowland Maya culture and society. To continue this same line of speculation, it is possible that such a horizon style as the Southern Cult of the southeastern United States is developmentally prototypical to Middle and South American great styles in the same way that southeastern Formative cultures are prototypical to the Mexican and Peruvian Classic civilizations.

Civilization has been characterized, both qualitatively and quantitatively, by Childe, Redfield, and others.[9] The chief requisites are city life with its concomitants of large population size and

9. Childe, 1946, pp. 82–105; Redfield, 1953; Braidwood, 1952.

density, formalized religions, class systems, craft specializations, the beginnings of codified learning and science, and great artistic traditions. Inferentially, it is our opinion that a consciousness of a larger social order is also a feature of civilization. In other words, the societal basis of a civilization differs from that of a culture, both quantitatively and qualitatively. In quantity, it is larger, it encompasses more people, it overrides community and tribal barriers. In quality, it demands beliefs in, and allegiances to, ideas and values that are abstract and remote from the individual and his tribal hearth.

The foregoing review of the various archaeological unit concepts in their social aspect has brought out several interesting but highly tentative possibilities. First, it appears that the basic units, component and phase, are theoretically capable of intelligibility in the social aspect on all the lower stages of development up through the Formative, but the difficulties of close equations are not to be minimized. Though the question of just what the social equivalents of these smaller units might be in the more highly organized Classic and Postclassic societies has not been investigated, it is nevertheless easy to foresee that the difficulties of doing so would be formidable. Second, while the integrative units, horizon and tradition, have been rather summarily dismissed because of apparent lack of completeness and self-sufficiency in both the cultural and the social aspects, this is a rather arbitrary exclusion which, needless to add, requires further investigation. Third, in testing rather more thoroughly the maximum units, culture and civilization, we seem to have stumbled upon a valuable insight which is at the same time a useful criterion for distinguishing between these units. For, while it has proved to be difficult to envisage any social equivalent for the culture, it appears that the really definitive characteristic of the civilization is that such a possible equivalent does exist.

Summary

In so far as the foregoing definitions and stated relationships can be formalized as a program for the integration of New World archaeological data on the descriptive level of organization, they may be summarized as follows:

1. The primary emphasis should continue to be placed on the formulation of basic units, component and phase, in local and regional sequences under stratigraphic control.

2. Phases should be studied intensively in their cultural and natural contexts.

3. Their external spatial and temporal dimensions should be kept within manageable limits of magnitude.

4. Their external relationships should be studied and expressed by means of the integrative units, horizon and tradition.

5. Large-scale integrating syntheses should be kept within the limits of the "area," as defined herein, and horizontal correlation of phases in such schemes should be effected so far as possible by means of independent extracultural data.

6. On the basis of these integrative studies, phases should be combined when possible to form the maximum units, culture and civilization.

7. Constant effort should be made to invest all units of whatever magnitude with the greatest possible intelligibility in both the cultural and the social aspects.

Part II

Historical-Developmental Interpretation

Chapter 3

The Historical-Developmental
Approach in American
Archaeology

TOWARD A SYNTHESIS OF NEW
WORLD PREHISTORY

Culture-historical integration, as we have seen, is the descriptive
process concerned with cultural forms, with plotting these forms
in space and time, and with defining their relationships and inferred
functions. There is, we think, common agreement that these are
archaeology's primary tasks, on the descriptive level of organization. It is with these tasks in mind that we have attempted to formu-
late intelligible archaeological "units" for study. The questions of
how such units may be named and defined and how they may be
related one to another are, we maintain, the foundation of theoretical formulations on the explanatory level of organization, i.e., in
the fields of culture-continuity and culture-change. Of the various
trial examinations and hypotheses that might be built upon this
foundation, a synthesis of New World archaeology as a whole is
one that falls short of the higher level of organization, occupying a
sort of gray borderland between description and explanation. The
historical-developmental interpretation presented in the following
pages is an attempt at such a synthesis.

We have already spoken of the tendency for large-scale area
chronologies to take on the characteristics of developmental
schemes. It might then be supposed that the difference between the

synthesis of an area and the synthesis of a continent, or a hemisphere, is just a matter of scale, but this does not seem to be the
case. Judging by the record, there seems to be a tacit agreement
among Americanists that, whereas archaeological reconstructions
of localities, regions, and areas may be treated in unified systems,
we are unable to extend these systems to continental or hemispheric
dimensions. This fact, in itself, is a highly interesting aspect of
New World culture-history. That the great American art styles
rarely, if ever, pass beyond the geographical limits of the areas of
their characterization is surely a key to cultural understanding.
Similarly, the relative scarcity of specific objects, "trade items,"
native to one area hearth and transmitted to another is a clue to the
areal isolation of New World cultures. What, then, is the nature
of the historical evidence that links the various American areas?

Let us narrow the question somewhat by asking which, if any,
of the large-scale unit concepts defined in the first part of this
study may be used to integrate archaeological data on an interareal
basis. Our so-called maximum units, *culture* and *civilization*, fail to
qualify, for the reason stated in the paragraph above. Archaeological areas in most cases owe their existence to previous formulations
of those maximum units with which their boundaries are, initially
at least, thought to be coterminous. Often, room has subsequently
to be made for other cultures and civilizations, and thus the areas
tend to be subdivided. Only rarely are they combined into larger
areas owing to a discovery of cultural distributions wider than first
supposed, and this again is a significant commentary on the isolable
nature of American cultures.

But what of the integrative units, *horizon* and *tradition?* The
horizon is characterized by its relatively limited time dimension and
its significant geographic spread. It is usually expressed by an art
style or a very specific complex of features of unmistakable historical uniqueness. As we have just noted, such phenomena do not frequently pass outside the major areas in which they originated. The
horizon clearly has little utility in multiple-area syntheses. What

then of the tradition? We have defined the tradition as "a (primarily) temporal continuity represented by persistent configurations in single technologies or other systems of related forms." Attention is called to the fact that, apart from the temporal factor—the essential characteristic of all traditions is persistence in time—this definition is extremely flexible. We were purposely vague about the behavior of traditions in the spatial dimension—and still are. Transmission of traditions through generations of people living in the same place is so obvious as to require no further comment, but how are they transmitted to other people living in other places? This is a question that is surely in need of further investigation. Does a tradition become diffused widely enough and rapidly enough to be usable as an integrating device in culture-historical schemes of larger than areal scope? American maize agriculture may be taken as an example of the sort of tradition we are talking about. It has distinctive content (*Zea mays* and its hybrids) as well as technical skills and utensils associated with its cultivation and preparation. Its tremendous spatial and temporal range in the New World makes it unsuitable for tracing out detailed interareal relationships; nevertheless it has an important historical unity. It is an American tradition whose diffusion has overridden areal boundaries and whose presence establishes common ties. Pressure flint-chipping and pottery-making are traditions of even broader scope, so broad as to be almost without historical significance. There are other traditions, however, whose range is more restricted and whose appearance might, therefore, be taken to indicate a higher degree of historical intimacy. The metallurgical techniques which extend from the south Andes northward to the southwestern United States furnish an example. They cross at least five major archaeological areas but are almost certainly a historical unit. The resist-dye painting of pottery (negative painting), the ceramic mold, curious and complex vessel forms such as the stirrup-mouth jar—all these are multiple-area phenomena, each presumably of single historical origin.

But can traditions, of whatever kind, be integrated into an effective historical system for the Americas as a whole? Horizons, as we have shown, enable us to equate local and regional phases in a reasonably precise spatial-temporal scheme for a particular area. Horizontal equivalence on the space-time chart means approximate contemporaneity. It might be supposed that traditions of the widespread sort referred to above would have a similar usefulness on a scale larger than that of the area, would operate in effect as superhorizons, but such does not appear to be the case. Maize agriculture, for example, did not commence at the same time, or even at approximately the same time, throughout its range of distribution; nor can the Peruvian and Mexican cire-perdue casting be established as contemporaneous. There is, in short, no device (except calendrical dating) by which cultures can be temporally equated on a continental or hemispheric scale. Traditions and horizons are, we repeat, the most effective units for the presentation and interpretation of intra-areal relationships, but this is the limit of successful spatial-temporal integration.

For larger syntheses, another type of formulation must be resorted to, one that is free from strict limitations of space and time yet has a general historical validity in the widest sense. The only possible kind of scheme that meets these requirements, so far as we can see, is a series of cultural stages in what we have chosen to call a historical-developmental sequence. These stages will of course be founded on common participation in important historically derived traditions, but their formulation is a procedure distinct from the methods of systematic historical (spatial-temporal) integration as laid down in the first part of this book. The historical-developmental sequence remains, however, as we shall attempt to demonstrate, essentially on the descriptive level of organization.

Possibly because of the strong reaction in this country against what is disdainfully referred to as "nineteenth-century evolutionism," overt developmental classifications are comparatively new in American archaeology. There were, however, perspicacious students who saw what was the true nature of area "chronologies" then current.[1] Such recognition is reflected in the increasing use of nomenclature emphasizing development, e.g., Frank Roberts' modification of the Pecos classification, using terms like "Developmental," "Great," and "Recessive Pueblo" in place of Roman numerals,[2] but these were still conceived as chronological periods, and archaeologists felt obliged to define them in strict calendrical terms. The Ford and Willey scheme for the eastern United States, published in 1941, was a succession of "stages" rather than periods, but these were based on "chronological profiles," and the style of the paper is narrative and historical.[3] James B. Griffin's slightly later synthesis of the same area showed no concern to differentiate between cultural development and chronology. "Successive *cultural stages* throughout the eastern United States can be erected on the basis of local stratigraphy, the interchange of specific cultural items and the common possession of definite cultural concepts at specific *chronological periods*."[4] The scheme put forward in the gigantic Cole Anniversary Volume, *Archeology of Eastern United States*, under Griffin's editorship, shows the same disinclination to differentiate between "stage" and "period." The terms are in fact interchangeable, as in this passage: "The description of these *periods* will emphasize a generalized cultural picture of the major features which characterize each of these *stages* by and large throughout the entire area."[5] About the same time, the authors of the first comprehensive textbook of North American archaeology organized the eastern data into four "chronological stages,"[6]

1. See Kluckhohn and Reiter, 1939, p. 159: "Probably the single fact of greatest general import which has emerged thus far from the Bc 50–51 excavations is that the various stages recognized by the Pecos Classification (and very commonly referred to as 'periods') do not, necessarily, represent separate and clear-cut time periods, *even in the same geographical locality*."

2. Roberts, 1936*b*, 1937.

3. Ford and Willey, 1941.

4. Griffin, 1946, p. 39. (Italics ours.)

5. Griffin's own contribution, "Culture Periods in Eastern United States Archeology," in Griffin, 1952*a*, p. 352. (Italics ours.)

6. Martin, Quimby, and Collier, 1947, p. 232.

thereby having it both ways. More developmental in terminology, and to a certain extent in implication, are a number of Middle American and Peruvian syntheses of more recent appearance.[7] With one exception, to which we shall presently return, these schemes are all on an areal scale and adhere to their supporting chronology more closely perhaps than the North American schemes just mentioned. Nevertheless, they show a new awareness of the possibility, not to say necessity, of distinguishing between stages in the development of cultures and archaeological periods. In his summary of the 1947 Conference on Peruvian Archaeology, at which a number of these syntheses were presented, Kroeber was impelled to say: "Another query that began to strike me as Bennett read his paper, and that kept recurring during our two days, was how far schemes of development like these also exemplify or imply general schemes of historic evolution of civilizations—the most famous and complete example, of course, being that of Toynbee."[8]

From the developmental standpoint, nearly all area schemes that have so far appeared are subject to the same difficulties. They have followed in the wake of archaeological chronologies and have found it impossible to break free of them. Their strength has derived largely from the supporting chronology, and this very fact has led to misunderstanding. Cultural development has a time dimension, but this dimension is not necessarily uniform for all localities or regions of an area. When stage and horizon (or period) lines are represented on a chart as straight and horizontal, confusion is inevitable. A similar difficulty arises when we attempt to extend developmental stages from one major area to another, except that within the area the time discrepancies probably will not be so great. Students of Andean and Middle American archaeology have rationalized the problem by insisting upon the homogeneity of the "area co-tradition" and by believing that developmental change will be more or less uniform throughout the area, with no re-

7. Armillas, 1948; W. C. Bennett, 1948; Larco Hoyle, 1948; Steward, 1948; Strong, 1948a; Willey, 1948a; Caso, 1953.

8. Kroeber, 1948, pp. 115–16.

gional retardations. This is an unlikely possibility, certainly not a demonstrated fact.[9]

The scheme for eastern North America, referred to above (Ford and Willey, 1941), employed stage lines rising obliquely from south to north, and, apart from the circumstance that some of these lines now appear to have been sloped the wrong way, it is likely that this conception better fits the facts of chronology and development. However, when all chronology is relative, as in this particular scheme, there are no firm landmarks for establishing relative rates of cultural change from region to region. This will be one of the important roles of true area chronologies based on independent dating.

When we shift from an areal to an interareal consideration of the New World data, we note that only two comprehensive developmental schemes have been formulated with recent archaeological evidence.[10] Julian Steward's "functional-developmental" classification of American high cultures is a scheme for equating the major developmental stages of Middle American and Andean civilizations. These equations are made on the basis of technology for the earlier stages and upon what might be called general configuration in development for the later. Although Steward's primary interest in this particular paper was the areas of American high cultures (or civilizations, as we have chosen to call them), his classification has much wider applicability. He defines six "periods" which are in effect developmental stages: (1) "Pre-agricultural"; (2) "Basic Agricultural Beginnings"; (3) "Basic or Inter-areal Developmental or Formative"; (4) "Regional Developmental or Formative"; (5) "Regional Florescent"; and (6) "Empire and Conquest." In a later article Steward proposes a similar classification of world-wide

9. Extension of the concept of area co-tradition to the North American Southwest by Martin and Rinaldo (1951) ran into immediate difficulties on this account. See critiques in Rouse, 1954; Willey, 1954.

10. Steward, 1948, and Krieger, 1953. Pedro Armillas has recently prepared a synthesis of New World culture-history for the "Program of History of the Americas" of the Pan-American Institute of Geography and History (MS of September, 1954).

scope. With some changes in terminology, and with a considerable expansion of later "eras," this revised scheme is basically the same as the first.[11] Steward, in effect, sees the following major stages (which he terms "eras") in the development of native American civilizations: first, a pre-agricultural hunting and gathering stage; second, the beginnings of agricultural experimentation; third, the establishment of agriculture and permanent village life with special ceremonial and political institutions; fourth, a climax of the agricultural pattern with resultant artistic and technical elaborations and the maximum development of "religious states"; and, fifth, the rise of urbanism, the secular state, and the formation of empires.

Alex Krieger has recently proposed a somewhat similar classification. At the International Symposium on Anthropology held by the Wenner-Gren Foundation in New York in 1952, he read an inventory paper on the archaeology of "Anglo-America," in which an immense amount of recent data was presented but without any formal chronological or developmental structure.[12] The latter he supplied in the discussion period in a statement, subsequently revised for publication, which not only presents the first adequate developmental scheme for North America as a whole but also contains the clearest discrimination between the concepts of stage and period that we have yet seen in print:

For present purposes, I will consider a "stage" to be a segment of a historical sequence in a given area, characterized by a dominating pattern of economic existence. The general economic life and outlines of social structure of past peoples can often be inferred from archaeological remains and can be related to similar phenomena, whether the dates are known or not.

11. Steward, 1949a. In this study the eras are listed as: (1) "Hunting and Gathering"; (2) "Incipient Agriculture"; (3) "Formative"; (4) "Regional Florescence"; (5) "Initial Conquest"; (6) "Dark Ages"; (7) "Cyclical Conquests"; (8) "Iron Age Culture"; and (9) "Industrial Revolution." Era 3 combines Periods 3 and 4 from the first classification. Era 4 is the same as Period 5 in the first classification. Eras 5, 6, and 7 parallel Period 6 of the first classification. Eras 8 and 9 are beyond the developmental range of New World civilizations.

12. Krieger, 1953.

The term "period," on the other hand, might be considered to depend upon chronology. Thus a stage may be recognized by content alone, and, in the event that accurate dates can be obtained for it in a given area, it could be said that the stage *here* existed during such-and-such a *period*. Further, the same stage may be said to appear at different times or periods in different areas and also to end at different times. A stage may also include several locally distinctive culture complexes and minor time divisions. A great deal of discussion is needed on these points.[13]

Krieger's scheme employs four major stage divisions: "Paleo-Indian";[14] "Food-gathering"; "Food-producing"; and "Urban Life." It will be noted that, although his main concern is still with "Anglo-America," i.e., North America north of Mexico, the classification is one that would accommodate Middle and South American data as well. His definitions parallel those of Steward rather closely. "Paleo-Indian" does not have any real counterpart in Steward's scheme, evidence of this order of antiquity in the high-culture areas being so slight at the time of Steward's formulation. Krieger's "Food-gathering" is approximately equal to Steward's "Pre-agricultural," with an overlap into "Basic Agricultural Beginnings" perhaps, depending on where one prefers to put the emphasis in cultures of mixed gathering–food-producing economy. Krieger's "Food-producing" would then take the rest of Steward's "Basic Agricultural Beginnings" and both his "Formative" stages, and Krieger himself has made it explicit that he would bracket Steward's "Regional Florescent" and "Empire and Conquest" together in the stage he has designated as "Urban Life."

A comparison of the two classifications brings out the somewhat different interests of the two classifiers. Steward was focusing his attention on the areas of "high civilization" in the New World. Krieger, while allowing for data of this type, was thinking in terms of the simpler cultures of North America. The discrepancy between his "Food-gathering" and Steward's "Basic Agricultural Beginnings" reflects this. Steward, with the Peruvian sequence data

13. Krieger, in Tax *et al.*, 1953, p. 247.

14. Krieger has recently proposed the term "Paleo-American" in place of "Paleo-Indian" (Suhm and Krieger, 1954, p. 15).

on the Huaca Prieta[15] premaize agriculturists in mind, conceived of this stage as a slow transition from hunting and gathering to agriculture. Krieger, to judge from his examples, was considering the California cultures and the Archaic cultures of the eastern United States as representative of the "Food-gathering" stage. Actually, either concept might accommodate both the South and the North American data. The Huaca Prieta culture of the Peruvian coast depended for food on gathering as well as on agriculture; and there is a reasonable possibility that some of the Archaic cultures of the eastern United States were experimenting with plant domestication.

To date, neither the Steward nor the Krieger scheme has been applied to New World data in complete detail. These authors may eventually do so. We make no claim that our effort here is a substitute for the particular interpretations of either. The ideas they have proposed, however, are of such wide and general interest to Americanists that additional points of view are desirable. In our previous paper we put forward our particular scheme and subjected it to a trial run by projecting a considerable amount of data against it. This we propose to repeat here with certain modifications that we will describe presently.

Before doing so, however, we think it necessary to enter the controversial domain of culture-evolutionary theory far enough at least to demonstrate our contention that ours is not an evolutionary scheme. In a paper written after the ones quoted above, Steward defined with considerable precision three evolutionary approaches in anthropology: unilinear, universal, and multilinear.[16] It does not seem necessary to support with long-winded arguments the statement that the developmental classification proposed in these pages conforms to neither of the two first-named approaches. The skeptical reader is advised to read Steward's paper, and if he still thinks that what we are describing is unilinear or universal evolution (as therein defined), then we have completely failed to explain what we

15. Bird, 1948a, 1948b.
16. Steward, 1953.

are about. Whether it be multilinear evolution is a more difficult question. In the general sense that we are concerned with a line of cultural development in one part of the world, while recognizing that there are other quite unrelated lines of development in other parts of the world, this might be called multilinear evolution.

But, if we understand Steward correctly, particularly his application of the theory in recent publications,[17] he is concerned with tracing multiple lines of evolutionary development leading to specific kinds of cultural features or whole cultures (his "culture types") wherever these may be found. His formulations are limited in scope, more so than ours perhaps, but they are universals in the sense that they are unrestricted geographically or chronologically. A "theocratic irrigation state" can be designated as such whether found in Peru or Mesopotamia, and the stages leading up to such a culture type—if truly parallel—are reflections of inherent cultural causality. Historical causality is important only in that it has to be eliminated from the equation. Thus, in terms of basic theory, as expounded in the introductory section of this book, Steward's multilinear evolution is on our explanatory level. We, on the other hand, as already hinted, are classifying cultures in a sort of theoretical twilight. Cultures A and B are classified as Archaic because they possess certain common denominators that we have chosen as criteria for that stage. Their common possession of these features may be the result of historical contact, environmental determination, homotaxis in a truly evolutionary sense, or any two or all three of these. In other words, the system, if it can be called a system, is not rigged to exclude any particular kind of explanation. This is why we have stated that, although it seems to lie outside the domain of culture-historical integration, above the descriptive level of organization, it cannot claim to operate on the explanatory level. This is also why we have chosen to call it "historical-developmental" interpretation, which sounds like a contradiction in terms but which expresses the fact that our stage concepts are not wholly abstracted from the historical matrix. Within the geographical

17. Steward *et al.*, 1955.

frame, large as it is, contact and diffusion may have played a larger role than set deterministic relationships within the province of culture alone. Man's biological and subcultural psychological and emotional reactions cannot be omitted from the equation, nor can the reality of the social groups in which he exists be denied its formative role. Environment and increases or decreases in size and distribution of population, reflected in cultural-ecological adaptations, are also significant factors exerting strong influences on the nature and direction of cultural change.

STAGE DEFINITIONS AND FORMULATIONS

In selecting criteria with which to define the stages of New World culture-history, it is obvious, from the foregoing review of the Steward and Krieger schemes, that there are but two broad divisions of a fundamental technological and economic nature: hunters-gatherers and agriculturists. This is analogous to the broad division in the Old World between the Paleolithic-Mesolithic stages, on the one hand, and the Neolithic and later stages, on the other. As in the Old World, these two general patterns of life have a sequence relationship, with the hunters-gatherers preceding the farmers. And, as is also the case in the Old World, there is a considerable chronological overlap, with hunting-gathering cultures persisting in some regions into periods of contemporaneity with farming cultures. It should be recognized that no other differentiation between stages with which we will deal has the same profundity and significance as this one. In this we are in agreement with Robert Braidwood[18] and Robert Redfield,[19] who see the Old World "urban revolution," or "dawn of civilization," as something that was made possible by the establishment of agriculture several millenniums earlier, but not as marking a technological and economic shift as profound as the one from food-gathering to food production. This point of view is reflected in our stage criteria and terminology. The criteria for dividing pre-agricultural stages are essen-

18. Braidwood, 1952.
19. Redfield, 1953.

tially technological. They refer to artifact types and traditions in technology. The criteria for dividing stages above the threshold of agriculture take reference in much more complex data. They pertain to social and political organization, religion, aesthetics—to the whole of what Redfield has termed the "moral order."

Our method of formulating stages was to review archaeological sequences from all parts of the New World in local and regional detail, on an area basis and with reference to cross-areal comparisons. Our first concern was to set up a series of trial stages by seeking for clues to generalization between areas. We drew generalizations, tested them by going back to primary sources on the regional and local levels, and thus came to recognize certain "common denominator" criteria for each of the stages. Needless to add, with a procedure of this kind, our trial stages and the criteria of definition changed constantly. This was true during preparation of the first published article,[20] and there is testimony to the fact that changes have continued in this present version. In 1955 we proposed six historical-developmental stages. We are now proposing five stages, with some changes in terminology and in criteria of definition. A quick comparison of the two schemes may be set down as follows:

1955	1957
Postclassic stage	Postclassic stage
Classic stage	Classic stage
Formative stage	Formative stage
Preformative stage	
Archaic stage	Archaic stage
Early Lithic stage	Lithic stage

The present "Lithic" corresponds almost exactly to the former "Early Lithic"; reasons for dropping the "early" will be given in the next chapter. The "Archaic" stage remains about the same, except for some modifications resulting from the elimination of the "Preformative." Phases and cultures formerly assigned to the "Preformative" have been divided between the "Archaic" and the

20. Willey and Phillips, 1955.

"Formative." Otherwise the "Formative," "Classic," and "Post-classic" are essentially unchanged in so far as archaeological content is concerned; in definition and emphasis upon criteria, there have been some changes.

Before we set forth our definitions of these stages, it may be well to consider briefly a difficulty that inheres in all developmental interpretation, to wit, the familiar problem of cultural lag. We have found it useful to differentiate between two kinds of lag situations: *belated* and *marginal*. The first is one in which a culture shows the essential characteristics of a given stage long after the time generally considered to be appropriate to that stage. This is in effect a temporal marginality, often referred to as a "late marginal situation." The second kind of situation, to which the term "marginal" applies primarily in a cultural sense, is one in which a culture shows significant characteristics of a given developmental stage in a configuration which, as a whole, fails to measure up to the definition of that stage. In the first, it is primarily a matter of persistence without change; in the second, it is a matter of change that, from the standpoint of the developmental criteria employed, is one-sided or incomplete. This second type of cultural, as opposed to merely temporal, marginality can also under certain conditions be the result of developmental regression, as we shall have many occasions to point out.

Marginal cultures are usually belated as well; so, in effect, the distinction we are trying to make is between cultures that are simply belated and those that are *both* belated and marginal, in the sense in which we are using these terms. Figure 2 is a very crude expression of the relationship, which may be clarified by the use of examples. Culture *A* in this figure is a belated Lithic culture, somewhat theoretical, it must be confessed, because our definition of Lithic is not so unrestricted temporally as some of the other stages. This would be a culture late enough to have received influences from Archaic (or later) stage cultures but sufficiently immune to such influences to permit us to classify it as Lithic without any qualifications beyond those implied in the term "belated." In simpler language, some Archaic elements may be present, but these are not sufficient to raise any classificatory difficulties. Certain late Lithic cultures in the North American Great Plains might be used as examples. Culture *B*, on the other hand, is marginal Archaic in the sense that it has incorporated sufficient Archaic elements to take it out of the Lithic category but not enough to qualify fully as an Archaic stage culture. Many, if not all, Plains Archaic cul-

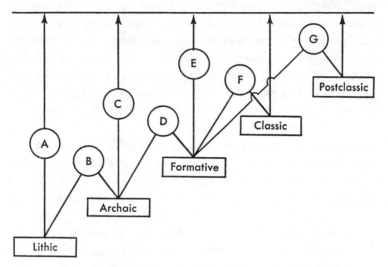

Fig. 2.—Belated and marginal cultures in relation to developmental stages

tures appear to be of this character. Culture *C* is a belated Archaic culture, and here we are on firm ground, for there are many examples available, some coming right down to very recent times. Most of the ethnographic cultures of the peripheral areas of North and South America could be classified as belated Archaic. Culture *D*, marginal Formative, is well illustrated by many of the Middle Woodland cultures of eastern North America, which received significant elements of the Formative Adena-Hopewell culture without profound modification of their essentially Archaic pattern. There are many marginal Formative cultures of the *regressive* type. Since Formative culture presupposes a stable economic base, usually agricultural, movement of cultures into areas unfavorable to that base or an unfavorable change of climate will often result in regression to an Archaic stage of development. Culture *E* on the diagram is belated Formative. This is the situation of many New World Formative cultures. Classic and Postclassic stage cultures are all so late that it does not add anything meaningful to distinguish some of them as belated, and so these are not shown on the diagram. Marginal Classic, *F* in the diagram, is well represented in lower Central America, in cultures such as Nicoya, Costa Rica, etc. Culture *G* is a rather special case intended to show that developmental marginality may, under certain conditions, "skip" a stage. An example is to be seen in the Quebrada de Humahuaca region of northwestern Argentina, where Inca influence operating on an essentially Formative level has produced a culture of marginal Postclassic type.

The point of this apparent hair-splitting is that a vast number of New World cultures are belated or marginal in the sense here given these terms, and in many cases their classification hinges on our ability to say which. There is probably no such thing as a pure belated culture, i.e., one that fails to show any elements of higher developmental stages whatever, and there is probably no such thing as a marginal culture that is not belated to some degree. So it usually comes down to the question of the number of developmentally significant elements and their relationships to the total configuration, which will in fact determine whether we classify a culture as a belated culture of a given stage or a marginal culture of a higher one. These qualifiers are designed to enable us to hedge on difficult classificatory decisions, and they will be used pretty freely in the pages to follow. This will perhaps contribute little in the way of culture-developmental understanding but will at least point up some of the difficulties of large-scale developmental interpretation.

The remaining pages of this book will be devoted to comprehensive definitions of the five stages enumerated above, to their identification, examination, and evaluation in terms of archaeological sequences and syntheses. Before we start this trial run, let us make it very clear that we are under no illusion that this is anything re-motely resembling a *natural* system. There is nothing inevitable about five stages; there might as well be four, or even eight. Nor is there any law, evolutionary or otherwise, that says that all New World cultures must pass through these stages one after the other in their proper order. We cannot even say, for example, that an Archaic stage culture will "in the natural course of events" pass on to the Formative stage. Whether or not it will do so depends on a multiplicity of factors, not all of which are in the domain of culture. As we have previously stated, our basic theoretical position is that culture is not an independent order of phenomena intelligible in terms of itself alone (the "cultural superorganic"), and from this it follows that there are no universal, irreversible processes of cultural development. We are not, in short, attempting to impose an evolu-tionary or any other kind of determinism on the data of New World archaeology. Nor can we accept the criticism that ours are not the "right" stages, if such criticism carries the implication that "right" stages are to be found. This attitude involves an important method-ological distinction between what we have called culture-historical integration and developmental interpretation, our present concern. The aim of the first was the organization of archaeological data in terms of a real world. However far short of attainment it falls, our object was the formulation of archaeological units that have (or rather had) a correspondent historical reality. It therefore seems possible that such units may be judged as to their "rightness." In developmental interpretation, on the other hand, we abstract, not only from the primary data but from the above-mentioned inte-grated units as well, certain characteristics that seem to have sig-nificance from the point of view of the general development of New World culture. In a general sense the sequence is historical as well as developmental, but the individual stages can have no correspond-ent historical unity or reality. Therefore the test of "rightness" is irrelevant. This also disposes of the idea that developmental stage formulations must not be "set" until we know all the archaeology—which will be never.

Finally, it is clearly impossible in the space available to survey the entire field of American archaeology. The most we can do is to sample liberally from all areas and periods in the hope that no significant block of data is overlooked altogether. It is not to be expected that the specialist in any area will be satisfied. We may plead in extenuation, however, that the purpose of our inquiry is not to effect a tight classification of New World cultures but to explore the possibilities of this kind of approach.

Chapter 4

Lithic Stage

DEFINITIONS

In our previous paper we designated and defined the earliest stage of American culture as "Early Lithic."[1] This stage was conceived of as embracing two major categories of stone technology: (1) unspecialized and largely unformulated core and flake industries, with percussion the dominant and perhaps only technique employed, and (2) industries exhibiting more advanced "blade" techniques of stoneworking, with specialized fluted or unfluted lanceolate points the most characteristic artifact types. At that time we hesitated to use this division as a basis for setting up two separate stages in our classification, because there seemed to be insufficient evidence of a time differential between them. The evidence is still inconclusive, although the case for a distinct and earlier core and flake stage is somewhat stronger than it was. We still adhere to our original decision to consider all these early evidences of man in America as a single stage, but we recognize the good possibility of an eventual division along the lines suggested above. In view of this possibility, we have modified our terminology and will refer hereinafter to this earliest New World stage simply as "Lithic," allowing for future separation into "upper" and "lower" Lithic stages, if such a course seems advisable.

"Lithic" is not entirely satisfactory as a name, but we have so far been unable to come up with anything better. Its sole merit is that the evidence on this stage is predominantly in the category of

1. Willey and Phillips, 1955, pp. 730–39.

stone technology (although there is an increasing number of early bone finds). The terms most commonly applied to this stage, "Paleo-Indian" or "Paleo-American," are open to a serious objection, in our view, in that they imply a grand twofold division of New World prehistory, with a "Neo-Indian" or "Neo-American" stage as a counterpoise. There *is* a grand twofold division, as we have shown, but the hinge comes later in the sequence, viz., between the Archaic and the Formative.

The Lithic stage cannot be defined without reference to geochronological considerations. Illogical as it may appear in a developmental scheme, we have to start with the flat assertion that the Lithic is the stage of adaptation by immigrant societies to the late glacial and early postglacial climatic and physiographic conditions in the New World. The effective working criteria are, therefore, associations of artifacts and other evidences of man's activity in geological deposits, or with plant and animal remains, reflecting these times and conditions. When types so established are found without such associations, which is more often the case, the relationships are inferred in the normal archaeological manner, with the result that an immense corpus of Lithic stage data is available in the literature but has not so far been subjected to effective integration and synthesis.

The nature of these finds has led to the assumption that the predominant economic activity in this stage was hunting, with major emphasis on large herbivores, including extinct Pleistocene forms, and that the general pattern of life, like that of the animals on which it depended, was migratory in the full sense of the word. The possibility of a measure of circularity entering into this assumption cannot be investigated here but certainly should not be ignored. In any case, upon this basis many American students have erected a simple historical and typological dichotomy: an early hunting stage followed by a gathering stage, each with its own characteristic technological traditions. In the present classification, although we have not been able to avoid this attractive simplification altogether, we will try to maintain a critical attitude toward it. An early non-agricultural society would presumably make the best possible use—within the limits of its culture—of whatever animal and vegetal resources were available; consequently, the relative importance of hunting and gathering would be a function of the ecological and technological balance in a particular place and time. Quite possibly, however, the natural conditions in the late glacial and early postglacial times postulated for the Lithic stage may actually have been more favorable generally to hunting than to gathering, and technological limitations (lack of milling techniques and implements?) may have contributed to tip the balance further. We would say, then, for purposes of definition, that the Lithic is pre-eminently a hunting stage, though other economic patterns were certainly present whose local dominance, under certain conditions, is not precluded.

Known details of culture in the Lithic stage are few. Lithic stone technology covers an immense range of rough- and chipped-stone traditions[2] but does not include the practice of grinding and polishing. Work in bone and horn is assumed to have been important, but the evidence has largely disappeared.[3] Settlement and habitation patterns were such as to leave few traces in the ground. Correlated with the absence of house remains is the scarcity of deep refuse deposits. Sociopolitical inferences for this stage are hazardous in the extreme. A small-scale kinship type of organization is postulated, but, within this generalization, great variability and a high degree of specialization must be allowed for. The data do not support the view that because Lithic cultures are relatively simple they are also uniform. Let us not forget that the major portions of both American continents were "pioneered" on this stage.

2. "Rough" refers to artifacts shaped by use rather than design; "chipped," to artifacts shaped by techniques ranging from crude percussion to controlled pressure flaking and fine-edge retouching.

3. Sufficient evidence of early bone finds has been summarized by Krieger (1951a; 1953, p. 242) and by Cotter (1954, p. 65) to suggest that, if conditions were more favorable for preservation, traditions of bone technology might rank with stone in the definition of Lithic stage culture.

Before considering the better-known Lithic cultures of the New World, we may as well first get the problem of the putative "lower" Lithic stage out of the way. There is considerable documentation for such a stage, but its evaluation is extremely difficult for the present writers, in whose fields of specialization stone technology plays a distinctly minor role. It seems to us that, if this is ever to be more than a theoretical stage in the development of American culture as a whole, certain questions have to be answered in the affirmative: (1) Have stone complexes of this nature been found unmixed in specific sites under controlled conditions? (2) Do they constitute true assemblages, i.e., can the possibility be ruled out that they represent only partial inventories of the total tool complex owing to special conditions? Tools from a quarry site or a butchering station, where only a segment of the total economic activity is represented, might be cases in point. (3) Finally, and most importantly, can it be shown that there is a time differential between these percussion industries and the more specialized industries that would be classed as "upper" Lithic if such a division were made? This does not mean, of course, that *all* percussion assemblages must be early but that some of them are is a minimum requirement.

The outstanding proponent among Americanists for this early percussion stage is Alex Krieger, who referred to some of the evidence in its favor in his paper at the International Symposium on Anthropology in 1952. More recently he summarized the evidence in greater detail at an informal meeting of American archaeologists held at Andover, Massachusetts, in April, 1956.[4] The finds regarded as significant by Krieger are briefly as follows: (1) Heavy percussion-flaked tools and sharpened bone splinters found at Tequisquiac in the Valley of Mexico in 1870, deep down in the Up-

---

4. We are grateful to Alex D. Krieger for allowing us to use this information and to Frederick Johnson, of the R. S. Peabody Foundation, who supplied us with a transcript of the meeting.

per Becerra formation only two feet above the *caliche* layer that separates it from the Lower Becerra—*caliche* estimated by geologists to be of mid-Wisconsin date.[5] (2) An obsidian flake, crude choppers and scrapers, and a split and pointed bone implement, from Tule Springs, Nevada.[6] Charcoal thought to be of human origin from this site was dated as older than 23,800 years.[7] Faunal associations included mammoth, horse, and (mostly) camel. (3) Worked bones including a bone tube from the famous Potter Creek Cave in northern California, excavated by paleontologists in 1870. The deposit contained an abundant middle to late Pleistocene fauna. After considerable controversy,[8] the finds were rejected as "water-worn bones," but they have been seen recently by Krieger, who declares them to be artifacts.[9] (4) Very crude chipped stones of *possible* human workmanship and a bone tube found with a rich late Pleistocene fauna in Friesenhahn Cave in south-central Texas.[10] The bone tube, found beneath the skeleton of a saber-toothed cat, is similar to the one from Potter Creek Cave and may, in Krieger's opinion, help to authenticate the otherwise dubious human origin of the stone objects. (5) Three rude sandstone heads found underneath twenty-six feet of gravel near Malakoff, Henderson County, Texas,[11] not generally accepted by archaeologists but believed by Krieger to be "probably" of human workmanship. If so, there is not much to be said for the skill of the workman. (6) Basin-shaped hearths on Santa Rosa Island, off the southern California coast, containing masses of split bones of dwarf mammoth but no un-

5. The artifacts are mentioned and illustrated in de Terra, 1949, pp. 46, 66, Pls. 9*f*, 10*b*. Radiocarbon dates earlier than 6000 B.C. have been obtained from the top few inches of the Upper Becerra formation; according to Krieger, the artifacts must be considerably older than this date.

6. Harrington, 1955.

7. Sample No. C-914 (Libby, 1954*b*).

8. For a selected bibliography of the dispute over the Potter Creek finds see Sellards, 1952, p. 123.

9. Krieger, 1953, p. 240.   10. Sellards, 1952, p. 94, Fig. 43.

11. Sellards, 1941; 1952, pp. 99–105, Fig. 47.

mistakable artifacts, which yielded a very early radiocarbon age of about 30,000 years (not yet published). A number of other finds of this putative pre–projectile-point category were rejected by Krieger because of uncertainty of their status as artifacts, lack of dating, or both. These include: G. F. Carter's La Jolla and San Diego finds;[12] the Imlay Channel finds in eastern Michigan;[13] the Black's Fork culture of southwestern Wyoming;[14] the Malpais industry of the Mohave Desert in southern California;[15] and the Death Valley finds in the same region.[16] This list might be extended to include the Albuquerque, Comanche Springs, and Rio Puerco finds in central New Mexico;[17] the Tolchaco complex of the Little Colorado River in Arizona;[18] and the Farmington complex in the foothills of the Sierra Nevada of central California.[19] It is manifestly unfair to list all these finds together without comment, as though they were all of equal standing. Some of them, especially the two last named, appear to be valid assemblages that are typologically "lower" Lithic, but confirmative evidence of early date is lacking.

Our timid conclusion is that none of the finds cited by Krieger, or those added by us, fully answers the requirements of the classificatory problem. Some of them indicate a strong probability of the presence of man on the North American continent at a considerably more remote period than the "end of the Pleistocene" usually attributed to the better-known "upper" Lithic cultures. But there is a possibility that these cultures, too, have to be pushed farther back into the past. Radiocarbon ages for the Sandia culture in excess of 20,000 years have been recently published though not generally credited.[20] Clovis, the earliest known culture sharing the fluted-point tradition, has not yet been satisfactorily dated, so far as the

12. Carter, 1949, 1950, 1952, 1954.

13. Baggerly, 1954.

14. Renaud, 1938, 1940.   17. Hibben, 1951.

15. M. J. Rogers, 1939.   18. Bartlett, 1942, 1943.

16. Clements and Clements, 1951.   19. Treganza, 1952.

20. Sample Nos. M-247, M-349 (Crane, 1956). Cf. p. 91, n. 47.

present writers are aware. A partial overlapping contemporaneity with Sandia is not an unreasonable hypothesis.[21] Even when this possibility is disregarded, however, and the temporal priority of the finds that Krieger has assembled is accepted, it nevertheless remains a fact that the evidence in the form of artifacts associated with these remote cultures is insufficient to support the assumption of a prior state of percussion technology. To be sure, there are no points or other artifacts that suggest a "higher" stage, but in no single instance among the datable occurrences is the artifact sample large enough to be conclusive.

One of the complications of this problem of dividing the Lithic into two stages is that, in the Greater Southwest and contiguous areas, where most of the early finds have been made, the percussive techniques and characteristic tool types seem to have persisted with little change (to our unpracticed eyes) and with continued dominance into cultures that we have classified on other grounds as Archaic. Thus, the precise classificatory difficulty is to distinguish between Archaic cultures and Lithic cultures that would be "lower" rather than "upper," if such a division were to be made. It is this, perhaps as much as the uncertainties of dating, that has kept us from making such a division.

We conclude, then, about as in our 1955 paper: The possibility of a "lower" Lithic stage of technology in the Americas remains an intriguing hypothesis. The case for temporal priority has grown stronger but remains to be proved, whereas persistence of such a percussion technology into post-Lithic times is more certain than ever. The general impression, from a world-wide standpoint, is one of marginal survival rather than technological regression, and we still feel that Linton's suggestion that the industries in question represent a belated survival of very early technological traditions distantly related to the lower Paleolithic cultures of Southeast Asia is an exciting possibility. Nevertheless, we are both unwilling

21. Compare the finds at the Lucy site, in central New Mexico, where Sandia points, including fluted examples, were found in the same "blowouts" with typical Clovis points (Roosa, 1956).

and unable to set up the "lower" Lithic as an independent stage in the present classification.

We move onto surer ground with the cultures that would be "upper" if a division of the Lithic were made. The best-known areas for finds on this stage are the central and southern North American High Plains and adjacent eastern foothills of the Rocky Mountains, home of a series of early cultures sometimes collectively referred to as Folsom-Yuma, on account of the highly specialized projectile points that bear those names. Available data consist of a few thin habitation sites, a larger number of game "kills" and butchering stations, and innumerable surface finds in "blowouts," where they are associated with other objects of all ages, and in isolated spots, without associations of any kind. The nature of the finds is such as to yield a fragmentary and incomplete view of the total archaeological culture and, except in one or two lucky instances, even of the total stone assemblage. The consequent emphasis on projectile points—the various types of which are used for identifying the "cultures"—and on knives, scrapers, and other tools supposedly used in butchering, skinning, and preparing skins, has undoubtedly resulted in a one-sided view expressed in the frequent designation "early hunting cultures."

The earliest cultures of this category are Clovis and Folsom, with their celebrated fluted projectile points and extinct faunal associations.[22] Clovis is not only stratigraphically older than Folsom[23] but is consistently associated with remains of mammoth and other Pleistocene fauna,[24] whereas Folsom is usually found with an ex-

22. The Folsom site in northeastern New Mexico will long be famous as the scene of the first association of human artifacts with remains of extinct fauna in an incontestable early postglacial geological context, probably the most important "breakthrough" in the history of American archaeology. See Cook, 1927; Figgins, 1927; Roberts, 1935, 1936a.

23. At Blackwater No. 1 site near Clovis in eastern New Mexico (Sellards, 1952, pp. 29–31).

24. Figgins, 1933; E. B. Howard et al., 1935; Sellards, 1952; Haury, 1953a; Roosa, 1956.

METHOD AND THEORY
IN AMERICAN ARCHAEOLOGY 86

tinct bison that differs only slightly from modern forms. Clovis points are more generalized in form and distribution; Folsom seems to represent a late climax of the fluted-point tradition that is confined to the Plains. The Folsom culture has been dated around 8000 B.C., a date which appears to be consistent with the geological and climatic conditions.[25] Since there is a rather complete shift in faunal associations between the two cultures, Clovis must be very considerably older. Thus we have to reckon with the possibility of a very early beginning and an immensely long time span for the fluted-point tradition in North America.[26]

Considerably more recent, but still on the Lithic stage, is the tradition of fine parallel flaking on points that used to be called Yuma but now are more often referred to as Eden-Scottsbluff. This culture, or cultures—it is difficult to apply consistent terminology to assemblages of which only the projectile points have been adequately described—is stratigraphically younger than Folsom,[27] and this relationship is to a certain extent confirmed by radiocarbon dates of 4000–5000 B.C.[28]

The older dichotomy between fluted and parallel-flaked traditions, expressed in the terms "Folsom" and (now largely super-

25. 7932 ± 350 B.C. at the Lubbock site in northwestern Texas (sample No. C-558 [Libby, 1951]).

26. An unexpectedly early radiocarbon date of 35000 B.C. plus for Clovis has been recently published (*Time* magazine, August 6, 1956, p. 42). This remarkable date was obtained by the Humble Oil Company laboratory on charcoal from a hearth at the Lewisville site, near Dallas, Texas. A typical Clovis point was found in close proximity to the hearth. Qualified archaeologists who have investigated the finds accept the association, but the date is altogether out of line with previous estimates, a consensus of which would give to Clovis an age of about 12,000 years.

27. At the Finley site in southwestern Wyoming (Moss *et al.*, 1951) and the MacHaffie site near Helena, Montana (Forbis and Sperry, 1952).

28. At the Horner site in northwestern Wyoming. Actual dates are 4925 ± 250 B.C. (sample No. C-302 [Arnold and Libby, 1951]) and 4966 ± 500 B.C. (sample No. C-795 [Libby, 1954a]). Scottsbluff-like points at the Ft. 41 and Ft. 50 sites in the Medicine Creek locality of Nebraska are dated considerably earlier, but the final report on the stratigraphy and association has not yet appeared (Schultz and Frankforter, 1948; Davis and Schultz, 1952; Davis, 1953).

seded) "Yuma," has given way before an increasing accumulation of typologically intermediate forms, which may have been intermediate in time also. We refer to various point types which at first were called "unfluted Folsom" because of their general resemblance to Clovis and Folsom in shape but which exhibit a flaking technique more like a crude approach to the fine parallel flaking of Eden-Scottsbluff. The best-documented points and "cultures" of this general intermediate category are: San Jon,[29] Plainview,[30] Long (or Angostura),[31] Portales,[32] and Milnesand.[33] A general continuity of these cultures with Clovis-Folsom, on the one hand, and Eden-Scottsbluff, on the other, is indicated by the other, less characteristic implements associated with these point types, which further suggests an intermediate temporal position, and the faunal associations and few available radiocarbon dates are in agreement.[34]

Thus we appear to have in the Great Plains an immensely long continuity of culture based primarily on the hunting of large mammals—from wholly extinct Pleistocene forms down to the modern bison—marked off into archaeological units mainly by changes in projectile-point forms. This obviously oversimplified picture masks an actual situation of great complexity that is in need of further organization.

Many of the point types referred to above, particularly those of the fluted-point tradition, have a near-continental distribution. The Clovis-like points have such general distribution that it is unsafe to specify any major unglaciated areas in North America where they are not found. They seem to be relatively scarce, however, on the Pacific Coast and in the nearby intermontane plateau and desert areas, and only doubtful specimens have been reported from Mexico and farther south. They also tend to diminish north-

29. Roberts, 1942.

30. Sellards, Evans, and Meade, 1947.   32. Sellards, 1952, pp. 72–74.

31. Hughes, 1949.   33. Sellards, 1955.

34. 5122 ± 300 B.C. for Plainview and Long (Angostura) points at the Allen site in southwestern South Dakota (sample No. C-604 [Libby, 1951]).

ward, a circumstance unfavorable to any theory of specific Asiatic origin. Perhaps the greatest total of fluted points have come from the Mississippi Valley and the East, but until fairly recently very little could be said about associated complexes. Now sites are being reported, and we can begin to speak of phases and cultures. In the Enterline culture of the Middle Atlantic subarea, we have Clovis-like fluted points and a complete stone assemblage with some characteristics that are not found in western fluted-point cultures.[35] The recently reported Bull Brook site near Ipswich, Massachusetts, shows relationships to both Enterline and Clovis along with individual features of its own.[36]. Some of the fluted points from Bull Brook are said to be practically indistinguishable from the points found inside the carcass of the Naco mammoth in faraway Arizona.[37] Fluted points from another New England site, the Reagan site in northwestern Vermont, show considerable variance from western norms, however.[38] An important center for surface finds, the lower Ohio Valley and Tennessee-Cumberland regions produced the first eastern fluted-point site, the Parrish site in western Kentucky,[39] and it seems possible that the well-known "Ohio" or "Cumberland" fluted point may be the marker type for another, as yet unformulated, culture which may also include recently discovered sites in northern Alabama.[40] It is commonly held by western archaeologists that the eastern distribution of the fluted-point tradition represents a belated extension of early western hunting societies forced out of the High Plains by the advent of arid conditions in the altithermal period. Since there are no extinct faunal associations and practically no dating of any kind for eastern fluted-point cultures, this theory is not directly refutable. However, the present trend of dating in the East is pushing the later Archaic stage

35. McCary, 1951; Witthoft, 1952.

36. Eldridge and Vacaro, 1952; Byers, 1954, 1955.

37. Byers, 1956, p. 9, citing personal communication from Emil Haury.

38. Ritchie, 1953.   39. Webb, 1951a.

40. Lewis and Kneberg, 1951; Lewis, 1953; Kleine, 1953; Soday, 1954; Mahan, 1954–55.

cultures back to a point that leaves little if any time for such a movement to have taken place.

Some of the point types that we have tentatively placed in an "intermediate" category, especially Plainview, also have been reported widely in the East, but, since the forms are more generalized, the nature of the relationship to their western counterparts continues to be questionable. Complaints of uncritical use of western point typology by eastern archaeologists usually have to do with this category of types. "Plainview" points, for example, have been reported from many sites and complexes in the East, often on the basis of superficial resemblances that may have no culture-historical significance whatever. The contexts are usually Archaic, which allows us to sidestep the problem momentarily.

Parallel-flaked points of Eden-Scottsbluff types are less often reported in the East. Their general distribution in North America seems to be more northerly than that of the earlier fluted-point types, which possibly reflects a northward drift of the early Plains hunting cultures and their quarry with the slow retreat of the late Wisconsin ice.

In the areas considered so far, most if not all of the early finds pertain to hunting cultures, and the relationship between hunters and gatherers is not a problem. On the other hand, when we turn to the Southwest and the contiguous Basin and California desert areas, we find an environment which, for a period that extends very far back into the past, fostered a gathering–small-game-hunting way of life, for which "Desert culture" is a commonly accepted term. For reasons that will appear later, we have relegated the Desert cultures en bloc to the Archaic stage, even though some of them show evidences, including radiocarbon dates, of comparable antiquity to Folsom and other Lithic cultures of the Plains. In the Southwest proper, the best-known Desert culture is the Cochise.[41] In our first paper we classified the earliest phase of Cochise, the Sulphur Spring "stage," as Early Lithic because of its extinct faunal associations and what at that time we regarded as early radio-

41. Sayles and Antevs, 1941.

carbon dates.[42] These dates are no longer too early for Archaic, and there is even some question about the association of the extinct fauna.[43] Furthermore, projectile points, formerly thought to be non-existent in Sulphur Spring, have since turned up in subsequent excavations, and these are the same Pinto-like points that occur in the later Chiricahua phase.[44] It appears that, notwithstanding the time gap indicated by carbon 14 dating between Sulphur Spring and Chiricahua—which is certainly Archaic—the continuity in artifact types is more pronounced than the differences.

That there is an indisputable Lithic stage in the Southwest, however, and that it is chronologically early is evidenced by the remains of hunting cultures similar to, and in some cases specifically related to, the "upper" Lithic cultures of the Plains and the East. Perhaps the earliest is the Sandia culture, first encountered in a cave in the Sandia Mountains near Albuquerque, New Mexico.[45] This culture, with its characteristic asymmetrically stemmed (Solutrian-like) points, was associated in the lower levels of the cave with a rich Pleistocene fauna in a geological context estimated by an eminently qualified geologist to be of Wisconsin interstadial age,[46] and was stratigraphically overlain by younger deposits containing a late Folsom or an "intermediate" stone complex that also had extinct faunal associations. Radiocarbon ages of over 20,000 years for mammoth ivory from the Sandia level have been recently published,[47] but, notwithstanding these combined evidences of high antiquity, the temporal position of Sandia is still in question.[48]

42. Dates for Sulphur Spring Cochise are: 5805 ± 370 B.C. and 4259 ± 450 B.C. (sample Nos. C-216 and C-511 [Arnold and Libby, 1951]).

43. Information by J. Charles Kelley given at the Radiocarbon Conference, Andover, October, 1956.

44. E. B. Sayles (verbal communication, 1955).

45. Hibben, 1937, 1941.   46. Bryan, in Hibben, 1941.

47. Sample Nos. M-247, M-349 (Crane, 1956). For an impression of the uncertainty surrounding these important dates see Hibben, 1955, and Crane, 1955.

48. Johnson, n.d.

Recent evidence from the Lucy site in central New Mexico suggests Sandia's possible overlapping contemporaneity with Clovis, Sandia's principal rival for the distinction of being the oldest projectile-point-bearing culture in the Americas.[49] From the standpoint of continental distribution, however, Sandia has proved a disappointment. Unlike Clovis and Folsom points (particularly the former), which, once properly recognized and defined, turned up in great numbers all over the country, Sandia points are still extremely rare, and occurrences outside the type locality are typologically dubious.[50]

Other evidences that the Southwest was not lacking in early hunting cultures classifiable as Lithic were found in the lower level of Ventana Cave in south-central Arizona—a somewhat impoverished Folsom-like culture with abundant extinct faunal associations, in a "humid" deposit referable to one of the later substages of the Wisconsin glaciation[51]—and in a large number of surface finds more specifically related to the Lithic cultures of the Plains.[52] More spectacular was the discovery of typical Clovis points inside the carcass of a mammoth at Naco in southwestern Arizona.[53] It has been suggested that such finds may reflect a seasonal hunting aspect of cultures which in their entirety would conform to the prevailing Desert pattern.[54] If true, this would be very embarrassing, because we would be found to have classified two activities of the same culture in separate developmental stages. As a hypothesis

49. Roosa, 1956.

50. Hibben, 1946; Wormington, 1949, p. 75. The difficulty of identification is that asymmetrically stemmed points or "knives" are found in many North American stone assemblages of various ages. Within the range of variability of this class of artifacts, individual specimens might easily approximate the Sandia type without any culture-historical significance. See M. W. Hill, 1953, Ritchie, 1953, Kleine, 1953, and Lewis, 1954b, for examples that come close to Sandia forms. There is also an early(?) Archaic lozenge-shaped point that tends to look like Sandia.

51. Haury et al., 1950.

52. Hurt, 1942; Haynes, 1955.

53. Haury, 1953a.   54. Cressman, 1951, p. 294; Haury, 1953a, p. 13.

it cannot be ignored; in a transitional phase like Sulphur Spring Cochise it might be a reasonable expectation. However, the present trend of dating appears to support the contrary view—that the finds really do pertain to an earlier, predominantly hunting stage of culture in the Southwest.

In a brief summary of our discussion of the Lithic stage thus far, the following points may be emphasized: (1) The principal stage criteria are rough- and chipped-stone artifacts. (2) The natural context is that of the late glacial and early postglacial environments of the New World. (3) The areas where these evidences are most complete are western North America, particularly the High Plains and the Southwest. (4) Two major technological traditions, or groups of traditions, are postulated: one characterized by pressure flaking and lanceolate blades, the other by percussion chipping and crude choppers and scrapers. (5) There are indications that the percussion chopper-scraper traditions may have earlier beginnings than the pressure-flaked-blade traditions, but this remains to be demonstrated as a fact. There is certainly good evidence that the two existed contemporaneously for a long time. (6) The pressure-flaked-blade traditions are clearly best adapted to the ancient grassland environment of the Plains and the East and to the hunting of large mammals now extinct, whereas the percussion chopper-scraper traditions seem more at home in the semiarid environments of the Greater Southwest, where they are associated with gathering economies. This is not an iron-clad separation, however, and in some instances both may be exemplified in the archaeological assemblage of a single culture. (7) It should be understood that both groups of traditions, the early forms of which are markers for the Lithic stage, show continuity into later cultures of the succeeding Archaic stage. This is particularly true of the percussion chopper-scraper traditions, which carry on into the Archaic Desert cultures of the Greater Southwest.

So far we have drawn examples from Lithic stage cultures in the Southwest and the Plains, with a brief side glance at the East. There are in the rest of North America, so far as we can see, no other Lithic cultures of comparable ponderability to Clovis, Folsom, Enterline, and Eden-Scottsbluff. A long catalogue of widely scattered finds of artifact types related to these better-known cultures could be compiled, but it would not add anything but distribution to the picture already given. The balance of our survey of the North American Lithic can be taken at a swifter pace.

The Great Basin area, comprising western Utah, all of Nevada, south-central Oregon, and large portions of southern California, has produced as many chronologically early finds as any other area of comparable size in the New World, but, for reasons which we hope will appear to be sound, we are putting most of them into the Archaic. The precise difficulty is that many sites with early radiocarbon dates show a dependence on gathering from the lowest levels on, with hunting in a secondary role and no remains of extinct Pleistocene fauna. If the dates are correct, the shift to modern conditions must have taken place earlier in the Great Basin than in other areas so far considered.[55] Extinct faunal remains have been found, however, in sites on the peripheries of the area. On the northern periphery, in south-central Oregon, at Paisley Five Mile Point, food bones in the lowest level of a cave included horse and camel, but there were no diagnostic artifacts in association.[56] At Lower Klamath Lake, in the same region but just over the California line, horse, camel, and probably mammoth were found, the last in direct association with fragmentary obsidian tools of indeterminate type. Not *in situ*, but believed to have come from the same geological deposit, were several beveled-bone foreshafts similar to the one found at Clovis, New Mexico, possibly a marker type of the Clovis culture. Unfortunately, manos and post–Lithic-type projectile points were also in this deposit.[57] No fluted or other Lithic stone types were found in either of these sites. On the southern periphery of the Great Basin, at Gypsum Cave in southeastern Nevada, ground sloth and possibly horse and camel were found in association with an artifact complex whose characteristic

55. Jennings and Norbeck, 1955, p. 4.
56. Cressman *et al.*, 1942, p. 93.   57. *Ibid.*, pp. 99–100.

"Gypsum point" is one of the marker types for the Archaic.[58] The problem of Gypsum Cave is aggravated by early radiocarbon dates well within the range of time assumed for the Lithic,[59] but we cannot regard the culture as anything but Archaic in terms of the definitions used here.

Other finds in the extreme southern part of the Great Basin and contiguous lower Colorado River and southern California desert and coastal regions confront the would-be classifier with even more vexing problems, but some of the cultures involved appear to be Lithic and cannot be overlooked. The San Dieguito–Playa (or San Dieguito I) culture seems to reflect a hunting pattern, notwithstanding its lack of characteristic point types,[60] and its close relationship with the Ventana culture indicates a date that would satisfy the chronological requirements of the Lithic stage.[61] In the Lake Mohave complex (which includes too many types for comfort) the San Dieguito–Playa percussion choppers, planes, scrapers, etc., are associated with points vaguely reminiscent of Sandia, Clovis, San Jon, and Plainview.[62] The Mohave and Silver Lake points have wide distribution but are not consistent or stable in their association.[63] An almost complete lack of milling stones in the Lake Mohave sites indicates a primarily hunting culture, and there is a good possibility that some, but certainly not all, of the material is early enough to qualify as Lithic.[64] A site subsequently reported by the same investigators, the location of which was not specified but was presumably in the same region, revealed a "pure" Folsom-like complex with rather striking similarities to Lindenmeier in

58. Harrington, 1933, 1934.

59. Dung of giant sloth from Gypsum Cave was dated at 8504 ± 340 B.C. and 6576 ± 250 B.C. (sample Nos. C-221, C-222 [Arnold and Libby, 1951]), but the association of dung and artifacts is not beyond question (Heizer, 1951a, p. 24; Cressman, 1951, p. 306).

60. M. J. Rogers, 1939.

61. Haury et al., 1950, p. 531.

62. E. W. C. Campbell et al., 1937.

63. Wormington, 1949, p. 85.   64. Brainerd, 1953.

artifacts other than points.[65] This, on typological grounds alone, we would classify as Lithic.

The relative infrequency of remains attributable to the Lithic stage on the Pacific Coast of North America appears to confirm the widely held assumption that early migration southward from Alaska was mainly in the intermontane and High Plains "corridors" on either side of the Rocky Mountains. Estimates of considerable antiquity have been made for the earlier manifestations of the La Jolla culture[66] and the Topanga culture,[67] of the San Diego and Los Angeles regions, respectively. The lowest level in the sequence at Malaga Cove, also in the Los Angeles region,[68] has been compared to Rogers' Dieguito and is thought to be early, but it includes a microlithic "flake drill" type that is remarkably similar to the characteristic "perforators" of the Poverty Point culture of the lower Mississippi Valley on a late Archaic or even Formative level.[69] The enigmatic Oak Grove culture of the Santa Barbara region[70] is also difficult to fit into our definition of Lithic. The four last-named cultures have been recently gathered together, along with material from the Little Sycamore site in Ventura County, under the designation "Early Milling Stone Cultures of Southern California" and have been assigned a guess date of 3000–2500 B.C.[71] This convenient generalization has encouraged us to put them all into the Archaic stage.

Farther north, in central California, well-developed sequences in the San Francisco Bay and Sacramento Delta regions have no Lithic phases; the earliest cultures are clearly Archaic in terms of the definitions used here. The Farmington complex has already been mentioned as a possible "lower" Lithic stage culture, but there is no dating to support the assumption. North of San Francisco Bay,

65. Campbell and Campbell, 1940.

66. M. J. Rogers, 1929, 1945; Harding, 1951; information given by Clement Meighan at the Andover Radiocarbon Conference of April, 1956.

67. Heizer and Lemert, 1947; Treganza and Malamud, 1950.

68. E. F. Walker, 1951.   70. D. B. Rogers, 1929.

69. Ford, Phillips, and Haag, 1955.   71. Wallace, 1954.

at the controversial Borax Lake site,[72] there seems to have been an early component that included rather dubious fluted points and Lindenmeier-like scrapers and gravers, but, if this existed as a complex, it was not clearly differentiated stratigraphically from a culture more like the milling-stone cultures referred to above. In view of this uncertainty, it would seem preferable to classify all of Borax Lake as Archaic.

From here on up the Pacific Coast, our sources of information on the Lithic diminish rapidly. In the northern California, Northwest Coast, and Plateau areas, finds attributable to the Lithic are very scarce, partly because of ignorance no doubt, partly because we are getting farther away from the bases of our criteria and are unable to recognize Lithic materials when we see them. A few possibly early sites have been reported but in no case fully published.[73] North Pacific archaeology is clearly not well enough known to permit generalization; nevertheless, it may be suggested that this is an area quite unsuited in nature to the migratory hunting-and-collecting way of life characteristic of Lithic cultures elsewhere.

This brings us to the Arctic. We can hardly expect to fit Arctic data into our scheme of classification without difficulty. As one of the outstanding Arctic specialists has recently said: "The pattern and development of Eskimo culture are the result of a combination of geographical, ecological and cultural factors that are truly unique."[74] This would apply equally to any cultural pattern in the Arctic, since the unique geographical conditions can be projected indefinitely into the past, and with them the special cultural adjust-

72. Harrington, 1948*b*.

73. The Lind Coulee site in eastern Washington may have a Lithic phase ("Notes and News," *American Antiquity*, **16**, 290; **17**, 281; **18**, 189, 297). A date of 6746 ± 400 B.C. (sample No. C-827 [Libby, 1954*b*]) certainly indicates that kind of occupation. Three fluted points found some time ago in Oregon and Washington have recently been identified as Clovis in type (*American Antiquity*, **21**, 451). In British Columbia a very good Eden-Scottsbluff point was recently received by the Provincial Museum, purportedly from the vicinity of Lake Windermere (Duff and Borden, 1954).

74. Collins, 1953*b*, p. 201.

ments required to make life endurable in such an environment. Apart from marginal phases of Indian cultures whose centers lie farther south, no major cultural configuration other than Eskimo has been conclusively shown to have occupied the area. The only culture that might represent a pre-Eskimo configuration is the well-known Denbigh "flint complex" first encountered at the Iyatayet site on the north Bering Sea coast of Alaska.[75] Denbigh shows connections of a tenuous nature with late Lithic stage cultures of the Plains, but its more significant affiliations appear to be with eastern Siberian cultures that are variously regarded as Mesolithic or Neolithic. The latter are assumed to be the source of the burin and microcore-and-blade ("polyhedral core and lamellar flake") traditions so characteristic of the Denbigh complex. These Mesolithic traditions, particularly the microcore-and-blade technique, are widely but erratically distributed in northern and eastern North America on a time level that is by no means early. The single fluted point from the Iyatayet site is a poor example that cannot be classified with any established type, but the fine parallel-flaked points would seem to be typologically related to the Eden-Scottsbluff culture of the Plains. Radiocarbon dates for the Denbigh level at Iyatayet, however, are considerably later than those for Eden-Scottsbluff.[76] This lends support to Henry Collins' belief that further information about the non-lithic aspects will bring out the essential Eskimo character of the Denbigh culture.

No other complex that might be considered Lithic has yet been

75. Giddings, 1951, 1952.

76. Radiocarbon dates for the Denbigh level at Iyatayet are: 1546 ± 230 B.C. and 2705 ± 220 B.C. (sample No. C-792 and C-793 [Libby, 1954a]). Giddings, who collected the samples, declined to accept the dates and adhered to his original estimate of 8,500 years ago (1955, p. 376). A good deal has been made of the date of 4042 ± 280 B.C. (sample No. C-560 [Libby, 1951]) obtained from a sample of twigs from the lower level of the Trail Creek Cave on Seward Peninsula which also contained Denbigh type material. According to Helge Larsen, who excavated the cave, these twigs could not be positively associated with the Denbigh artifacts and might even have been brought into the cave by hibernating bears (statement made at the Andover Radiocarbon Conference, October, 1956).

reported in the Arctic area. A few scattered fluted points have bee reported from various localities in Alaska, but most are without associations and reliable dating criteria.[77] The general impression is that they are relatively late and marginal to the main centers of the fluted-point tradition farther south. 'In the Canadian subarctic, an area of extreme difficulty for archaeology, the Yukon and Mackenzie valleys are crucial because they are the most likely diffusion routes in the Lithic stage. A few significant finds have been made,[78] but, in so far as they can be related to Lithic traditions elsewhere, they seem to be relatively late in the scheme of things. We have to conclude that remains pertaining to the earliest immigrants from Asia either have not been found or, if found, have not yet been recognized. The origins of Lithic cultures in North America are still completely obscure.

MIDDLE AND SOUTH AMERICA

We can, therefore, hardly expect clarification of the problem of Lithic origins in Middle and South America. Any theory of population-spread into these areas must assume north-to-south movements of peoples and cultures in a Lithic stage of development. In Middle America there is now ample confirmation of the presence of man with extinct fauna, including mammoth, in upper Pleistocene formations in the Valley of Mexico, but the associated artifact assemblages are incomplete and the relationships with North American Lithic cultures remain to be worked out. The San Juan "industry" of Helmut de Terra, consisting of ten artifacts from three sites,[79] has received some slight reinforcement from finds associated with the two Iztapan mammoths, among them three classifiable points, of the Eden-Scottsbluff, Angostura, and Lerma types, respectively.[80] The fact that these types are relatively late and heretofore not associated with mammoth may indicate that the

77. Hibben, 1943; Solecki, 1951; Collins, 1953b.

78. Johnson, 1946; MacNeish, 1951, 1953, 1954a.

79. De Terra, 1949.

80. Aveleyra and Maldonado-Koerdell, 1953; Aveleyra, 1956.

mammoth survived in central Mexico long after its extinction in the United States. It may also give slight additional meaning to the fact that good fluted points have not so far been found south of Durango. The poor example from Costa Rica is of doubtful significance.[81] Another important evidence of Lithic stage culture in Mexico is to be seen in the Canyon del Diablo sequence of southern Tamaulipas,[82] of which the first two phases, Diablo and Lerma, are said to represent hunting cultures; but the material has not yet been thoroughly described, and comparisons with Lithic material north of the border cannot be made. The occurrence of a Lerma point with the second Iztapan mammoth, referred to above, is a strong indication that both Diablo and Lerma belong in the Lithic stage. From Mexico on south through the Maya area and lower Central America, scattered and isolated evidences of man's presence in late glacial or early postglacial times could be cited, but they do not add up to anything of cultural significance and may be omitted here.

Identification of Lithic remains in South America is beset with difficulties. Technological similarities between North American Lithic traditions and those presumed to be of comparable date in South America are, for the most part, of a very general kind. An even greater source of trouble is the limited geological and paleontological criteria for temporal equation with North American Lithic cultures. Nevertheless, there are a number of finds in South America that may be considered relevant. One of the best-substantiated claims for a South American Lithic stage is to be found in the Magellanic sequence.[83] The lowest level, Period 1, in the Palli Aike and Fell's caves on the north side of the Straits, contained, along with remains of horse and sloth, pressure-flaked points of ovate triangular shape with broad tapering stems, a single unstemmed Plainview-like point, crude chopping tools, bone flakers and awls, and some rude disk-shaped pieces of lava. Bird's original

81. Swanger and Mayer-Oakes, 1952.

82. MacNeish, 1950.

83. Bird, 1938.

modest estimate of 1000–3400 B.C. for this culture has been considerably extended by a radiocarbon date of 6688 ± 450 B.C.[84]

Other researches into the problem of early man in the southern part of the South American continent may be compared and contrasted with the Palli Aike and Fell's caves Period 1 discoveries. In some instances there are indications of even earlier materials. M. A. Vignati's stratigraphy on the Argentine coast of Tierra del Fuego[85] reveals a three-part sequence in which the earliest phase has only retouched cores and flakes or bifacial percussion-flaked blades and choppers. In the second level, he recovered a "knife" or point similar to those of Bird's Period 3, and in the third, or top, cultural layer there was a point similar to those of Bird's Period 4.[86] It is to be noted, however, that crude bolas stones are found even in the first period of the Vignati sequence.[87] Along the Atlantic coast of Patagonia, Menghin has correlated site occupations with a series of rising coast lines and has defined an earlier Oliviense complex, characterized by retouched flakes and scrapers, and a later Solanense complex, featuring single-notched-base projectile points.[88] Geological dating here suggests that both these complexes antedate Bird's Period 1. Menghin has also described Patagonian cave stratigraphies the lowest levels of which (Toldense complex) appear to correlate with Palli Aike–Fell Period 1, on the basis of lanceolate Plainview-like points, though they include also crude bolas stones.[89] The upper levels in these same caves (Casapadrense complex) resemble Bird's Period 2 at Palli Aike in the absence of stone points and the presence of numerous bone implements along with crudely retouched scrapers and blades. This order, of course, tends to reverse the percussion chopper to pressure-flaked point

84. Sample No. C-485 (Libby, 1952).   85. Vignati, 1927.

86. This last identification was made by Bird (personal communication, 1956).

87. It is interesting to note that the rude percussion industries of southern and Baja California have "charmstones" which may also have been bolas stones, although the similarities to South American types are not close.

88. Menghin, 1952b.   89. Menghin, 1952a, 1952b.

("lower" to "upper" Lithic) sequence. This Casapadrense phase is dated, in relation to volcanic activity in the region, as subsequent to 6000 B.C. It appears to relate to a somewhat similar phase (Tandilense) in Buenos Aires Province.[90]

Possibly within the range of our Lithic definition is the Ayampitín phase of the Córdoba and San Luis hills in northwestern Argentina. Here A. R. González has obtained a stratigraphy at the Gruta de Intihuasi in which the Ayampitín assemblage, with its lanceolate points and crude grinding utensils, underlies the later, Archaic-like Ongamira phase. The Ayampitín projectile points are closest to Bird's Period 3, but the radiocarbon dating supports a Lithic assignment.[91]

We cannot leave Argentina without commenting on Ameghino's claims for the antiquity of man in Buenos Aires Province.[92] The geological basis for these claims of what seems an excessive age is still in dispute, and the characteristic artifacts, battered and splintered pebbles suggestive of crude hand-ax or chopper forms, have uncertain associations. In some of Ameghino's sites they seem to have been found with pressure-flaked points, grinding stones, and even pottery. Bird has reported similar implements from northern Chile in contexts that are relatively late.[93]

In Brazil the artifacts associated with the longheaded Lagoa Santa skeletal type,[94] also found in some of the *sambaquís* of the southern coast,[95] have been considered relevant to the problem of early man's presence in South America, but we have relegated them to the Archaic stage for reasons given in the next chapter.

From the great corpus of archaeological data pertaining to Peru and Bolivia, few finds could conceivably be on the Lithic stage. The only possibilities that might be mentioned are: (1) the long

90. Menghin and Bormida, 1950.

91. González, 1952. A recent radiocarbon date on the Ayampitín phase is in the neighborhood of 6000 B.C. (A. R. González [personal communication, 1956].

92. Ameghino, 1911.

93. Bird, 1943.

94. Walter, 1948; Evans, 1950.

95. Serrano, 1946.

tapered-stem points and other implements from the Chicama Valley, which seem to have no connection with later preceramic and ceramic phases in the region;[96] (2) the seemingly unrelated complex featuring stemless and diamond-shaped points found in the nonceramic refuse of certain inland rock shelters near Huancayo;[97] (3) the chipped-stone complex which Strong has reported from the south coast;[98] and (4) recent discoveries from Viscachaní in the Bolivian highlands.[99] From the northern Andes there is even less. Discoveries have been claimed as evidences of man in geologically early periods, such as the Punín skull,[100] or the Alangasí mastodon[101] (this claim recently demolished by Gross),[102] but no artifact complexes that can be measured against our criteria for the Lithic stage. In Venezuela, J. M. Cruxent and Irving Rouse have recently reported a quartzite assemblage from sites in the locality of El Jobo in the northwestern part of the country. This has not yet been formally described, but specimens from it have been examined by a number of North American authorities; the consensus is that the assemblage definitely represents an early culture—the specimens are closely related to artifacts found with the second Iztapan mammoth—with more distant but probably significant relationships to some of the later Lithic cultures of North America.[103]

In this résumé of South American data two things stand out: first, the tendency for Lithic finds to be concentrated in the temperate (southern) and arid portions of the continent, perhaps the only favorable areas for cultures primarily based on hunting;[104] second, the fact that there are few specific resemblances to early cultures in North America, and those that do appear are with projectile-point forms of the later post–fluted-point cultures of the Lithic stage.

96. Larco Hoyle, 1948, pp. 11–12, Pl. 1.

97. Tschopik, 1946.

98. Strong, 1954.

99. Menghin, 1953–54.

100. Sullivan and Hellman, 1925.

101. Uhle, 1930.

102. Gross, 1951, p. 104.

103. Cruxent and Rouse, 1956.

104. Bennett and Bird, 1949.

Archaic Stage

DEFINITIONS

Our previous use of the concept "Archaic" for the second stage of
New World historical-developmental interpretation is here retained in its essentials. The term was introduced into the archaeology of eastern North America by William A. Ritchie, who applied
it to his Lamoka phase in central New York.[1] Soon after, the rich
preceramic culture of the northern Alabama and Kentucky shell
middens was revealed by the extensive excavations of W. S. Webb
and his associates. Relationships to Lamoka were noted, and the
term "Archaic" was extended accordingly, with a "pattern" significance in the Midwest taxonomy.[2] About the same time, re-
examination of earlier shell-midden investigations in the far Southeast[3] and excavations on the Georgia coast[4] expanded the Archaic
still further geographically and also slanted it toward the concept
of a "Shellmound" culture. Similar extension was going on all over
eastern North America, and there were suggestions that cultures
as far away as California were somehow related.[5] However, it was
also becoming clear that the concept had outgrown its specific
historical implications, and Griffin in his first synthesis of eastern

1. Ritchie, 1932. Alanson Skinner had previously designated certain projectile points from shell middens in the vicinity of Manhattan as "archaic"
(1919, 1920), but Ritchie was apparently first to use the term in a full cultural sense.

2. Webb and DeJarnette, 1942.   3. Wyman, 1868, 1875; Claflin, 1931.

4. Unpublished work by Preston Holder and A. J. Waring, Jr.

5. Haag, 1942; Beardsley, 1948.

archaeology made an attempt to jettison it.[6] Failing in this, he and his co-workers reinstated it as a "period" in what might be referred to as the new midwestern chronology.[7] As it was our contention—and still is—that periods in area chronologies of wide geographical scope lose their temporal significance and become, in effect, developmental stages, we have chosen to use "Archaic" as a stage designation, making use of its broad typological implications and expanding the concept to its ultimate hemispherical limits.[8]

For some time North American archaeologists have found it convenient to speak of "early" and "late" Archaic, but there is a remarkable lack of agreement about what these terms mean. In preparing our first classification, we considered making a similar division into "upper" and "lower" Archaic stages but abandoned the idea for two reasons: (1) the difficulty of finding criteria that would hold for all major areas of New World archaeology and (2) the belief that the concept of a Preformative stage following the Archaic would take care of many of the cultures generally regarded as "late" Archaic. This did not work out quite as expected—the precise difficulties will be discussed later on—and, with the elimination of Preformative in the present scheme, the need for subdivision of Archaic seemed more pressing than before. There had also taken place in the interval the conference of North American archaeologists at Andover in April, 1956, at which a twofold subdivision of the Archaic was generally agreed upon. We tried very hard, therefore, in preparing the present version of our classification, to follow this lead—and failed again.

6. Griffin, 1946.   7. Griffin, 1952a.

8. "Archaic" was used much earlier in American studies by Boas (1913), Spinden (1928), and others to refer to the beginnings of settled agricultural village life in Mexico and Central America. This connotation is, of course, entirely different from the use and meaning here. Our "Formative" is the approximate equivalent of the Boas and Spinden "Archaic." Our decision on this terminology was influenced by the current and firmly intrenched North American usage of "Archaic" and by the fact that such names as "Formative" and "Preclassic" have now replaced "Archaic" as the designation for early New World village agriculture.

The Andover classification, if we may call it such, is of narrower scope than ours. The problem was limited culturally to stone technology and geographically to North America. Within this frame of reference it seemed possible to a majority of the conferees to distinguish two broad stages of Archaic technology, with the presence or absence of ground- and polished-stone artifacts as the governing criterion. We made a serious effort to expand these technological stages culturally and geographically but finally concluded that expansion was neither possible nor desirable. In the perspective of New World archaeology as a whole, polished-stone technology does not seem to have any consistent developmental or even temporal significance. One must conclude that polished-stone artifacts were desirable things to have, perhaps even essential in certain environments, but that many groups got on very well without them. For example, the first successful efforts toward agricultural food production seem to have been made in cultures lacking polished stone. To have to call such cultures "lower" Archaic would be disconcerting. On this point we were better off with our Preformative.

Even in the restricted frame of reference of North American stone technology, it may be questioned whether subdivision of the Archaic along the lines suggested at Andover is entirely feasible. It is, of course, a methodological principle that developmental classifications and chronological classifications do not of necessity march together, but, when we compare concepts of "early" and "late" Archaic in the literature with concepts of "lower" and "upper" Archaic proposed at Andover, we find scarcely any agreement at all. It seems best, therefore, to leave Archaic as a single stage allowing for the use of qualifiers, "lower" and "upper" (or "early" and "late"), by area specialists according to whatever criteria seem best to fit the case.

To define Archaic as a single stage, however, is not without its difficulties. So far as we can tell from the meager remains characteristic of most early Archaic cultures, there is no important shift in economic and social patterns from the previous Lithic stages. It would be convenient if, following the lead of some Americanists, we could simply designate the Lithic as the stage of early hunting and the Archaic as the stage of early gathering cultures. We have already inveighed against this simple division. For purposes of large-scale integration, concepts of hunting versus gathering cultures are useful only as convenient rubrics. We found that we had to accommodate both in our definition of Lithic, and we are obliged to do the same for the Archaic. Nevertheless, it does seem possible to see a shift in emphasis between hunting and gathering, in favor of the latter, and there certainly were differences in the plants collected and the animals hunted.

With these points in mind, we may briefly define the Archaic as the stage of migratory hunting and gathering cultures continuing into environmental conditions approximating those of the present. With the extinction of the large Pleistocene mammals hunted by Lithic stage peoples—and this extinction is assumed to have been virtually complete by the beginning of the altithermal period—there is now a dependence on smaller and perhaps more varied fauna. There is also an apparent increase in gathering; it is in this stage that sites begin to yield large numbers of stone implements and utensils that are assumed to be connected with the preparation of wild vegetable foods. In most Archaic cultures these are shaped by use rather than design and do not, therefore, fit into the category of ground and polished stone, which is one of the often-referred-to criteria of the Archaic stage. The specialized techniques of gathering and preparation of wild foods, especially in areas where these consisted mainly of hard-shelled seeded forms, suggest a medium in which early experimentation in plant domestication could take place. As a result, it is in some rather primitive, and surprisingly early, Archaic cultures that the first evidences of New World agriculture are to be found. These we designated as Preformative in our first classification. We have since come to the reluctant conclusion that the mere presence of agriculture, though of enormous importance historically in terms of the growth of particular American patterns of culture, is not of primary significance from a more abstract, developmental point of view. It becomes so only when it can be seen as dominant in the economy and integrated socially to produce the stable settlement patterns that we have postulated as the *sine qua non* of the Formative stage. Furthermore, certain cultures that we classified as Archaic in our first paper because they had no agriculture appear to have achieved stable settlement patterns and other prerequisites of the Formative without that stimulus. Lack of agriculture, therefore, is no longer a negative criterion in our formulation of the Archaic stage.

The point of departure for the description of Archaic stage culture in North America is commonly a level of stone technology marked by the addition of grinding and polishing to the earlier techniques of percussion and pressure flaking. This is no longer an adequate approach, for archaeologists tend increasingly to consider the possibility of an "early" Archaic prior to the adoption of ground and polished stone. Although we are not attempting to set up such a stage, for reasons already given, we shall refer to many cultures in the following pages that lack ground and polished stone altogether. Nevertheless, it is appropriate to begin our description with this category, which certainly represents a technological innovation of immense significance.

Of primary interest as stage criteria are the heavy ground-stone woodworking tools generally regarded as prerequisite to the successful occupation of forest environments—axes, adzes, wedges, gouges, etc. Highly characteristic, but less useful as criteria, are implements and utensils used in the preparation of vegetable foods— milling stones, metates, mortars, manos, pestles, pounders, etc. Some of these have already appeared in the Lithic but usually in the guise of rough-stone artifacts, i.e., objects fashioned principally by use rather than design. These carry over into the Archaic, but there is an increasing tendency toward more specialized forms and careful workmanship. Particularly characteristic of the Archaic in some areas are stone vessels, precursors of pottery. Their presence reflects the greater stability of occupation postulated for some of the later cultures of this stage. Migratory peoples are not partial to stone vessels for obvious reasons. Other Archaic elements of significance in particular areas are ground slate points and knives; polished atlatl weights of various forms; plummet-like objects (variously referred to as "plummets," · "charmstones," *"fusos"*); stone tubes, which may in some cases have been smoking pipes; stone beads; and an array of other objects of purely ornamental or problematical function. Thus, the addition of a new way of handling stone resulted in an immense increase in variety and complexity of the archaeological inventory.

In the chipped-stone category it is noteworthy that the high standards characteristic of many Lithic cultures are not generally maintained in the Archaic. Many of the older forms, however, persisted with little modification, particularly in the chopper and scraper categories. A new tool that seems to have had little if any significance in the Lithic is the drill. Drills are found in some Archaic cultures in great profusion and variety, a matter doubtless related to the fact that many of the ground and polished forms mentioned above are perforated and to the emphasis on beads and pendants of stone, bone, shell, and other materials that is a common feature in this stage. In some areas the older lanceolate projectile forms of the Lithic are carried over into the Archaic, but in general there is a greater variety of points, with emphasis on stemmed, corner-notched, and side-notched forms, roughly in that order. In areas where ground- and polished-stone artifacts are rare or absent, such points are of crucial importance in classification. Certain specific types, such as Pinto and Gypsum, have been used, perhaps too freely, as markers for the Archaic in many parts of North America. The increased variety of forms is matched by an increase in the variety of materials used. In some areas, notably eastern North America, Archaic cultures tended to specialize in the use of stones other than flint.

We would be able to record a number of Archaic determinants in the rough-stone category if we had this class of objects under better control. Plain, pitted, and faceted hammerstones, anvil stones, notched pebbles (usually called "sinkers"), saws, abraders, whetstones, polishing stones, etc., are consistently reported from Archaic sites. We know little about the history of these forms—some of them probably go back to the Lithic—but the association of a number of forms together, and in quantity, is a fairly reliable general criterion of the Archaic stage. Finally, of doubtful status as artifacts but extremely characteristic of Archaic sites in the Americas are masses of fire-cracked stones used in pit roasting and stone boiling. In areas where stones were unobtainable, objects of baked clay were used for the same purpose.

Artifacts of bone, horn, and ivory, present but not abundant in the Lithic stage—a fact partly due, no doubt, to unfavorable factors of preservation—assume a major importance in assemblages of the Archaic. These materials, for the first time, vie with stone as materials for many implements and ornaments, such as points, knives, scrapers, tubes, beads, and pendants, but in the main they were used for objects that have no counterparts in stone. Most important numerically are awls, perforators, and needles, generally regarded as adjuncts to the technologies of basketry and work in skins. An equally large number of forms—gorges, leisters, harpoons, fishhooks—testify to the importance of fishing and marine hunting activities for which there is little evidence in the previous stage. Shell makes its first significant appearance as a material, largely in articles of personal adornment, especially beads and pendants, except in certain coastal and island areas where it was used for implements normally made of stone. Other materials that seem to have made their first appearance in the Archaic, but only in regions near the sources of supply, are copper and asphaltum. Finally, although the word "Archaic" is often used interchangeably with "preceramic," many of the cultures classified as Archaic in this study have a well-developed pottery technology.

The above-named artifacts are found in village-site refuse and with burials, and in a very important sense these conditions are themselves criteria of the Archaic. In suggesting that burials first appear on this level, we do not mean to imply that Lithic peoples had no formalized modes of disposing of their dead but simply that it is only in the Archaic and later stages that we can say what they were. There is, as might be expected, too much variety to permit generalization on a hemispherical scale, but certain modes and features, such as flexed inhumation in round graves, partial cremation, and the use of red ocher in burial rites, have wide distribution on this level.

Habitations do not appear to have been any more permanent than in the Lithic, though, possibly, greater use was made of caves and rock shelters, where accumulations of refuse from (probably) brief and intermittent occupations suggest a degree of stability and continuity that may be illusory. Houses of sufficient durability to leave traces in the ground are still generally lacking, as are storage pits and other appurtenances of settled existence. Settlements are characteristically small in extent, but the depth of deposit often indicates considerable temporal continuity, from which a sedentary or at least seasonal type of occupance may be inferred—quite different from the nomadic way of life assumed for the Lithic stage. This, of course, could be made possible only by the development of specialized subsistence economies in favored localities. As an example, it seems to be in the Archaic that fishing, and especially shellfish-collecting, became important in the economic picture, an adaptation to coastal and interior waterside environments clearly evidenced by the distribution of Archaic cultures. Another sharply contrasting example is the widespread seed-gathering or "Desert" economy of the North American Great Basin and Southwest, which also, to a lesser extent perhaps, tended to anchor populations in favored localities and, by conditioning them to greater dependence on vegetal foods, prepared the way for the adoption of agriculture at a later time.

NORTH AMERICA

It seems appropriate to begin our survey of Archaic cultures in eastern North America, where the concept originated, but it must be confessed that the task of organizing the masses of available data is entirely beyond our competence. Use of the concept in a broad developmental sense is going to oblige us to call many cultures Archaic that have not been so designated before, but we will leave these aside for the moment in order to concentrate on those about whose status there can be no serious disagreement. Of these, we will start with the cultures that would be "early," or "lower," Archaic if we had chosen to make such a division. Even here there is an embarrassment of riches, so far as raw data are concerned, but a remarkable paucity of organization.

An initial difficulty, which will surprise no one who has tried to classify cultures in this way, is the separation of Archaic from Lithic, or "Paleo-Indian" as this stage is most frequently called in the East. "Paleo-Indian" has been indiscriminately applied to all sorts of cultures that are (1) reasonably early and (2) not "Archaic" in the older and narrower sense of "Eastern Archaic." The trouble is not all semantic, however. Lithic stage artifact types, including fluted and parallel-flaked points practically indistinguishable from their western counterparts and with characteristic basal grinding, have a disconcerting tendency to turn up in Archaic complexes in the East, and it is usually not clear whether they originated there or not. The explanation that they were "picked up" from earlier Lithic stage sites by thrifty or curious Archaic hunters does not seem to cover the situation. The fact that some of the marker types for early Archaic cultures in the East—such as Nebo Hill, Dalton (Meserve), Starved Rock, or Guilford—continue the lanceolate-point tradition of Lithic cultures on the Plains is a further indication that the criteria for the separation of Lithic and Archaic stages have to be sought outside specific point typology. For this we are obliged to fall back on more tenuous criteria, such as (1) increased variety in point types and the inclusion of stemmed and corner-notched forms that are not in the lanceolate tradition and (2) increased evidence of gathering activities in the form of milling stones, mortars, cupstones, etc.[9] Geochronological criteria are almost entirely lack-

9. The presence of heavy chipped ax- or adz-like tools that could be regarded as forerunners of the ground and polished axes and adzes of the "later" Archaic has been suggested as a criterion for the Archaic beginnings, but the proposition requires further investigation.

ing; faunal associations, when known, are invariably confined to modern forms; and radiocarbon dating is not extensive enough to be helpful but has in fact increased our classificatory difficulties, as we shall see.

The above remarks apply particularly to cultures in the eastern Plains and the prairie borderlands of the Middle West,[10] sometimes referred to as "Late Paleo-Indian." Pending better stratigraphic separation of these mixed Lithic-Archaic cultures than we now possess, it seems advisable to classify them all as Archaic. The lower levels of the Starved Rock site on the Illinois River,[11] the Modoc Rock Shelter in southern Illinois on the Mississippi,[12] the Hidden Valley Shelter on the Missouri side of the river below St. Louis,[13] and Graham Cave in central Missouri[14] are by no means identical in content, but they are examples of the transitional or mixed Lithic-Archaic cultures and are in all cases overlain by deposits containing what we shall have less difficulty in identifying as typical "Eastern Archaic."

Although dating is not supposed to be of crucial importance in a developmental scheme, we cannot refrain from mentioning the problem raised by the early radiocarbon dates from some of these middle western sites. The Modoc site yielded dates ranging from about 7000 B.C. to over 9000 B.C. for the middle and lower levels— with the earliest dates actually in the middle.[15] Dates from Graham Cave are only slightly later.[16] These dates fall well within the time

10. Evidence that the prairies formerly extended farther east and that this was significant in the spread of late "Paleo-Indian" cultures is given by Lewis, 1953, 1954a.

11. Mayer-Oakes, 1951.   12. Fowler and Winters, 1956.

13. R. M. Adams, 1941; Chapman, 1948, pp. 140–42.

14. Logan, 1952; Chapman, 1952.

15. Dates in question are: 8993 ± 900 B.C. for Level B2; 9246 ± 800 B.C. for Level B3; 8697 ± 650 B.C. for Level C1; 7147 ± 440 B.C. for Level C2 (sample Nos. C-904, C-905, C-907, C-908 [Libby, 1954b]).

16. Dates in question are: 7744 ± 500 B.C. and 6874 ± 500 B.C. for Level 6 (6–7 ft.) and 5944 ± 500 B.C. for Level 4 (4–5 ft.) (sample Nos. M-130, M-131, M-132 [Crane, 1956]).

range of Lithic stage cultures in the Plains. Nevertheless, on the basis of the preliminary reports available, a considerable portion of the materials associated with these dates is typical of fully developed Archaic cultures elsewhere in the East. In short, all these dates seem excessively early. It will not do to discount them entirely, however, because we are going to run into the same problem in other areas, notably in the Great Basin, where comparable dates have been obtained for cultures that we are also cheerfully classifying as Archaic.[17]

The early Archaic picture in the East is further complicated by the fact that, east of the Appalachians, such dubious late or transitional Lithic cultures are scarcely in evidence, and instead there is a series of cultures showing a preference for non-flint materials,[18] with a ruder aspect in consequence, not unlike the Desert cultures of the Great Basin and the Southwest, and a bewildering array of projectile-point types. Prominent among the latter as possible stage markers are lozenge-shaped points vaguely reminiscent of Gypsum and single-shouldered, Sandia-like points (or knives). Testimony to the complexity and long duration of the Archaic in this part of the East is provided by the well-known but as yet undocumented Badin site on the Yadkin River in the North Carolina piedmont.[19] Here in a deep (eighteen feet) stratigraphic column, a deposit containing the long, narrow Guilford point was underlain by a succession of levels, each with its own characteristic point type and all within the Archaic stage as defined in this study.[20]

17. Since the above was written, a popular account of excavations in Russell Cave in northeastern Alabama has appeared (Miller, 1956). Projectile points from the bottom level, dated as 6204 ± 300 B.C. (laboratory not given), are clearly Archaic in type, not unlike material from Graham Cave and the Modoc Shelter.

18. An example is the Old Quartz "industry" of the South Carolina piedmont (Caldwell, 1954).

19. Excavations at the Badin site have been briefly reported by Joffre Coe at meetings of the Southeastern Archaelogical Conference, and the final report is awaited with great interest.

20. There was no "Paleo-Indian" level in the Badin site, but fluted points were found in the St4 site directly across the river.

Turning now to the later and more typical Archaic cultures of the East, we are still plagued by a plethora of unorganized information. Everyone will agree that the cultures we are about to consider are Archaic, but probably no two easternists would organize them in the same way. One possibility would be to set up the old "Eastern Archaic"[21] as a major cultural continuum, but our feeling is that too much time and space have been built into this unit and that ultimately a considerable number of separate cultures will have to be formulated within it. A "Southeastern Archaic," preferably with another name, could be organized around the well-documented shell middens of the Tennessee River in northern Alabama[22] and the Green River in Kentucky.[23] Temporal phases of this continuum will have to be worked out, however, for there is a good possibility that more than one major cultural unit is represented even here. "Southeastern Archaic" is generally understood to include also the fiber-tempered pottery traditions on the Savannah River,[24] Georgia coast,[25] and St. Johns and Indian rivers in Florida,[26] but it might prove to be more sensible to make fiber-tempered pottery the basis for a separate far Southeastern Archaic culture. The St. Johns and Indian River phases also show the influence of the very distinctive Glades culture of lower peninsular Florida, which remained on an essentially Archaic level throughout most of the span of its existence.[27] The spread of Southeastern Archaic culture from the nuclear Kentucky-Tennessee region eastward up the Tennessee River seems to have been slight.[28] To the north and west it includes the

21. Ford and Willey, 1941.

22. W. S. Webb, 1939; Webb and DeJarnette, 1942, 1948a, 1948b, 1948c, 1948d; Webb and Wilder, 1951.

23. W. S. Webb, 1946, 1950a, 1950b, 1951a; Webb and Haag, 1939, 1940, 1947.

24. Claflin, 1931; Fairbanks, 1942; Miller, 1950.

25. A. J. Waring, Jr. (personal communication).

26. Goggin, 1952; Rouse, 1951b.   27. Goggin, 1949.

28. Kneberg, 1952. A thorough survey of the Norris Basin of the Tennessee River in eastern Tennessee failed to reveal any Southeastern Archaic sites (W. S. Webb, 1938).

early Eva phase on the lower Tennessee River,[29] perhaps the Faulkner phase,[30] and the phase represented by prepottery sites near Carbondale[31] in southern Illinois. So far, no Southeastern Archaic sites have been reported from the lower Mississippi. The Tchefuncte phase[32] has often been mentioned in this connection and is certainly Archaic in terms of our definition, but it would be better to leave the cultural affiliation of this phase in suspension until its relationships with other early cultures in the lower Mississippi have been clarified. How far up the Ohio River the concept of a Southeastern Archaic culture can be carried is hard to say—probably as far as the extensive but poorly documented shell middens about the falls of the Ohio at Louisville.[33]

Chronological estimates for Southeastern Archaic, formerly held within modest limits, have been very considerably extended by radiocarbon dating. It now appears that the culture was well established by 3000 B.C. and may have begun a good deal earlier.[34] Its terminal date is less easy to fix, some authorities maintaining that the culture persisted locally down to a late prehistoric period.

The idea of a "Northeastern Archaic" culture is sometimes referred to in the literature but does not seem to have found favor with the archaeologists of that area. The pioneer Archaic phase, the Lamoka of central New York,[35] is still rather isolated as far as direct relationships are concerned. It also remains the earliest

29. Lewis and Kneberg, 1947; Kneberg, 1954.

30. MacNeish, 1948; Cole et al., 1951.   32. Ford and Quimby, 1945.

31. Maxwell, 1951.   33. E. Y. Guernsey, 1939, 1942.

34. Radiocarbon dates from two sites of the Green River phase of Southeastern Archaic are as follows: 5423 ± 500 B.C., 3198 ± 300 B.C., and 2949 ± 250 B.C. from the Annis site (sample Nos. C-180, C-116, and C-251 [Arnold and Libby, 1951]); 3351 ± 300 B.C. from the Indian Knoll site (sample No. C-254 [Arnold and Libby, 1951]). The sample dated 5423 ± 500 B.C. from Annis was from a higher level in the midden than the other two samples dated from that site, and the date is therefore considered to be in error (Webb, 1951b, p. 30). However, a recently published date (5194 ± 500 B.C.) from the Eva phase on the lower Tennessee River is comparable (sample No. M-357 [Crane, 1956]).

35. Ritchie, 1932.

manifestation of the Archaic in the Northeast, with radiocarbon dates somewhat later than those for Southeastern Archaic referred to above.[36] A broader, if somewhat insubstantial, formulation is the later Laurentian, which, as the name implies, is thought to have been intrusive into New York from the St. Lawrence Valley[37] and also into New England, where it incorporates the famous Red Paint phase of coastal Maine.[38] To the west, Laurentian has relationships of an uncertain character with the Old Copper culture of the upper Great Lakes region.[39] Until recently regarded as little more than a technological tradition, the Old Copper culture has now become one of the most intriguing Archaic cultures in eastern North America, as a result of radiocarbon dates of surprising antiquity, which if substantiated would make this the earliest metal-using culture in the Americas and one of the earliest in the world.[40] Laurentian is also of interest because of a special flavor contributed by ground- and polished-stone gouges, rubbed slate points, and semilunar knives, formerly attributed to Eskimoan influence but now thought of as relating to an ancient circumpolar distribution.[41]

A coastal "substratum" extending from southern New England down through the Middle Atlantic states has been suggested as a possible point of departure for another Archaic continuum.[42] There may be another "Boreal Archaic" culture, or series of cultures, in the Northeast (which would include the Red Paint phase already

36. Radiocarbon dates from the Lamoka site are as follows: 2418 ± 200 b.c. and 3432 ± 250 b.c. (sample Nos. C-288 and C-367 [Arnold and Libby, 1951]); 2484 ± 400 b.c. and 2574 ± 400 b.c. (sample Nos. M-26 and M-195 [Crane, 1956]).

37. Ritchie, 1944, 1951a.

38. Willoughby, 1898, 1935, pp. 16–31; Moorehead, 1922b; B. L. Smith, 1948.

39. Ritzenthaler and Scholz, 1946; Miles, 1951; Wittry, 1951; Ritzenthaler and Wittry, 1952; Wittry and Ritzenthaler, 1956.

40. 3646 ± 600 b.c. and 5556 ± 600 b.c. (sample Nos. C-836 and C-837, C-839 [averaged] [Libby, 1954b]).

41. Gjessing, 1944; Spaulding, 1946; Ritchie, 1951b.

42. MacNeish, 1952; Sears, 1954.

mentioned), based on the taiga of northern New England, the Maritime Provinces, Newfoundland, and southern Labrador, but the idea is still in an unformulated state.

This by no means exhausts the material that has been called "Archaic" in the eastern United States, but it is enough to serve as a basis for the concept of an Archaic stage. There are other cultures in the area, however, that we are compelled by the logic of our definitions to relegate to this stage. About these there may be some disagreement. Lack of space forces us to hypothesize in a rather sweeping fashion. As a vehicle for generalization we will use the current Griffin chronology.[43] This scheme, in brief, classifies eastern cultures into a series of "periods," which are at the same time large-scale cultural units, as follows: Paleo-Indian, Archaic, Early Woodland, Middle Woodland, and Mississippi (which includes Late Woodland).

Our hypothesis starts with the assumption that the basic adaptation to the modern forest and waterside environments is represented by the various Archaic cultures already considered and that their ultimate sources lie in the boreal cultures of the Eurasiatic Mesolithic and Neolithic stages. Upon this substratum, we further hypothesize, was grafted one or several pottery traditions, also of northern Eurasiatic origin, resulting in the Early Woodland cultures of the Griffin scheme. Whether the same northern influences were responsible for the introduction of the earliest burial mounds is not yet clear. Certainly, at this time we can see evidence of the gathering together of mortuary ceremonialism that climaxed later in the mound-building (Middle Woodland) cultures of the Ohio Valley.[44] The incorporation of pottery (and possibly burial mounds) did not bring about any changes of significance from a developmental point of view. For the most part these Early Woodland cultures must be regarded as Archaic in terms of the definitions used here.[45] We also have to reckon with the possibility that

43. Griffin, 1952a.   44. Ritchie, 1955.

45. This is by no means a new idea (cf. Griffin, 1952a, p. 356). The suggestion made by William H. Sears (1948) that Archaic is merely Woodland

agriculture, already present in northeastern Mexico and the Southwest for a long time, was beginning to percolate into the East in the Early Woodland period, but, if so, its effect on the general cultural pattern was plainly insufficient to shift the cultures into the Formative stage. Examples of middle western Woodland cultures that we would be inclined to classify as Archaic may be seen in the Black Sand and Red Ocher phases of the Illinois Valley,[46] the Crab Orchard and Baumer phases of southern Illinois,[47] and the Glacial Kame "culture" of Ohio.[48] On the other hand, the Adena culture, often designated as Early Woodland in the literature, we are going to designate as Formative for reasons that will be developed later. Examples from the Southeast might include the Watts Bar and Candy Creek phases in eastern Tennessee,[49] Mossy Oak in Georgia,[50] and Deptford in Georgia and northwestern Florida.[51] In a strictly taxonomic sense these Early Woodland cultures are transitional from Archaic to Middle Woodland, but in the developmental terms used here they lack all the essential characteristics of the Formative.

The Middle Woodland period of the Griffin scheme is marked by the rise of a number of traditions, mainly from local sources but with outside contributions, the origins and extent of which are still obscure. We assume that diffusion from the Eurasiatic north is still going on, but there are now influences from the south to be reckoned with. These are of overriding importance for us, because now

---

without pottery arose from the same observation that we have made above, to wit, that the addition of pottery had little if any effect on the configuration of the culture as a whole. We are simply turning his statement around to read: Early Woodland is merely Archaic with pottery. Fairbanks was expressing the same idea in pointing out that Early Woodland cultures in the Southeast are in effect merely transitional from Archaic to Middle Woodland and that no change in basic economy was involved (1949, p. 59).

46. Cole and Deuel, 1937; Cole, 1943; Wray, 1952.

47. Maxwell, 1951; Cole *et al.*, 1951.

48. Cunningham, 1948; Morgan, 1952.   50. Fairbanks, 1952.

49. Lewis and Kneberg, 1941, 1946.   51. Willey, 1949.

certainly they are involved with the spread of agriculture and associated elements, and they do involve significant changes in the older cultural and economic patterns. Middle Woodland, then, marks the shift to the Formative stage in eastern North America, but, since it is primarily a temporal period, it does not necessarily follow that all cultures classified as Middle Woodland in the Griffin scheme are Formative in ours. Wherever Middle Woodland cultures came into contact with pre-existing Archaic or Early Woodland cultures, they tended to dominate in the resulting acculturation, except on the peripheries where this dominance was incomplete, resulting in cultures that would be classified here as marginal Formative. Excellent examples of this kind of developmental situation are to be seen in the Middle Woodland cultures of the upper Ohio Valley[52] and New York State.[53] Such acculturation was not only incomplete but decidedly impermanent, it seems, and there followed a re-emergence of simpler Woodland patterns, the Late Woodland of the Griffin scheme. This late regressive marginality is, of course, complicated by influences from the Mississippi cultures of the Formative stage, which by this time were flourishing to the south; it is to be noted that Mississippi and Late Woodland are essentially the same period. How to classify these Late Woodland cultures developmentally is a rather tricky question. Are they belated Archaic or marginal Formative? Beyond this uncertain and probably fluctuating dividing line, which is in effect an expression of the northern and eastern limits of successful maize agriculture, are the vast forest areas in which the culture remained on an Archaic level down to the ethnographic present.

Classification of Archaic stage cultures is even more difficult in the Plains than in the East, owing to a conservatism that probably reflects a long persistence of ancient hunting traditions and a reluctance or inability to take up the features, especially ground- and polished-stone technology, that characterize the Archaic stage in

52. Mayer-Oakes, 1955.

53. Ritchie, 1938, 1944, 1951a. Specific reference to the New York Hopewellian or Geneseo phase.

other areas.[54] Practically all Plains Archaic cultures show a mixed Lithic-Archaic typology, and in some cases the specific Archaic relationships are with the later "typical" Archaic cultures in the East. Nevertheless, owing to the conservatism postulated here, the general configuration of these cultures, so far as it can be discerned in the meager remains, is closer to our concept of Lithic. For example, Signal Butte I and II in western Nebraska show a persistence of lanceolate-point types of generalized Lithic stage character in a context that includes Archaic stemmed and notched forms, drills, and a few ground-stone implements.[55] A bison-hunting economy is indicated, and there can be little doubt that the culture reflects a strong continuity from the ancient Lithic stage cultures of the area. At the same time there are definite affiliations with Eastern Archaic, and the only available radiocarbon date is well within the time range of such cultures.[56]

The same general observations apply to the Frontier complex found at the Medicine Creek (Allen) site in south-central Nebraska, with interesting affiliations, on the one hand, to certain Desert cultures in the Great Basin and, on the other, to the Clear Fork culture in Texas, both of which will be classified as Archaic when we get to them.[57] The deeply buried Lime Creek sites in the same locality, not yet adequately reported, may be in the same Archaic category, although some of the points are said to be more

54. In emphasizing cultural continuity in the Plains, we are in effect rejecting a very attractive theory proposed by Krieger (1953), to wit, that the altithermal was a period unfavorable to hunting in most of the Great Plains. The Pleistocene mammals were gone. Only with the return of favorable conditions in the medithermal period was man able to occupy the Plains again, living off the great herds of bison that now roamed the area, but with a different culture, a much larger range of implements, many of them comparable to Eastern Archaic forms. It seems to us that the evidence suggests rather a gradual replacement of the older fauna by modern forms and that the life of the later hunters differed little from that of the earlier.

55. Strong, 1935; Bliss, 1950.

56. The Signal Butte I phase is dated at 1494 ± 120 B.C. (sample No. L-104A [Kulp, Feely, and Tryon, 1951]).

57. Holder and Wike, 1949.

specifically related to Lithic stage types (Plainview and Eden-Scottsbluff).[58] Radiocarbon dates from both Medicine Creek and Lime Creek sites are of the same order of magnitude as those for Archaic sites in the Middle West, i.e., well within the range of Lithic cultures in the Plains.[59] If they are correct, and if they date the material described—which is uncertain in the case of the Medicine Creek site—we have here a significant instance of temporal overlap of Lithic and Archaic stages in the same area.

The diffusion of Woodland pottery into the central Plains, though assumed to have taken place later than in the East, does not seem to have marked any significant advance in cultural development. The very large number of sites in the Valley phase, for example, indicate an intense and widespread occupation of the stream valleys at this time, but their small size and meager refuse deposits suggest a continuation of the migratory hunting-gathering economy of the area.[60] The distinctive Sterns Creek phase of eastern Nebraska is also designated as Woodland of this same "Middle" period; it furnished evidence at the Walker-Gilmore site of squash and gourds (no corn), but otherwise failed to present a configuration that we could classify as Formative.[61] This is the first of many examples we shall consider in which limited agriculture is present in cultures that otherwise remain essentially on an Archaic level. Not until the later emergence of the Plains Village type of culture beginning about A.D. 1200 can we begin to speak of a Formative stage in the central Plains.

The sequence for the northwestern Great Plains, recently proposed by William Mulloy,[62] fits our classification very neatly. In

58. Schultz and Frankforter, 1948; Davis, 1953.

59. Site Ft-50 (Medicine Creek) has a date of 8542 ± 1500 B.C. (sample No. C-470 [Arnold and Libby, 1951]), but the sample came from below the occupation zone (Roberts, 1951, p. 21). Average of two runs on a sample from Site Ft-41, one of the Lime Creek sites, was 7573 ± 450 B.C. (sample No. C-471 [Arnold and Libby, 1951]).

60. Hill and Kivett, 1940; C. S. Smith, 1949, pp. 298–99; Kivett, 1952; Wedel, 1953, p. 506.

61. Sterns, 1915; Strong, 1935; Champe, 1946.   62. Mulloy, 1954.

his "Early Prehistoric" period the area was occupied by small, migratory, hunting groups with a Folsom or Yuma-type culture, i.e., our Lithic stage of development. Following an interval of uncertain length for which evidence is lacking, the "Middle Prehistoric" shows an economy more strongly oriented toward plant-gathering and small-animal-hunting. The big bison have disappeared, but the modern American buffalo (*Bison bison*) is not yet in evidence. The two levels at the McKean site in northeastern Wyoming reflecting early and late phases of this Middle Prehistoric culture are related to Signal Butte I and II, respectively, and are plainly Archaic in general configuration and typology.[63] Mulloy's "Late Prehistoric" seems to reflect, in part at least, a culture rooted in the ceramic-agricultural traditions of the East, whose bearers, on moving out into the High Plains, abandoned agriculture and took to a nomadic hunting way of life, the modern buffalo having now appeared. Here seems to be an example of the regressive type of marginality described in chapter 3. Whether such cultures should be regarded as Archaic or marginal Formative is a question of emphasis, and its determination is a matter for the area specialist.

On the eastern border of the central Plains, lanceolate points continue to predominate in "Plains Archaic" cultures, but there is a greater admixture of Eastern Archaic forms. For example, the Nebo Hill assemblage, known from surface sites in the vicinity of Kansas City, has points that are very closely related typologically to some of the unfluted, Lithic stage types (Plainview, Angostura, etc.) but includes grooved axes.[64] If the association is valid, this would be a very difficult culture to classify. Farther east, in central Missouri, the distinctive trianguloid Dalton point is associated with lanceolate forms of the same general character.[65]

The archaeology of the Ozark Plateau, a region with a highly

63. The single radiocarbon date of 1333 ± 600 B.C. (sample No. C-715 [Libby, 1954a]) from the upper level compares closely with the date for Signal Butte I, cited above. Both would be late in the time range of Eastern Archaic cultures.

64. Shippee, 1948.   65. Chapman, 1948.

characteristic environment, has important bearings on the concept of an Archaic stage, but is a little difficult to generalize upon. Excellent survey reports by Carl Chapman and others afford an abundance of data, but they are organized in terms of the midwest (Griffin) sequence, a classification which is imposed on the material instead of deriving out of it.[66] Better for our purposes is the formulation of David Baerreis, in which the evidence, largely drawn from open sites in northeastern Oklahoma (the Grove focus), has been interpreted as reflecting a long continuity of basic stone artifact types, notwithstanding an apparent shift in the economic base from hunting and gathering to horticulture.[67] The later phases of this Grove continuum are thought to pertain to the famous Ozark Bluff-dweller culture, which, thanks to conditions unusually favorable for the preservation of perishable materials, is known in great but insufficiently documented detail.[68] This has led to spurious comparisons with the Basket Maker culture of the San Juan Anasazi region of the Southwest, another instance of fortunate preservation. Baerreis believes that the more significant relationships are with the Archaic cultures of the East. The preceramic Bluff-dweller culture is overlain by a later ceramic phase, not covered in Baerreis' summary, in which can be seen faint emanations of influence from the late Formative stage in the Mississippi Valley. This ceramic phase corresponds to Harrington's "Top-Layer"[69] and Robert Bray's "Marginal Mississippi."[70] For our purposes it is sufficient that the entire Ozark Bluff-dweller culture, notwithstanding the abundant remains of domesticated plants in the later phases, remains essentially on the Archaic stage of development as defined in this study. It is a remarkable fact that the culture of a region so close geographically to the centers of maximum intensity of Forma-

66. Chapman, 1948, 1954, 1956; Chapman, Maxwell, and Kozlovich, 1951.

67. Baerreis, 1951.

68. Harrington, 1924; Gilmore, 1930; Dellinger, 1936; Dellinger and Dickinson, 1942.

69. Harrington, 1924.

70. Bray, 1956.

tive development in the Mississippi Valley has been so impervious to cultural influences from those centers. This would provide an extremely nice frame for a study of culture-environmental interaction.

Identification of an Archaic stage in Texas is easy enough—where would Texas archaeology be without it?—but we are confronted with the same difficulty, reference to which is beginning to sound repetitious, of separating it from Lithic. Conditions favoring a predominantly hunting type of economy persist in much of the area, and there is the same disconcerting tendency for Lithic point types, specifically Plainview and Angostura, to turn up in Archaic contexts. Further, there is an almost complete lack of ground and polished stone in Texas Archaic cultures; so we are deprived of this handy criterion. An outstanding example is the Edwards Plateau culture of central Texas, known from open camp sites and "burned-rock middens" (accumulations of fire-cracked hearth stones) containing refuse indicating a hunting-gathering economy with more dependence on deer than on bison. Plainview and Angostura points are found too consistently in these sites to be regarded as accidental intrusions.[71] Otherwise the chipped-stone assemblage is typically Archaic, with a wide variety of stemmed points, knives, axes, choppers, picks, and large drills (mostly made-over projectile points). Ground milling stones and manos are common, and there are a few minor artifacts of polished stone, including crude boat-stone atlatl weights. It is evident that this culture persisted for a long period of time. Of the three documented foci of this culture, the Clear Fork, featuring a specialized end-scraper (the "Clear Fork gouge"), has long been the center of a dating controversy, with estimates running as early as 8000 B.C., but general typological considerations favor the more conservative figures of 4000 or 2000 B.C. (depending on certain alternative geological correlations) to about A.D. 1500.[72] The Round Rock focus is thought to have

71. Suhm and Krieger, 1954, pp. 104–5; Suhm, 1955.

72. Kelley, 1947a. More recently Suhm and Krieger have extended the beginning date of Clear Fork to "not later than 4000 to 5000 B.C." (1954, p. 106).

been approximately coeval with Clear Fork,[73] but the Uvalde focus occupied only the last two or three centuries of this long interval of time.[74] The important point for us here is that this continuum comes down to a very late period—late enough to receive intrusive types from east Texas cultures on the Formative level—without departing significantly from the original Archaic pattern. The Trinity culture of north-central Texas, nearer to the source of east Texas intrusives, is nevertheless equally Archaic in its general configuration.[75]

The belated character of Texas Archaic is perhaps even more conspicuous on the coast, where, in the Tonkawa, Karankawa, and Coahuiltecan tribes comprising the so-called ethnological sink, we have an opportunity of viewing a low-grade Archaic way of life in ethnohistorical detail.[76]

The Big Bend aspect of the trans-Pecos region, in the extreme western part of Texas, is known from rock shelters as well as open sites and has in consequence a larger cultural inventory, including many perishable items, and a more southwestern flavor.[77] The early Maravillas focus of this culture has been compared with Ventana-Amargosa I of south-central Arizona; the intermediate Pecos River focus has Gypsum-type points; and the later Chisos focus has Pinto and San Pedro types.[78] In other respects the stone assemblages compare closely with that of Edwards Plateau, and the time range is thought to be similar, except that the terminus of the Big Bend culture may be slightly earlier. This is a culture extremely important, from our point of view, as a bridge between the Archaic cultures of the East and the Desert cultures in the Southwest, which we are about to designate as Archaic.

Before doing so, however, it might be well to pause at this point to consider at greater length a general classificatory question already touched upon in connection with the Plains and the Ozark

73. T. N. Campbell, 1948.

74. Kelley, 1947b.

75. Suhm and Krieger, 1954, pp. 76–80.

76. Swanton, 1924; Newcomb, 1956.

77. Kelley, Campbell, and Lehmer, 1940.

78. Kelley, 1947b.

Plateau. With regard to the Big Bend culture, which we have considered as essentially Archaic, it should be noted that two of the later foci, the Chisos and the Livermore, have furnished evidence of agriculture. In our previous paper we classed these two later foci as "Preformative." Our concept of a Preformative stage had been developed to take care of the many cultures that possessed domesticated maize but do not yield substantial evidence that this possession was of primary, or even significant, economic importance. In the present classification we have dropped the Preformative, admitting the presence of domesticated food plants on Archaic levels where it is reasonably obvious that such agriculture was not of importance in the development of stable, sedentary village life. In this connection it is of interest to note that these early occurrences of plant domesticates in North America are mostly from the arid or semiarid areas of the continent. The fortuitous factor of favorable conditions for preservation may be involved here, but it is also likely that the seed-gathering and seed-grinding cultures of these areas assimilated a trait like maize as they would numerous wild plants and with little more immediate cultural effect. Hence we classify these Texas cultures possessing corn as Archaic, because in all other respects they seem to have that kind of conformation. This is a preview of a situation that will be encountered again in discussing the cultures of the Southwest and northern Mexico.

Generalization about the Archaic in the Great Basin and the Southwest involves a continuation of the difficulties foreshadowed in the Lithic section. These have to do with that great continuum of basin and range Desert cultures,[79] which, because of the prevalence of grinding stones in the archaeology, are so often contrasted with the early hunting cultures in the literature. In our first attempt at classification we chose to play down this division between hunters and gatherers and, without really committing ourselves, suggested that the earliest phase of this Desert continuum in the Southwest, the Sulphur Spring phase of the Cochise culture of southeastern Arizona and southwestern New Mexico, might be regarded as

79. Jennings and Norbeck, 1955.

Early Lithic—or Lithic, as we would now call it. We have already given reasons for abandoning this position[80] and now prefer to call all three phases of the Cochise culture Archaic. Chiricahua is involved in another division, that between gatherers and farmers,[81] and this antithesis too has probably been overdone. The early corn in Bat Cave, on the St. Augustin Plains of west-central New Mexico, was associated with a stone assemblage that differs little from Chiricahua Cochise.[82] Radiocarbon dates from corn-bearing levels in the cave run as early as about 4000 B.C.,[83] but data on the association of the corn and the charcoal samples dated have not yet been published. The earliest Bat Cave corn is exceedingly primitive—it cannot be said with certainty that it is not a wild variety—but reliable evidence of domestication comes early in the sequence, and we can infer that it was well advanced by 2000–3000 B.C. The same story of evolving corn in a retarded Chiricahua-like culture is seen in the Tularosa Cave in the same region of New Mexico.[84] There are said to be evidences of a renewed importance of hunting in the late San Pedro phase of Cochise,[85] which might be taken as further evidence that agriculture was not decisive in the patterning of Cochise culture. Cochise appears to have been the basis for both the Mogollon continuum of the mountain region of southeastern Arizona and southwestern New Mexico and the Hohokam of the southern Arizona desert, which we shall classify later as Formative.

To the west, in the lower Colorado River and California desert regions, the Amargosa continuum parallels Cochise with some differences, but these are not significant from a developmental stand-

80. See p. 91.   81. Kirchhoff, 1954.

82. Mangelsdorf and Smith, 1949; Dick, 1952.

83. Earliest of a long series of dates are: 3654 ± 290 B.C. and 3980 ± 310 B.C. (sample Nos. C-571, C-573 [Libby, 1951]).

84. Martin et al., 1952. Radiocarbon dates on Tularosa corn are: 272 ± 200 B.C., 194 ± 160 B.C., 349 ± 200 B.C. (sample Nos. C-584, C-585, C-612 [Libby, 1951]).

85. Campbell and Ellis, 1952.

point. Amargosa II, or Pinto-Gypsum as it was formerly called,[86] correlates roughly with Chiricahua Cochise in time[87] but shows no signs of agriculture and not much of collecting; hunting is still (or again) the dominant mode. Stone types are what we have come to regard as Archaic in character. Whether or not it is correct to equate Gypsum and Pinto temporally is a question we do not have to go into. Both types seem to be widespread horizon markers on the Archaic level for large portions of the Southwest and Texas and on into the eastern United States. How this is to be reconciled with the extinct faunal associations at Gypsum Cave and the early radiocarbon dates of sloth dung in the cave deposits is difficult to see.[88] Amargosa III, equating roughly with San Pedro Cochise, is also classified here as Archaic.

At Ventana Cave, in south-central Arizona, Amargosa and Cochise traditions mingled in an excellent stratigraphic sequence that has provided most of the evidence for the correlations referred to above.[89] Above the deposit containing the Lithic stage Ventana complex and the discontinuity that is believed to mark a long period of erosion and abandonment of the cave was a thin, red-sand deposit containing artifacts of the Amargosa I phase, previously postulated but not isolated in the lower Colorado River region. The characteristic broad, stemmed points, somewhat similar to Borax Lake points,[90] are well within the typological range of Eastern Archaic forms. This was followed by thick midden deposits, the lower portion containing both Amargosa and Cochise types, called Chiricahua-Amargosa II, the upper portion containing San Pedro Cochise. The upper terminus of this midden was marked by another disconformity, followed by deposits containing Hohokam of the Colonial and Sedentary periods. Amargosa I, Chiricahua-Amargosa II, and San Pedro are Desert cultures on an Archaic stage, and the Hohokam phases are Formative. In this cave we have

86. M. J. Rogers, 1939.   87. Haury *et al.*, 1950, p. 534.

88. Harrington, 1933. The sloth dung has been dated at 8504 ± 340 B.C. and 6576 ± 250 B.C. (sample Nos. C-221, C-222 [Arnold and Libby, 1951]).

89. Haury *et al.*, 1950.   90. Harrington, 1948*b*.

in vertical stratigraphy the full range of our developmental sequence from Lithic through Formative.

A number of other cultures would have to be considered in any complete description of the Archaic stage in the Southwest, a few of which may be briefly mentioned. The San José culture, found in fossil sand dunes in the Grants region in northwestern New Mexico, has points in the Pinto tradition.[91] The dunes are associated with the altithermal period, a date which agrees with the general time position of other early Archaic cultures in the Southwest. Closely related to San José is the Concho complex from undated surface sites about one hundred miles away in east-central Arizona.[92] The general character of the artifacts and many of the specific forms are also Archaic as defined in this study.

Pinto-type points have been recently reported from the San Juan Anasazi region.[93] It may be assumed that when the elusive Basket Maker I is finally run to earth it will be a culture of Archaic type. Basket Maker II, formerly classified as Preformative, we are now obliged to demote to the Archaic. Although agriculture was well developed—there is nothing comparable here to the primitive corn of Bat Cave—it does not seem to have become the central theme of the culture, perhaps was not even the principal food resource. Hunting and collecting are still much in evidence. Characteristic settlements are small, unorganized groups of very crude, unstandardized-surface, or shallow pit-houses of "brush and timber masonry" and stone-slab-lined storage cists. There are as yet no specialized religious structures (kivas) and in general only the faintest indications of developing ceremonialism. Thanks to favorable conditions for preservation in those regions where dry caves and shelters were utilized as storage, burial, and camp sites, there is an unusually large body of information about basketry, cordage, finger-woven bags, sandals, wooden implements, and weapons, in-

91. Bryan and Toulouse, 1943; Bryan and McCann, 1943.

92. Wendorf and Thomas, 1951.

93. Reported by J. Charles Kelley at the Andover Radiocarbon Conference, April, 1956.

cluding the atlatl but not the bow. Pottery, however, has not yet appeared, though presumably already in use in the Mogollon and Hohokam regions. In sum, as a cultural phase that has adopted agriculture without profound modifications of settlement patterns or other branches of technology, Basket Maker II remains essentially on the Archaic level.[94] Basket Maker III, on the other hand, also classified as Preformative in our first effort, is now promoted to Formative; so we can again face our southwestern colleagues without fear of personal violence.

In sum, the general southwestern picture in the Archaic stage is one of basic uniformity, reflecting an over-all environmental homogeneity, with collecting as the most characteristic economic pattern. There are marked local and temporal variations in the role of hunting and, in the southeastern portion of the area, an early appearance of maize agriculture unaccompanied by any recognizable changes in the technological inventory.

An impressive accumulation of finds in the central and northern Great Basin relates to another, perhaps even more fundamental, Desert continuum, for which the name "Bonneville" has been suggested.[95] The cultures involved appear to be on an Archaic level. These include Deadman,[96] Promontory and Black Rock,[97] and Danger[98] caves in the Great Salt Lake region; Lovelock Cave[99] and Leonard Rock Shelter[100] in the Humboldt Sink region of western Nevada; and Catlow, Roaring Springs, Paisley Five Mile Point, and Fort Rock caves in south-central Oregon.[101] General typological affiliations are with the Amargosa and Cochise cultures already discussed, but the remarkably early radiocarbon dates for some of these sites, running as early as 9500 B.C. at Danger Cave, raise

94. Kidder and Guernsey, 1919; S. J. Guernsey, 1931; Amsden, 1949; Morris and Burgh, 1954.

95. Jennings, 1953, p. 208; Jennings and Norbeck, 1955.

96. E. R. Smith, 1941, 1952.

97. Steward, 1937, 1940.   99. Loud and Harrington, 1929.

98. Jennings, 1953.   100. Heizer, 1951*b*.

101. Cressman *et al.*, 1942; Cressman, 1951.

some very serious classificatory problems.[102] Until the discrepancies between some of these dates and the local geological correlations are resolved, and until the temporal phases of this "long and placid" continuum have been worked out and described, our relegation of practically all these Basin cultures[103] to the Archaic stage must be regarded as tentative. If the dates are correct, it would follow that the Desert pattern was already in existence in the Great Basin in a period occupied by Lithic cultures elsewhere and, if so, was probably basic to all the Desert cultures in the Greater Southwest. Whether this would negate the assumption of temporal priority of Lithic over Archaic stage cultures in western North America is a question that can be neither settled nor ignored. We have already referred to certain eastern "lower" Archaic dates that pose the same problem.

Archaic cultures in the southern part of the Great Basin have already been touched upon. The assemblage at Gypsum Cave in southeastern Nevada,[104] notwithstanding the possible extinct faunal associations and early radiocarbon dates, seems to represent a typical Desert culture and provides in the Gypsum point a useful marker type for wide areas in North America.[105] The Pinto point, which takes its name from a series of surface finds in the Pinto Basin of southwestern California,[106] has an even wider distribution on the same level. The temporal relationship of Gypsum and Pinto has been hotly debated; for our purposes it is sufficient that both are in the Archaic stage. Farther north, the Little Lake (Stahl) site in Inyo County, California, with Pinto, Lake Mohave, and Silver

102. The first radiocarbon dates from the lowest culture-bearing levels at Danger Cave were: 9502 ± 600 B.C. and 9200 ± 570 B.C. (sample Nos. C-609 and C-610 [Libby, 1951]). These were subsequently confirmed by dates of 9044 ± 700 B.C. and 8444 ± 700 B.C. (sample Nos. M-118 and M-119 [Crane, 1956]). Sandals from the Fork Rock Cave gave a date of 7102 ± 350 B.C. (sample No. C-428 [Arnold and Libby, 1951]).

103. A few possible exceptions have been mentioned above in the Lithic section.

104. Harrington, 1933.

105. Hurt, 1953, p. 215.   106. Campbell and Campbell, 1935.

Lake points, has provided one of the rare evidences of house construction on the Archaic level in North America.[107] The association of Pinto with Lake Mohave and Silver Lake points on this site throws a little extra doubt upon our tentative classification of the Lake Mohave complex as Lithic. Possibly Lake Mohave ought to be called Archaic as well.

Turning to the southern California coast, we have already discussed a number of finds, thought to be early, and dismissed their claims to be considered Lithic. These are the "Early Milling Stone" cultures,[108] a "culture type" which includes the Little Sycamore site in Ventura County,[109] Oak Grove in the Santa Barbara region,[110] the Topanga culture from the Tank site just north of Los Angeles,[111] Level 2 at the Malaga Cove site near Redondo Beach in Los Angeles County,[112] and the La Jolla complex localized near San Diego and extending for an uncertain distance into Baja California.[113] Somewhat more distantly related are Buena Vista Lake near the south end of the San Joaquin Valley[114] and the controversial Borax Lake site north of San Francisco Bay.[115] Relationships outside the California area are said to be with Pinto Basin, Chiricahua-Amargosa II, and Chiricahua Cochise, which we have already defined as Archaic. These coastal California milling-stone cultures have some polished-stone artifacts, specifically consisting of simple and rather crude charmstones and discoidals; there are said to be remains of houses in at least one of them, the Oak Grove; and in several of them burials assume a considerable importance in the archaeological record. It is not unlikely that early gathering communities on the California coast were somewhat more stable than those of corresponding development in the interior. This was certainly the case in later times.

107. Harrington, 1948a, 1948c, 1951.
108. Wallace, 1954.
109. *Ibid.*   111. Treganza and Malamud, 1950.
110. D. B. Rogers, 1929.   112. E. F. Walker, 1951.
113. M. J. Rogers, 1929, 1945; Harding, 1951.
114. Wedel, 1941.   115. Harrington, 1948b.

Among the best-documented archaeological cultures of North America are those of the Sacramento–San Joaquin Delta and San Francisco Bay regions of central California.[116] It is mainly in reference to these that comparisons with Eastern Archaic have been made,[117] but such discussions have usually had to do with the possibility of historical connections, which is not germane to our present purpose. The relationships from the culture-developmental point of view are indubitable, whatever the causes may have been.[118] According to Beardsley, the elements that support the theory of an actual historical connection are for the most part in the early and middle "horizons" of the three-part central California sequence.

The California late horizon, particularly in its climax Cosumnes phase,[119] shows a density of population and relatively advanced level of cultural development made possible by a stabilized food supply in the form of a highly specialized acorn complex. In our first paper we took note of this economy in the following terms: "This might be regarded as an alternative to agriculture in its capacity to produce conditions for a Preformative or even Formative stage," but we were bound by the logic of our classification and consigned the late horizon, along with the early and middle, to the Archaic stage. Now, with the shift of emphasis consequent upon the elimination of the Preformative, amounting to a downgrading of agriculture as the indispensable economic basis for Formative stage culture, we are inclined to think that some at least of the late central California cultures should be ranked as Formative. The same

116. Schenck, 1926; Gifford and Schenck, 1926; Schenck and Dawson, 1929; Heizer and Fenenga, 1939; Lillard, Heizer, and Fenenga, 1939; Heizer, 1941, 1949; Belous, 1953.

117. Haag, 1942; Beardsley, 1948.

118. "Although basing their description of an Archaic stage primarily on eastern data, Willey and Phillips (1955) have presented a summary which conforms in nearly every detail to the California picture as well" (Clement Meighan, in "A Review of the California Archaic," read at the Andover Radiocarbon Conference, April, 1956).

119. Lillard and Purves, 1936.

METHOD AND THEORY
IN AMERICAN ARCHAEOLOGY 134

possibility must be extended to the final phase of the parallel three-part Canalino sequence in the Santa Barbara region of southern California.[120] This late phase has been identified with the historic Chumash occupation of the region. Village populations, according to estimates of the early discoverers, were as high as one thousand people living in eighty houses, which suggests a degree of concentration a good deal more intensive than we think of as characteristic of the Archaic. It must be noted, however, that both this and the Cosumnes phase mentioned above are climax phases; it by no means follows that all late California cultures had advanced beyond the Archaic level. The significant thing about these climactic food-gathering cultures is that they seem to have been the end products of extremely long and gradual internal development, without observable stimuli from outside. They have become Formative the hard way, so to speak. This situation offers an interesting comparison to what seems to have happened farther up the Pacific Coast.

Revision of our scheme of 1955 also gives us an opportunity to renege on our classification of all Northwest Coast cultures as Archaic, a position which elicited some not entirely unanticipated criticism. W. C. McKern put the case in the clearest possible manner, and it must be acknowledged that his intervention had something to do with our change of outlook:

The authors' difficulty would seem to be that of selecting agriculture as the most significant culture criterion everywhere; selecting a measuring device for Middle America and attempting to apply it universally. The real contributions of agriculture, a sedentary life and security, can be provided, within certain developmental limitations, by patterns of life other than the agricultural. I submit that the Northwest Coast fishing-gathering pattern produced for its peoples a richer, more complex social and economic manner of existence than that enjoyed by the importantly agricultural Iroquois.[121]

120. P. C. Orr, 1943, 1952.

121. McKern, 1956, p. 361. McKern's further suggestion that an ecological variant must be taken into account in developmental taxonomy has undeniable merit but would involve an operation entirely different in scope and level of abstraction from what we are attempting here. The object of the present inquiry is to see whether a gross classification of all New World archaeological

On taking a second look at some of the Northwest Coast archaeology for the purpose of this revision, however, we have the same impression of its essentially Archaic flavor. Unlike the archaeology of California, it does not seem to provide a deep and adequate basis for the climax development that we know ethnographically as Northwest Coast culture. The latter we are now prepared to call Formative, but it remains an interesting problem to locate in the rather meager archaeological record the shift from Archaic to Formative configurations. The best available data seem to be in the Gulf of Georgia region, where a number of sequences[122] have revealed substantially the same general pattern of cultural change: an early chipped-stone culture (lacking ground and polished stone) with evidence in some localities of a land-hunting economy, followed in at least one locality by a maritime sea-mammal-hunting "Eskimoid" culture with emphasis on ground slate, followed again by an "Intermediate" period featuring the reintroduction of land hunting and the use of ground-stone tools testifying to a well-developed woodworking industry of presumed interior origin, and finally the amalgamation of this with the earlier maritime culture to produce a culmination. According to Bryan, it was in the "Intermediate" period that the culture became adapted to *all* the natural resources of the area, both land and sea, and it is here that he would place the first evidences of culture configurations classifiable as Formative.[123] Substantiation of this hypothetical sequence must await further investigation.

In the meantime, while agreeing perfectly with McKern in theory, we continue to feel uneasy about the classificatory situation. We cannot escape a feeling of unreality about the discussion, a sense of factors missing from the equation. All developmental interpretation is subject to this malaise, but it is especially apparent

data into a small number of broad developmental stages is possible and, if possible, useful. Introduction of the ecological variant would result in a classification of entirely different nature which would answer neither of these questions.

122. King, 1950; Borden, 1951, 1954; Carlson, 1954; A. L. Bryan, 1955.

123. A. L. Bryan (personal communication, October, 1956).

when we move out to, and possibly beyond, the limits of what might be called the nuclear American "diffusion sphere."[124] The sad fact is that our definition of the Formative stage has only nominal value in peripheral situations. Whatever we think of the importance, or lack of importance, of agriculture as a criterion, the concept is nonetheless based very largely on configurations near the center. This is particularly true in the case of Northwest Coast cultures, the sources of which, wherever they ultimately turn out to be, were almost certainly not to the south. The present tendency seems to be to discount the role of Asiatic and Oceanic elements, emphasizing rather the possibility of old Eskimo-Aleut connections.[125] It seems to us, from the vantage ground of more or less complete ignorance, that Kroeber's views on this question have not been superseded. "From both the northward centering and recent northward trend of the climax of the whole Northwest Coast, it is expected that more refined analysis will confirm the conjecture that Asiatic influences perhaps were more potent than Nuclear (Middle) American ones in the specific shaping of Northwest Coast culture. If direct Oceanic influences have ever to be reckoned with, they may complicate the picture."[126] Archaeology, it appears, has not yet been able to provide the "more refined analysis" mentioned by Kroeber, perhaps never will, because the presumed Asiatic elements are such as to leave few traces in the ground.[127] In any case, whatever may be the true explanation, one senses here the presence of forces more stimulating than mere abundance of food—forces definitely outside the range of the more familiar (to us) patterns of New World cultural development. It is something like the explosive climax of Plains culture after the introduction of the horse, a development which would be equally hard to classify.

124. This term was suggested by Christopher Hawkes (personal communication, 1953).

125. Borden, 1954; Drucker, 1955; M. W. Smith, 1956. Borden has a date of 476 ± 163 B.C. for his "Eskimoid" phase in the lower Fraser River region (University of Saskatchewan, sample No. 5-3).

126. Kroeber, 1939, p. 31.   127. De Laguna, 1947, p. 12.

In line with what has just been said, it might be better not to mention the Archaic stage in the Arctic. Here we are dealing with cultural traditions and configurations so unique as to make comparisons appear faintly ridiculous. There is a rapidly accumulating corpus of finds in the Arctic that are earlier than, and possibly distinct from, the Eskimo cultures, but the only adequately formulated unit in this category is Denbigh, which, on the basis of extraordinarily fine chipping techniques and specific point types, we have already considered as a possible Lithic culture. However, we have found similar late Lithic point types (Plainview, Angostura, Eden-Scottsbluff, etc.) turning up repeatedly in contexts that we have classified without hesitation as Archaic, with radiocarbon dates considerably older than those obtained for Denbigh.[128] Since the original discovery at Iyatayet, burins and the associated microcore-and-blade tradition that seem to us to be more characteristic of Denbigh than the Lithic traits mentioned above have turned up in many new sites and old collections in Alaska,[129] the Aleutians,[130] the Mackenzie Valley,[131] and the eastern Arctic and Canada,[132] as well as Greenland,[133] in contexts that are variously labeled "Early Man" and "Paleo-Eskimo." The geographical and temporal dimensions of this tradition are not yet sufficiently understood to make it useful as a criterion in developmental classification, but we have a strong impression that its first appearance in New World archaeology and subsequent associations are with cultures of the Archaic stage, although something rather like it is found farther south in the Formative stage.[134]

With these exceptions out of the way it is surprising how many

128. Cf. chap. 4, n. 76.

129. See Daugherty, 1956, for summary of recent Alaska finds, and Irving, 1955, for reappraisal of Alaska Campus material.

130. Laughlin, 1951; Laughlin, Marsh, and Leach, 1952; Laughlin and Marsh, 1954.

131. MacNeish, 1954a.

132. Harp, 1951, 1952; Collins, 1953b.   133. Melgaard, 1952.

134. In Hopewellian cultures of Ohio and Illinois and the Poverty Point culture of the lower Mississippi Valley. Cf. pp. 156–59.

of the criteria of our definition of Archaic are applicable to Eskimo and Paleo-Eskimo cultures. This is particularly noticeable in the Dorset culture of the eastern Arctic,[135] whose relationship with northeastern Archaic cultures is a perpetual subject of discussion.[136] But even such climactic phases as Old Bering Sea and Ipiutak[137] would, if the specifically Asiatic elements were subtracted and if the finds were subjected to the same unfavorable conditions for preservation, appear to be on the same level of development as many of the well-known Archaic cultures farther south. Not only is there a basic conformity in stone and bone technologies but there are a great many shared artifact types of a specific nature. Until fairly recently the tendency was to attribute the presence of such traits in Archaic contexts to Eskimoan influence. Now, with the far greater time depth allowed to North American Archaic, this interpretation is no longer tenable.

MIDDLE AND SOUTH AMERICA

The case for an Archaic stage in Mexico and Middle America is similar to that outlined for the southwestern and Great Basin areas of the United States. In Tamaulipas, the Nogales phase, which follows the probable Lithic stage Diablo and Lerma phases, is characterized by teardrop- and triangular-shaped points, large oval blades, chipped-stone hoes or celts, and frequent crude hammerstones, manos, and metates.[138] The subsequent La Perra phase is characterized by the appearance of a primitive maize, but, otherwise, the Archaic culture continuum is essentially unchanged.[139] By

135. Jenness, 1925; Rowley, 1940; Leechman, 1943; Collins, 1953a.

136. Strong, 1930; De Laguna, 1946; Ritchie, 1951b; Hoffman, 1952.

137. Collins, 1937; Larsen and Rainey, 1948. The settlement of Ipiutak is altogether exceptional from the point of view of village plan and size (575 located house pits!). The excavators themselves were able to account for this only by supposing that the village was occupied seasonally, with new houses being built each year in preference to reoccupation of those previously used (ibid., p. 47).

138. MacNeish, 1950, p. 92.

139. MacNeish, 1947; MacNeish, 1950, p. 87. The radiocarbon date for La Perra is 2490 ± 280 B.C. (sample No. C-687 [Libby, 1952]).

extension, the preceramic Chalco complex of the Valley of Mexico is assigned to the Archaic upon the basis of its artifact similarities to Nogales. Quite probably, the Abasolo and Repelo complexes of the Tamaulipas coast fit into this bracket. In Coahuila the Cienegas complex and the later Coahuila complex, both defined by Taylor, are Archaic cultures in the Desert tradition.[140]

On the Chiapas coast, at Islona de Chantuto, the preceramic levels of the shell middens have yielded little in the way of distinctive artifacts[141] and may, possibly, pertain to anything from Lithic to Archaic; however, the nature of the site deposit suggests the Archaic.

In Panama, a non-ceramic and probably preceramic complex, the Cerro Mangote, has been discovered on an old shoreline of the Bay of Parita on the Pacific coast.[142] Artifacts include crude pebble choppers and grinders, rubbing stones, and scrapers. The subsequent Monagrillo phase of the same region sees the addition of rather simple plain, incised, and red-painted pottery to this Cerro Mangote complex. A third phase, the Sarigua, which may be later than Monagrillo, lacks the stone chopping and grinding tools but possesses pottery of a simple kind, though in a style quite different from Monagrillo. The location of all these sites on abandoned shorelines and lagoons and the nature of their refuse argue against the presence of agriculture; and their general configuration is that of the Archaic.[143]

In South America there are several possibilities for an Archaic stage. Among these is the culture, or culture continuum, represented by the deep preceramic levels at Huaca Prieta, in the Chicama Valley on the north coast of Peru.[144] Formerly, we discussed this Huaca Prieta phase as Preformative, basing our judgments on the abundant remains of domesticated squash, peppers, gourds, and

---

140. Kelley, MS presented at Andover, October, 1956. Radiocarbon dates on Cienegas range from 6920 to 5450 B.C. The Coahuila radiocarbon date is 1670 B.C. See also Martinez del Rio, 1953.

141. Drucker, 1948.   143. Willey and McGimsey, 1954.

142. McGimsey, 1956.   144. Bird, 1948a, 1948b.

cotton, and seeing in this early agriculture something of a parallel with Chiricahua Cochise or La Perra. The Huaca Prieta stone complex, which consists only of crude flakes and choppers, offers few clues for comparisons with North America or anywhere else. Tentatively, we may consider Huaca Prieta as being on the Archaic level, an assignment which is fairly consistent with its radiocarbon dates of 2500–1250 B.C.[145]

In northern Chile, at Arica and Pichalo, the Archaic is well represented by two sequent periods or phases. Shell fishhooks, cigar-shaped stone sinkers, composite stone fishhooks of stone and bone, stone mortars, and stone bowls are among the distinctive artifact types. Rough percussion-flaked artifacts are found all along the Chilean coast, but these are clearly associated and contemporaneous with pressure-flaked and ground- and polished-stone implements. In brief, there is no evidence of Lithic stage cultures antedating those of the Archaic along the Chilean littoral.[146] At both Arica and Pichalo, maize agriculture and ceramics follow the Archaic periods. In the Arica sequence there is some slight indication that maize may have preceded pottery, but this is not certain.

In southern South America, in the Straits of Magellan sequence, Archaic stage cultures follow the Lithic stage Periods 1 and 2.[147] In the Archaic artifact assemblages some of the stemmed projectile points are not unlike Archaic points of North America. Bolas stones, showing up in Periods 3, 4, and 5, mark the use of ground-stone implements in this Magellanic sequence. Subsequent to this, pottery appears as a part of the historic Tehuelche artifact complex in this far southern region. There is little doubt that the pottery trait spread southward into the Pampas and Patagonia in prehistoric times, probably diffusing from foci on the lower Paraná River. Arroyo Sarandí and El Cerrillo, near the delta of the Plate, are representative of these pottery-making Archaic cultures of the northern Pampas.[148] Bone implements and objects, chipped and ground stone, and incised and punctated pottery of simple vessel

145. Bird, 1951.   147. Bird, 1938.
146. Bird, 1943.   148. Lothrop, 1932.

forms make up the artifact assemblages. As yet, preceramic Archaic phases have not been stratigraphically demonstrated for the Pampean or Paraná regions, although certain site collections suggest them. In general, aboriginal life on the Pampas and in surrounding regions is revealed by both archaeology and ethnohistory as varying between nomadism on the open flat country and relatively stable small sites along the rivers. Land game and riverine foods were the staples.[149] Only in very late times, with the occupation of sites like Arroyo Malo in the Plate Delta by Guaraní Indians, was an agricultural village pattern tentatively established in the area.[150]

In eastern Brazil, in some of the Lagoa Santa caves, chipped- and ground-stone celts, handstones, pitted anvils, and bone projectile points are found in levels preceding pottery and pottery pipes. Serrano defines an early coastal shellmound, or *sambaquí*, culture as having an artifact complex very similar to that of the Lagoa Santa caves.[151] Later *sambaquí* phases (the "Middle" and the "Southern")[152] are characterized by numerous ground- and polished-stone artifacts, including plummet-like stones (*"fusos"*), bolas, mortars, axes, celts, and elaborate fish-shaped dishes. As such, they are reminiscent of the Archaic stage in North America.

Preceramic cultures of Archaic appearance are reported from Manicuare,[153] in Venezuela, and from the various islands of the West Indies.[154] The Venezuelan Archaic resembles that of the Antilles in the possession of conch-shell tools, and resemblances of this nature are also noted northward into Florida. West Indian preceramic levels are rather unique in their specific artifact forms, and

149. Howard and Willey, 1948.

150. Lothrop, 1932.

151. Serrano, 1940a, 1946. The Araujo II *sambaquí*, in Paraná, has an early phase (Culture A) in which stone-grinding and stone-polishing are less well developed than in later phases (B and C) (Orssich and Orssich, 1956).

152. Serrano, 1940b.

153. Manicuare radiocarbon dates: 1615 ± 130 b.c. and 1095 ± 80 b.c. Yale Natural Radiocarbon Measurements III, 1956, Nos. Y-295 and 296g.

154. Rouse, 1941, 1948, 1949, 1951a; Osgood, 1942.

there is considerable variation from island to island. The preceramic levels of Puerto Rico and the Guayabo Blanco phase of Cuba, along with the Manicuare of Venezuela, lack polished-stone forms.[155] On the other hand, in such phases as the Couri and the Bay of Conch in Haiti and the Cayo Redondo in Cuba, peg-shaped ceremonial stones, stone dishes, and axes all reveal stone-grinding and stone-polishing techniques.

To summarize briefly, the Middle and South American cultures classed as Archaic in this discussion represent numerous historical lines whose origins and connections have not been, or cannot be, traced. In Mexico there appear to be connections with early cultures in the southwestern United States and in Texas. The Chilean coast, another principal center of Archaic-type developments, shows an amazing number of parallels to the Archaic units of the southern California coast.[156] In the far south, what we have designated as Archaic seems to have deep roots in the old Patagonian and Fuegian hunting cultures of the Lithic stage, although in its later periods it undoubtedly assimilated various traits, including pottery, from the Archaic cultures in the areas to the north. In eastern Brazil, as well as in the northern Pampas and Paraná River section, there are a number of parallels to the Archaic of the eastern United States.[157] Archaic cultures in the Antilles, which could have formed a convenient link between those of the eastern United States and those of Brazil, are rather distinctive and highly localized, although there are some similarities both with Venezuela and with Florida.

155. Rouse, 1952; Alegria, Nicholson, and Willey, 1955; Rouse, 1948.
156. Bennyhoff, 1950; Lathrap, n.d.
157. Baerreis, 1950; Willey, 1951a.

Chapter 6

Formative Stage

DEFINITIONS

In discussing the Archaic, we have already indicated the kind of changes we have to make in our original concept of the Formative. The latter was defined "by the presence of maize and/or manioc agriculture and by the successful socioeconomic integration of such an agriculture into well-established sedentary village life."[1] As we pointed out at the time, this definition introduced specific diffused, i.e., historically derived, agricultural traditions as criteria in a developmental classification. We were not unmindful of the ambiguity of this procedure, but were constrained to follow along the lines of conventional thinking in both New and Old World archaeology.

We were well aware of the possibility of sociocultural patterns of comparable complexity being sustained by economies other than agricultural. We thought of cultures such as those already discussed in the California and Northwest Coast areas as marking a sort of florescence within the limits imposed by their hunting-fishing-gathering economies; we were quite prepared to admit that they might have attained the essential demographic characteristics of the Formative stage, but we preferred to call them Archaic, for two reasons: (1) they might be said to represent the "older" (developmentally speaking) pattern and (2) it could be argued that they lacked the potentialities for demographic increase that agricultural food production normally provides. That is to say, they were not Formative in the sense that they might go

1. Willey and Phillips, 1955, p. 765.

on to a Classic stage. This is a perfectly defensible position. It is substantially that taken by a majority of Old World archaeologists at a similar juncture. It is well known that certain Mesolithic sites in northern Europe exceed in size and material richness sites of the later Neolithic cultures in the same area.[2] On the other hand, in making a survey of "Preformative" cultures in our first paper, we found that agriculture per se was not the explosive stimulus to cultural development we had supposed it to be. The early evidences of plant domestication seem to be associated with cultures that we would be inclined to think of as "lower" Archaic if we had such a division, and in the one area where we have fairly reliable chronological control, the North American Southwest, there was plant domestication for a remarkably long time before any spectacular development followed.

This "slow-footed agricultural revolution" was actually the principal theoretical basis for our "Preformative" stage. It was the stage of *emerging* agriculture prior to its "successful integration into well-established sedentary village life." This also is a perfectly defensible formulation, but in practice it did not work very well. At the lower border of "Preformative," i.e., when one is trying to distinguish "Preformative" from Archaic, the mere presence of agriculture is detectable archaeologically only under unusually favorable conditions; at the upper border, the termination of emerging and beginning of "successful integration" can be established only by inference from settlement patterns and other indirect evidence. Practically speaking, then, the settlement patterns, etc.—not the agriculture—are the effective criteria for classification. Such being the case, it seems unreasonable to ignore the evidence of stable sedentary organization in those instances in which an agricultural basis cannot be inferred, either because there is no evidence or because the environment was unsuited to agriculture. Thus, the elimination of "Preformative" may be seen as largely a practical consideration, but a change of outlook is involved, not in regard to the importance of agriculture in New

2. Clarke, 1936, 1952.

World archaeology, but in regard to its place in developmental interpretation. We are not retreating from the position that agriculture was the principal *formative* agent in the development of Formative cultures, but only from a rigidity that makes it the indispensable agent. In so doing, we have shifted the emphasis somewhat away from the historical toward the developmental side of our hybrid "historical-developmental" scheme. If, as we believe, it is thus more consistent and workable, the change may be an improvement.

Therefore, we now define the New World Formative by the presence of agriculture, or any other subsistence economy of comparable effectiveness, and by the successful integration of such an economy into well-established, sedentary village life. We are dealing with societies of a certain minimal complexity and stability whose population sizes and gross groupings have been made possible by specific food economies, but, since these are preponderantly agricultural, we are also dealing with a historical phenomenon— the diffusion, or diffusions, of native American agriculture. Pottery-making, weaving, stone-carving, and a specialized ceremonial architecture are usually associated with these American Formative cultures. These elements are not linked to American agriculture through any inner causality, and some of them are often found in contexts that are non-agricultural. Seldom, however, are American agricultural societies lacking in all of them. There are insufficient data as yet to establish the relative chronological appearances of these trait complexes in the various New World areas, but it is unlikely that they exploded concurrently in one locality to effect a sudden and sweeping cultural revolution. Their significance is less one of origins than of function. It is a practical certainty that the origins of Formative stage cultures will be found to be extremely complex and diverse—the gradual assemblage of elements over considerable periods of time and over wide areas to produce cumulative and patterned results.

Cultures of the Formative stage occupy a geographically central position in the Western Hemisphere. They are found throughout much of Middle America and most of Andean South America. From these areas they extend northward, with some lacunae, into the southwestern and eastern United States, and in South America they run down the Cordillera to central Chile and eastward along the Amazon and Orinocan drainages of the lowlands. Their chronological span would appear to go back to the second millennium B.C. in Middle America[3] and almost that far back in Peru.[4] As noted above, there are early occurrences of maize in New Mexico and Tamaulipas, but there is no indication that agriculture was the primary basis of life in these cultures or that populations were organized into sizable, stable villages.

Not until the first centuries A.D. were Formative-type cultures established in the Southwest. Most authorities would agree on this same approximate date for the Southeast. In lower Central America, Colombia, and Ecuador, it is possible that agricultural village life is of an age with that of Middle America and Peru, but there is still little in the way of proof. In the South Andes the Formative threshold may be as late as A.D. 1000.[5] Caribbean and Amazonian archaeological sequences suggest considerable time depth for Formative-type cultures in some regions, but, as yet, there are few means by which to correlate these with Mexican or Peruvian chronologies.

MIDDLE AMERICA

In Middle America[6] the earliest known pottery-and-agriculture phases of several different archaeological regions are representa-

3. The date of 1359 ± 250 B.C. for Early Zacatenco in the Valley of Mexico is consistent with the Valley of Mexico stratigraphy and with the majority of the other carbon 14 dates (sample No. C-196 [Libby, 1952]).

4. Radiocarbon date of 714 ± 200 B.C. for Coastal Chavín culture in northern Peru (sample No. 75 [Libby, 1952]).

5. This would be true if agriculture and ceramics were introduced into northern Chile and northwestern Argentina on a Derived Tiahuanaco level. It is more likely, however, that these events antedate Tiahuanacoid diffusions from Peru (see Bird, 1943).

6. An area to be defined approximately as Kirchhoff (1943) defines 'Mesoamerica."

tive of Formative stage culture. A definition of all the regional culture sequences of Middle America is beyond the scope of this book, but any one of several will serve to demonstrate the rise and growth of Middle American civilization in the Formative stage. In the Valley of Mexico and its environs the El Arbolillo I[7] and the Early Zacatenco[8] phases are the earliest Formative manifestations. These phases are represented by large village sites of deep and extensive refuse. Handmade figurines, incised or white-on-red decorated ceramics, and metate and mano stones are characteristic artifacts. There follow the successive Middle Zacatenco, Tlaltilco, Ticoman, and Cuicuilco phases.[9] Although there is continuity from one phase to the next, this should not be misconstrued as a wholly local development. Outside influences came into the Valley of Mexico during these phases. One of the most striking of these "foreign" waves is reflected in the Tlaltilco pottery and the associated Olmec-style figurines. Toward the close of the Formative stage in the Valley of Mexico, the trait of platform-mound construction appears—Cuicuilco is the outstanding example[10]—as does monumental stone sculpture. The end of the Formative in the Valley of Mexico is marked by the beginning of the Teotihuacán II, or Miccaotli, phase of the Classic Teotihuacán civilization. This Mexican highland Formative sequence is, apparently, paralleled by the Mamom-through-Chicanel sequence of the lowland Maya,[11] the series of Formative stage phases at Kaminaljuyu in the Guatemalan highlands,[12] those of the Huasteca,[13] and various other sequences of southern Mexico.

In all these Middle American regions there are general technological and aesthetic similarities which link the Formative cultures. Ceramics show a competence of manufacture. They tend to be plain or monochrome, or, if decorated, the decorative techniques are frequently incision, scoring, punctation, rocker-stamping, or

7. Vaillant, 1935.
8. Vaillant, 1930.
9. Porter, 1953.
10. Cummings, 1933.
11. R. E. Smith, 1955.
12. Shook and Kidder, 1952.
13. Ekholm, 1944; MacNeish, 1954b.

a rather uncomplicated use of painting. Handmade figurines are a hallmark, and there are stylistic details which serve to establish cross-regional ties. A village community, probably consisting of from a dozen to several hundred households, was the basic living situation of the Middle American Formative cultures. In some regions there is evidence that this kind of settlement, alone, preceded the appearance of sites marked by public or religious architecture in the form of pyramid platforms. Wauchope has termed such a subdivision of the stage as the "Village Formative."[14] This was followed by an "Urban Formative" in which ceremonial centers, consisting of pyramid-mounds, were constructed in addition to the ordinary villages.

This distinction, between a purely village life and a village life plus ceremonial-center participation, poses a problem in stage classification. In so far as the archaeologist is able to read a prehistoric record, there can be little argument but that the ceremonial center, with its public works, stands for multivillage co-operation and for the beginnings of relatively large-scale politico-religious organization. These, presumably, were patterns which had not existed before. Should we not, then, fix upon this change as a stage division by lowering the upper limits of the Formative? We admit the validity of this reasoning but hesitate to follow it up. For one thing, the concept of the "Formative," the "Developmental," the "Preclassic," or the "Archaic"—all terms which have been applied to more or less the same span of culture development in Middle America—is rather deeply established in the existing literature.[15] This, in itself, is not cause to perpetuate the terminology and classification; but we feel there are other arguments. The name "Formative," as we use it, implies the *formation* of the New World agricultural village pattern. At the same time, it carries with it the connotation that this pattern was basic to and *formational* toward later and more advanced developments. The era that we think of

14. Wauchope, 1950.

15. Caso (1953) makes the distinction referred to by calling the earlier, or "Village Formative," the "Archaic" and the later division the "Formative."

as the late Formative in Middle America was a time of rapid growth, of new ideas and their material implementation in the form of community construction projects. It was, in this sense, part of the stage still *formational* to what we will define as the Classic.

The extent to which the similarities between the regional culture sequences of Middle America can be attributed to inter-regional diffusion or to developmental parallelism is not always clear. Some cases, such as the presence of the Olmec figurine style at Tlaltilco, in the Valley of Mexico, and Tres Zapotes, in Veracruz,[16] or the resemblances between Formative stage pottery of the lowland Maya Mamom and Chicanel phases and that of Veracruz and of the Huasteca, are undeniably the results of diffusion. But such a phenomenon as the apparent increase of populations during the Formative cannot be explained by historical forces alone. The idea of the platform- or pyramid-mound was undoubtedly widely diffused in Middle America during the late Formative, but the conditions for its acceptance from region to region were locally developed. This suggests the hypothesis that Middle American Formative stage culture, as it developed in its various foci, proceeded steadily but somewhat unevenly.

Most of the great achievements of the subsequent Classic stage are presaged by the Formative, but there is no significant regional clustering of these elements. Ambitious stone sculpture is featured in one region, elaborately decorated ceramics in another, and what appear to be the beginnings of a glyphic system elsewhere.[17] Certain regions may have evolved particular features because of peculiar natural environmental circumstances or advantages. Other cultures lacking settings with these specific potentialities may have turned to different courses. Geographical proximities and distances or physiographic barriers undoubtedly influenced the workings of diffusion, allowing an innovation or an acceleration of a trend here, delaying it there. With such cultural growth, which we cannot yet follow and may never be able to follow in all its complexity of detail, the Formative cultures of Middle America

16. Drucker, 1943.   17. Caso, 1947.

gradually assumed what archaeologists have come to call a "Classic" status.

Surely, one of the reasons that Classic cultures could be developed in Middle America was that there was a multiplicity of regional traditional antecedents. The intertwining of the many varied strands of the Formative produced the Classic. Individually, these strands would have supported nothing of greater moment than a culture like the Mississippian of the eastern United States, with its temple mounds, or the Coclé culture of Panama, with its fine pottery and metal craft. Together, they emerge as Middle American civilization. This does not mean that the Middle American Classic stage was characterized by a single, homogeneous culture or civilization. Regionalism persisted, but it was a regionalism in which the various Classic cultures had assimilated enough from each other so that all drew upon a common fund of great depth and richness.

NORTH AMERICA

Northwest of Middle America the distinctive patterns which characterize that area become attenuated and eventually disappear. A well-developed Formative stage, however, was attained in all three principal subareas of the North American Southwest. Middle American Formative elements are abundantly present in the later phases, but even before this the general configurations are distinct and characteristic Formative entities in their own right. It is in the southwestern setting, in fact, that archaeology can offer the most detailed view of continuous cultural development from Archaic into Formative, and it was because of this that our previous exposition of a Preformative stage relied heavily upon data from this area.

We are inclined to agree with J. O. Brew[18] that Anasazi, Hohokam, and Mogollon can no longer be considered self-contained cultural continuities; instead, as sequence formulations of a scope somewhere between what we have designated as regional se-

18. Brew and Smith, 1954, p. 588.

quences and area syntheses, they offer the best opportunity for testing our developmental hypotheses without losing us in the superabundance of detail that southwestern archaeology offers. Let us begin with the Mogollon subarea. We have already spoken of the early corn in Bat and Tularosa caves of southwestern New Mexico and their story of a protracted Archaic-with-corn stage of development. The point at which this ends and Formative begins is more than usually difficult to establish. Five separate "branches" (regional sequences in our terminology) of the Mogollon subarea have been correlated by Joe Ben Wheat, in two recent publications, into a sequence of five numbered periods covering a span from about 300 B.C. to A.D. 1500.[19] He gives excellent summaries of developments in various technological categories but not much idea of changes in total configuration. This kind of information is also rather hard to get from the primary sources.[20] All writers emphasize the continuity from Cochise into Mogollon, and, apart from the incorporation of elements derived from Hohokam and, later, Anasazi sources, the subsequent history seems to have been one of slow and uneventful change. On the other hand, it appears that, in the Pine Lawn, Hilltop, and possibly other early phases of the Mogollon sequence, there were already small villages of pit-houses clustered around a larger, presumably ceremonial, structure.[21] It would seem that we have to accord Mogollon I a qualified Formative status, but it is not until considerably farther along in the sequence that the settlement patterns and general configurations are comparable to Formative developments in other parts of the Southwest, and by this time it is a moot question whether the culture is still Mogollon.

In the Anasazi subarea, Basket Maker III of the Pecos Classifi-

19. Wheat, 1954, Fig. 1; 1955, Fig. 12.

20. Haury, 1936; Martin and Rinaldo, 1947, 1950a, 1950b; Martin, Rinaldo, and Antevs, 1949; Martin et al., 1952, 1956.

21. Wheat, 1954, p. 580.

cation (or Modified Basket Maker, as it is alternatively called)[22] is essentially a continuation of Basket Maker II with new features, such as additional varieties of corn, beans, domesticated turkey, pottery, the bow, the grooved ax and maul—none of decisive significance perhaps from a developmental point of view, but the general configuration is suggestive of the Formative. There is now widespread use of substantial slab-lined pit-houses of standardized types, with antechambers, ventilators, and other special features that became embalmed in the small kivas of later periods. There are also, in some localities, ranges of contiguous one-story surface rooms of crude masonry and jacal construction that foreshadow the agglutinated unit-type house structures of the Pueblo II and III periods. More important, perhaps, from our point of view, is the fact that the villages attain considerable size in Basket Maker III, up to one hundred and fifty rooms or more, and that in some cases large circular structures are associated with them, presumably of religious or ceremonial import and possibly prototypical of the Great Kivas of Pueblo III.

In the succeeding Pueblo I period, although there is progressive development of masonry architecture, there is a tendency for villages to be smaller.[23] Without knowing whether these seemingly small settlements were organized into larger communities, we cannot readily evaluate this kind of change. At any rate, in Pueblo II[24] the trend toward larger villages, which started in Basket Maker III, is resumed and is accompanied by pronounced architectural improvement, both in planning and in construction. All the specialized features of the kiva attained their characteristic forms in this period and began to be incorporated into the village plan in a manner that indicates foresight and design. The Anasazi phases of the great Pueblo III and IV periods represent a climax of Formative stage culture in the Southwest as a whole. Athabascan incursions and Spanish conquest had serious effects upon Anasazi culture, and the towns decreased in size and number; nevertheless,

22. Roberts, 1929; Martin, 1939; Amsden, 1949; Lancaster et al., 1954.
23. Roberts, 1931, 1939, 1940   24. Morris, 1939; Brew, 1946.

the culture remained viable, and a Formative type of life persisted —and still persists—in the modern pueblos.

Like the Mogollon, the Hohokam of the Gila Basin and Tucson regions of Arizona appears to have grown out of the earlier Cochise, but with the difference that the later phases of Cochise in this subarea have not yet furnished evidences of agriculture. As in the Mogollon sequence, the earliest phases of the Hohokam are a sort of incipient Formative in that it is as yet difficult to judge the significance of agriculture as a means of promoting sedentary village life. We are inclined, however, to place the Formative threshold in the Vahki phase of the Pioneer period[25] at an estimated date of 300 B.C. Population increase and such features as ball courts, canal irrigation, and a presumed step-up of agricultural production in the succeeding Colonial period phases[26] mark the crystallization of full-fledged Formative stage culture. Undoubtedly the ball-game idea, along with many other elements, passed into the Southwest from Middle America, but its adoption and the construction of large community works in connection with it indicate that Hohokam societies were developing sufficient size and co-ordination to exploit such an idea. In the Hohokam Sedentary period[27] irrigation systems were enlarged and improved; ball courts were still in use but were reduced in size; villages became compactly planned settlements of adobe houses, in some cases inclosed by walls to form compounds. In the Classic period, beginning about A.D. 1000, the innovations were largely architectural, culminating in the massive, multistoried adobe structures of Casa Grande[28] and Los Muertos.[29] To some extent these architectural and settlement changes of the Sedentary and Classic periods may be attributed to diffusion, and even actual migration, from the Anasazi regions to the north; yet the continued expansion of the irrigation systems would seem to suggest steadily increasing populations. Thus, although the form and style of the new settlements may have been

25. Gladwin *et al.*, 1937.
26. Woodward, 1931; Haury, 1932.   28. Gladwin, 1928.
27. Gladwin *et al.*, 1937.   29. Haury, 1945.

Anasazi (or "Salado," whatever that term may mean), the social and cultural conditions which they reflect were, at least in part, engendered within the Hohokam culture. The causes of the breakup of Hohokam culture after A.D. 1400 are not fully understood. Soil depletion and irrigation difficulties, internal warfare and external pressures, are cited as possibilities. Whatever the course of events, the prosperous agricultural villages could no longer be maintained, and Hohokam culture slipped back from its Formative level to a condition reminiscent of an earlier and simpler stage.[30]

In summary, the Formative stage cultures of the Southwest, in contrast to those of Middle America, are seen in their earliest beginnings and show the gradual steps by which marginal agricultural societies may achieve full agricultural status. In an internal sense, southwestern culture could be said to have reached a Classic stage in such manifestations as Pueblo Bonito of the Chaco Canyon[31] or Casa Grande of the desert region of southern Arizona.[32] But from an external point of view, in the perspective of New World culture-history, these achievements are meager in their over-all architectural, artistic, and intellectual attainments when compared to Classic Middle American or Peruvian civilizations. It has been a commonly held opinion that southwestern native cultures lagged behind Middle American cultures because they were geographically remote from the sources of American agriculture and therefore started their climb toward a higher culture much later. But the early dates for Bat Cave corn in the Southwest force us to re-examine this rationalization. We have argued that a varied natural environment and multiple regional-cultural centers in Middle America were significant stimuli for cultural growth in that area. It is likely that the limitations of the Southwest in this regard were the most important deterrents to the rise of a native American Classic stage in that area.

In our discussion of the Archaic in eastern North America, we placed the Formative threshold roughly on the division between

30. DiPeso, 1951, 1953.
31. Kidder, 1924; Judd, 1954.   32. Gladwin, 1928.

Early and Middle Woodland in the Griffin chronology.[33] It remains only to give examples and the reasons for calling them Formative. First, however, we must dispose of some exceptions to the corollary generalization that all "Archaic" (in the Griffin terminology) and Early Woodland cultures are below that threshold. The Poverty Point culture of the lower Mississippi[34] is generally designated as "late Archaic," because it has stone technology of that level, baked clay objects highly reminiscent of the central California Archaic, soapstone vessels, and no pottery. On the other hand, there are mounds of unascertained function up to seventy feet high, and the type site in northeastern Louisiana has a great sixfold system of concentric octagonal earth embankments three-quarters of a mile in diameter. The function of this remarkable earthwork is likewise problematical. The only investigators who have seen something of these embankments from the inside have found them to be composed largely of refuse, and argue therefrom that they represent a planned village of these extraordinary proportions.[35] The temporal position of Poverty Point, now fairly well established by no less than ten radiocarbon dates ranging from about 1300 to 200 B.C. with the majority clustering around 800 B.C., would be more appropriate to an Early Woodland culture, but, from our point of view, the possibility of Formative status must be allowed for. On the basis of the sheer size of the mounds and earthworks, we have to infer a concentration of population, or at least a concentration of control over a large population, backed up by a stable food supply. So far there has been no evidence of agriculture, but it is quite impossible to imagine any other adequate economic basis in the geographic setting.

The second exception to the generalization that Formative in the East begins with Middle Woodland is the Adena culture of the

33. Griffin, 1952a. For those who prefer the Ford and Willey scheme (1941) the line would be between the Burial Mound I and II periods.

34. C. H. Webb, 1944, 1948b; Haag and Webb, 1953; Ford, 1954d; Ford, Phillips, and Haag, 1955; Ford and Webb, 1956.

35. Ford and Webb, 1956.

Ohio Valley.[36] Adena has been designated as "Early Woodland" in the Griffin classification, and is so regarded by most easternists, on the basis of an assumed priority over Hopewell, the main anchor of the Middle Woodland concept in eastern archaeology. This assumption, based largely on typological and distributional grounds without stratigraphic confirmation, was badly shaken by the first published radiocarbon dates, which appeared to invert the relationship.[37] More recent dates have substantially restored the original chronology,[38] however, and it has received additional support from recent stratigraphic studies in the upper Ohio Valley.[39] Thus, if we set aside Poverty Point as a developmental enigma clearly in need of further explanation, Adena probably represents the earliest reorientation of eastern Archaic culture along lines that we can designate as Formative. All available information comes from the excavation of burial mounds and small sections of village sites beneath them, and thus very little can be said about the settlement patterns. However, the great size of mounds,[40] the nature and complexity of mortuary practices (suggestive of social

36. Mills, 1902; Greenman, 1932; Webb and Snow, 1945; Spaulding, 1952.

37. Griffin, 1951.

38. There are now too many Hopewell and Adena dates available to be listed here, and they are too erratic for summary generalization. The significant dates from the point of view of this discussion are 696 ± 170 B.C. (sample No. C-759 [Libby, 1954a]) and 826 ± 410 B.C. (sample No. C-942 [Libby, 1954b]) from Adena sites in Kentucky and Ohio, respectively, both of which are substantially earlier than 545 ± 300 B.C. (sample No. M-15 [Crane, 1956]) and 385 ± 250 B.C. (sample No. C-152 [Arnold and Libby, 1951]), two of a fairly neat cluster of Illinois Hopewell dates. The Ohio Hopewell dates so far obtained run slightly later than those from Illinois.

39. Information given by John Witthoft at the Andover Radiocarbon Conference, October, 1956.

40. The Grave Creek Mound, near Wheeling, West Virginia (Squier and Davis, 1848, Fig. 56), and the Miamisburg Mound near Dayton, Ohio (Shetrone, 1931, Fig. 100), each approximately seventy feet high, and the Great Serpent Mound of Adams County, Ohio, though they have not been satisfactorily excavated, are all considered on fairly good evidence to be Adena. They may, therefore, date as early as 500 B.C. From the standpoint of mass, these monuments will stand comparison with any other New World structures of comparable date.

stratification), the large and substantial houses, and the high artistic quality of some of the artifacts permit us to infer stable settlements and an effective economic base.[41]

When we turn to cultures that have been classified as Middle Woodland, it is impossible to avoid beginning with Hopewell. Adena is a reasonably well-defined archaeological unit; not so with Hopewell. The name has been much abused in the literature. There are at least two primary centers of concentration, one in southern Ohio, the other in the Illinois River and Mississippi River valleys in Illinois and adjacent states, and there are a great many so-called Hopewellian phases or cultures farther afield that we shall speak of presently. Dates for Illinois and Ohio Hopewell range from about 500 B.C. to A.D. 1, the Illinois sites being slightly older at the present time. The nature of the relationship between them is a problem about which there might be considerable diversity of opinion, but all would agree that the climax of the culture is represented by the "big four" Ohio sites: Hopewell,[42] Mound City,[43] Seip[44]—all three in the Scioto Valley in the vicinity of Chillicothe —and the Turner Mounds,[45] on the Little Miami River near Cincinnati. This climax development cannot be placed accurately within the time span indicated above, but we may assume it was toward the end, say, in the last one or two centuries B.C. The technological skill and artistic sensitivity attested by some of the objects in stone, obsidian, tortoise shell, bone, copper, silver, and meteoric iron were unapproached anywhere else in North America at this time and hardly surpassed in Middle and South America. The same may be said of the energy expended in the complicated construction of huge burial mounds, ceremonial earth inclosures, and fortifications.[46] In our first paper we reluctantly assigned this

41. Spaulding, 1955, pp. 19–21.

42. Moorehead, 1922a; Shetrone, 1926.

43. Mills, 1922.   44. Mills, 1909; Shetrone and Greenman, 1931.

45. Willoughby, 1922.

46. The great Fort Ancient, its name given erroneously to a later culture, is now recognized as a hilltop sanctuary of the Hopewell period (Morgan, 1952, p. 93).

classic Hopewell phase to a "Preformative" status on the grounds of insufficient evidence of large, stable villages—excavations in Ohio Hopewell sites have been almost entirely confined to burial mounds for understandable but not altogether praiseworthy reasons—and only very occasional direct indications of maize agriculture. Under our present less rigorous standards we can redress that injustice. As in the case of Poverty Point and Adena, it seems unlikely that the large populations we are obliged to infer could have been supported and organized for public works of such magnitude without a stable and efficient economic base. The Ohio Valley lies well within the known historic orbit of maize agriculture; in later aboriginal periods maize was of primary economic significance. We find it difficult to conceive of an alternative wild food supply of sufficient dependability in this region. In any case, maize or no, the configuration of the culture is fully Formative, as we now define the stage.

Whether the many Hopewellian manifestations scattered widely throughout the East should be regarded as units of a major Hopewell continuity or as phases of other unformulated cultures linked by a Hopewellian horizon is a complicated question that we do not have to go into here. Our casual impression is that the various phases in Illinois,[47] Indiana,[48] Wisconsin,[49] Michigan,[50] and perhaps New York[51] might be drawn in with Ohio Hopewell into a Hopewell "culture" without stretching the formulation unduly, but whether these also, in all cases, could be regarded as Formative is another question. Hopewellian manifestations farther away from the nuclear centers, particularly in the South, while possessing individual elements (horizon markers?), show markedly differ-

47. Cole and Deuel, 1937; Griffin and Morgan, 1941; Deuel *et al.*, 1952.

48. Lilly, 1937; Quimby, 1941*a*.

49. McKern, 1931*b*; L. R. Cooper, 1933.

50. Greenman, 1927; Quimby, 1941*a*, 1941*b*, 1952.

51. Ritchie, 1938.

ent configurations. Marksville,[52] Troyville,[53] and Issaquena,[54] for example, are more intelligible as phases in a lower Mississippi continuum that has yet to find a name. It does not contribute any cultural understanding to call them Hopewellian. The kind of excavations required to permit judgment as to whether this Marksville-Troyville culture is classifiable as Formative have not been made or at least have not yet been published. It would, however, be very surprising if such were not the case.

Similarly, on the Florida Gulf Coast, Hopewellian traditions, chiefly ceramic, entering perhaps by way of the lower Mississippi, have combined with resident traditions to form a regional development of great vitality and individual flavor. In its early Santa Rosa–Swift Creek phase[55] this regional development lacks sufficient site documentation for developmental interpretation, but, in the later Weeden Island[56] and Kolomoki[57] phases, particularly the latter, it would qualify as Formative.

Many other instances of Hopewellian intrusion into the Southeast could be mentioned. The elements that reveal such a connection are often striking, as in the famous Crystal River mound in Florida,[58] but there is always the question whether they reflect a serious orientation of pre-existing Early Woodland patterns or merely some sort of trade relations. The same developmental uncertainty attaches to Middle Woodland cultures in the Southeast which seem to have been more resistant to Hopewellian influences. An example is the Copena (COPPER-galENA) of the Tennessee River

52. Fowke, 1928; Ford, 1936; Ford and Willey, 1940.

53. W. Walker, 1936; Ford, 1951. The Troyville and Greenhouse sites covered by these reports are multicomponent sites. The ideal type site for the Troyville phase (Baptiste, or Av-25, on the Marksville Prairie, Louisiana) has been dug but not reported.

54. Greengo, 1957.

55. Willey and Woodbury, 1942; Willey, 1949.

56. Moore, 1901, 1902, 1903, 1918; Fewkes, 1924; Willey, 1945b, 1949.

57. Sears, 1951a, 1951b, 1953, 1956.

58. Moore, 1903, 1907a; Greenman, 1938; Willey and Phillips, 1944; Willey, 1948b.

Valley in northern Alabama.[59] Here again, our information is confined to burial mounds of modest proportions and their contents, which show a level of sophistication comparable to Adena and Hopewell, but little can be said about the kind of settlements or the economic base.

Middle Woodland period cultures in Georgia and contiguous portions of adjoining states are likewise difficult to classify. These are unified by common participation in the southern Appalachian or Complicated Stamp pottery tradition, a ceramic development grounded in the simple and checked stamp styles of the Early Woodland phases such as Mossy Oak and Deptford (already classified as Archaic), which attained a sudden climax from the aesthetic point of view in the beautiful curvilinear style of the early Swift Creek phase of south-central Georgia.[60] A parallel development, possibly derived out of the Mossy Oak simple stamped type, resulted in a complicated rectilinear style the best-known example of which is called "Early Napier."[61] Both curvilinear and rectilinear styles went through a number of phases and reacted upon each other in a very complex fashion, their influence spreading far beyond the borders of Georgia, but the associated cultures, so far as we can see, remained on a relatively low level of development, until the Etowah and Lamar phases, which will be referred to later.

Cultural development in peninsular Florida tended to pursue a course of its own which renders terms like "Early Woodland" and "Middle Woodland" somewhat meaningless. Cultures of the St. Johns River, Indian River, and Glades regions, where we have excellent sequences, seem to have remained on an Archaic level throughout most of the long spans of their existence. Elements derived from Formative culture to the north appear in considerable strength in some of the later phases, but there are few signs of accompanying socioeconomic changes. This is almost certainly

59. W. S. Webb, 1939; Webb and DeJarnette, 1942.
60. Kelly, 1938; Fairbanks, 1952.
61. Sears, 1952.

due to the conservative influence of a highly characterized environment which offers an abundance of fresh- and salt-water foods but is not, generally speaking, favorable to agriculture. We are frankly at a loss to say where Formative begins in these Florida sequences. St. Johns II, as represented in sites like Mount Royal and the Grant Mound,[62] would probably qualify, as would, possibly, the corresponding Malabar II phase of the Indian River region.[63] The climax of the Glades III phase, as exemplified in the famous Key Marco site, is perhaps another instance of attainment of at least a marginal Formative status on an economic base that almost certainly did not include agriculture.[64]

Middle Woodland cultures in the upper Mississippi Valley, the Great Lakes region, and the Northeast generally failed to reach an unquestionable Formative level. Exception to this facile generalization might perhaps be taken in favor of the Effigy Mound culture of Wisconsin and portions of adjacent states,[65] in which a remarkable amount of energy was expended in raising monuments to the distinguished dead. Excavations have disclosed that in some cases an effigy or linear mound several hundred feet long contains no more than the body of a single individual. Unfortunately, artifacts seldom accompany the burials, and we know next to nothing of the more prosaic aspects of the culture. It has been suggested that this unique florescence of mound-building in what otherwise appears to be an essentially Archaic context may have been made possible by a subsistence economy based on the abundant supplies of wild rice in the region. If so, perhaps Effigy Mound should be added to the short list of debatable instances of Formative cultures based on economies other than agriculture.[66]

To generalize briefly on the Middle Woodland cultures of the

62. Goggin, 1952.   63. Rouse, 1951b.

64. Cushing, 1897; Goggin, 1949.

65. Barrett and Hawkes, 1919; McKern, 1928, 1930, 1931a; Nash, 1933; J. W. Bennett, 1952.

66. Cf. discussion of late phases of central California, the Northwest Coast, and the Florida Glades.

East, we are conscious of the marginal nature of most of them with respect to our concept of a Formative stage and of the inadequacy of the data upon which we are basing our opinions. Actual settlement data are extremely scanty. For certain phases, such as Ohio Hopewell and other closely related manifestations, the earthworks and burial mounds attest to population densities and sociopolitical organization of a sort consistent with sedentary life based upon established agriculture, but even here the direct evidences of such a life and such an economy are very weak. In other regions, as we have acknowledged on numerous occasions, it is difficult even to infer settled economies and village life. Evidently our statement that Middle Woodland marks the beginning of Formative in the East requires a great deal of qualification. The fact is that some of the inferred splendor of the climax Ohio Hopewell phase has rubbed off on related and even unrelated (but contemporaneous) cultures, which, examined coolly on strictly developmental criteria, fail to come up to Formative standards. We are semantically embarrassed at this juncture, because, if such cultures are not Formative, or at least marginal Formative, we have to call them "Archaic," and the term has a more restricted meaning in eastern archaeology.

The situation, fortunately, is rather different in the succeeding Mississippi period. The features of this period that seem reliably reflective of an intensive agricultural village life, i.e., a full-blown Formative stage, are the rectangular "temple" or "town-house" mounds, the arrangement of these mounds around a central plaza, compact villages of substantial pole-and-thatch or wattle-and-daub houses with deep and extensive refuse (other than shell middens), and the frequent and abundant finds of maize itself. Such features, along with certain characteristic pottery styles and artifact types, are known to be associated with, though not confined to, the Mississippi (or "Middle Mississippi") culture. Many of these elements appear to have derived from Middle American sources. They are clearly post-Hopewellian arrivals in the eastern United States. The mechanisms and routes of their presumed diffusion from Middle America are still completely unknown, although there has been no lack of speculation on the subject.[67]

Mississippi is probably the best-known culture in the East, yet one looks in vain for an integration of its manifold phases and a description of the whole. The chief difficulty, perhaps, has been our inability to nucleate the culture geographically. This in turn is partly, if not wholly, due to the belief expressed above that the source of most of its diagnostic elements is Middle America and that we might therefore expect to find its nucleus in the Gulf coastal, lower Mississippi Valley, or Caddoan regions. Such expectations have not, in our opinion, been fulfilled.[68] Certain elements that have been identified closely with Mississippi culture, notably the above-mentioned rectangular temple mounds, do enter into certain Gulf, lower Mississippi, and Caddoan area cultures, but, whenever the really diagnostic Mississippi features appear in these regions, they seem to have intruded from the north. This has led to the hypothesis that the nuclear area for the Mississippi culture is somewhere in the central Mississippi Valley (from the mouth of the Missouri to the Ohio) and lower Ohio Valley or Tennessee-Cumberland regions.[69] It is only in this general area that the culture

67. Swanton, 1924; Spinden, 1931; Beals, 1932; Vaillant, 1932; Mason, 1937; Phillips, 1939, 1940; Griffin, 1944; J. W. Bennett, 1944; Krieger, 1945, 1948.

68. This is admittedly a matter of opinion. Alex Krieger, for one, is confident that such a nuclear center has been found, in the Alto phase of the Caddoan area (Newell and Krieger, 1949; Krieger, 1951b, 1952). His arguments in favor of the proposition have considerable appeal, and he has one radiocarbon date of A.D. 398 ± 175 on corncobs from the Davis site (sample No. C-153 [Libby, 1951]), but this would require drastic revision of dating in other areas that archaeologists working in those areas have so far been unwilling to make (Griffin, 1950; Phillips, Ford, and Griffin, 1951; Ford, 1951, 1952).

69. This statement appears to be at variance with opinions previously expressed by one of the present authors (Phillips, Ford, and Griffin, 1951, p. 451) because we are now attempting to take a more precise view of the Mississippi culture. We now prefer to think of some of the "centers" of Mississippi development, referred to in the publication cited, in terms of Mississippi influence upon units that in the main belong to other cultures, e.g., Etowah-Lamar, Fort Walton, Coles Creek–Plaquemine, etc.

seems to have any appreciable time depth. A number of "Early Mississippi" phases have been identified, but the stratigraphic evidence is rather tenuous.[70] Examples are: the Old Village phase at the great Cahokia site in East St. Louis,[71] the Obion phase in western Tennessee,[72] and the Hiwassee Island phase in the Chickamauga Basin of eastern Tennessee.[73] The Macon Plateau phase of central Georgia[74] is early Mississippi in type but is clearly an intrusion into a region dominated by cultures of the Complicated Stamp pottery tradition.[75] Following closely upon these scattered early phases, the climax period of the Mississippi culture is seen in such phases as Monks Mound,[76] named after the big mound at Cahokia, Illinois, largest rectangular platform-mound north of Mexico; Kincaid and Angel, on the lower Ohio;[77] Cairo Lowland, in southeastern Missouri;[78] Nodena and Parkin, or "St. Francis," in northeastern Arkansas;[79] Cumberland, in the Nashville Basin of central Tennessee;[80] Dallas and Mouse Creek, in eastern Tennessee;[81] and Moundville, on the Black Warrior River in north-central Alabama,[82] including the closely related Bessemer site near Birmingham.[83] Many more phases could be cited, but these are the most intensively Mississippian and seem to define the nuclear area as outlined above. Here is more than sufficient material for a com-

70. One of the puzzling anomalies of eastern archaeology is the fact that dating estimates are as incongruent and unreliable in the later periods as in the earlier, if not more so, a condition which is only beginning to be remedied by radiocarbon dating.

71. Kelly, 1933; Griffin, 1949. The recently published Cahokia date of A.D. 1156 ± 200 (sample No. M-33 [Crane, 1956]) refers, we assume, to the Old Village component in the site.

72. Kneberg, 1952, p. 193.   74. Kelly, 1938.

73. Lewis and Kneberg, 1946.   75. Fairbanks, 1952; Willey, 1953*b*.

76. Moorehead and Leighton, 1923; Moorehead *et al.*, 1929; Titterington, 1938.

77. Cole *et al.*, 1951; Lilly, 1937; Black, 1944.

78. Williams, 1954.

79. Phillips, Ford, and Griffin, 1951; Griffin, 1952*c*.

80. Phillips, 1939.   82. Moore, 1905, 1907*b*.

81. Lewis and Kneberg, 1946.   83. DeJarnette and Wimberly, 1941.

prehensive definition of Mississippi culture, but it is sufficient for our purposes to note that all these phases, both early and late, are on the full-blown Formative level as defined in this study.

During or perhaps slightly after the climax period of the Mississippi development, an outstanding horizon style, the "Southern Cult," spread throughout the Southeast far beyond the boundaries of the Mississippi culture as understood here.[84] This style is exemplified in certain designs and motifs on embossed copper plates, on engraved shell, and on modeled, engraved, and negative-painted pottery, as well as in a number of highly specialized artifact types commonly associated with these designs. The style is almost certainly of Mississippi origin and serves to measure the extent of Mississippi influence in the late pre-contact period. It poses some very interesting questions in culture dynamics, in that some of the strongest centers for Cult material are not, strictly speaking, in the Mississippi tradition. At Etowah, in northern Georgia,[85] the Cult material seems to be intrusive in a culture that is dominated by the Complicated Stamp pottery tradition of that region and is doubtless a thrust from the nearby Tennessee-Cumberland region; and Spiro, on the Arkansas River in eastern Oklahoma,[86] which yielded the gaudiest Cult material of all, is entirely outside the Mississippi orbit in all other respects, as are Mount Royal (St. Johns IIb) and other Cult centers in Florida.[87] The horizon-style concept appears to fit the situation admirably but of course is not an explanation.

Getting back to the problem in hand, most of the remaining late Formative stage cultures in the East can be interpreted on the basis of some sort of relationship with the Mississippi culture. This usually takes the form of a blend with earlier, or at least resident, cultures, as in the mixed (Woodland-Mississippi) Fort

84. Phillips, 1940; Krieger, 1945; Waring and Holder, 1945; Griffin, 1952b.

85. Moorehead et al., 1932.

86. Burnett, 1945; K. G. Orr, 1946, 1952; Griffin, 1952b.

87. Goggin, 1952.

Ancient, in the Ohio Valley,[88] and Owasco-Iroquois of central New York,[89] though it may take the form of an attenuated Mississippi-like ("Upper Mississippi") culture, of which the Oneota furnishes a most interesting example. This protohistoric culture, which has a very wide distribution extending from central Wisconsin through Iowa and Minnesota to Missouri and even Kansas and Nebraska, has been identified with the Chiwere Sioux in the period of their migration from east of the Mississippi River out onto the Plains.[90] From our point of view, it is of interest that throughout this very extensive movement the culture retained its homogeneity and remained on a Formative level.

In Georgia, as already indicated, Mississippi blended with the Complicated Stamp tradition to produce a culture which, in the late Etowah and Lamar phases in northern and central Georgia,[91] and in the Savannah and Irene phases on the coast,[92] was on its way to becoming one of the strongest and most pervasive Formative cultures in North America. On the Florida Gulf Coast, Mississippi combined with Weeden Island to produce the Fort Walton phase,[93] which may certainly be classified as Formative; in the lower Mississippi Valley, it blended with the Coles Creek–Plaquemine culture in the late Deer Creek[94] and Natchez phases[95] to an extent that makes it difficult to say which predominates. The native cultures of the Caddoan area of eastern Texas and northwestern

88. Griffin, 1943. Fort Ancient is perhaps not a good example. The earlier phases, such as Baum, show a mixture of Woodland and Mississippi elements, but the later Madisonville phase is practically all Mississippi. Nevertheless, it differs in essential respects from the nuclear Mississippi culture as defined here.

89. Ritchie, 1934, 1944, 1949, 1952; Ritchie and MacNeish, 1949; Ritchie *et al.*, 1953.

90. Hill and Wedel, 1936; Griffin, 1937; Keyes, 1942; Berry and Chapman, 1942; H. G. Smith, 1951.

91. Fairbanks, 1952.

92. Caldwell and McCann, 1941.

93. Willey, 1949.

94. Phillips, n.d. (MS in preparation).   95. Quimby, 1942.

Louisiana were strong enough to resist effectively the inroads of Mississippi culture. Whether this is because the Alto[96] and other phases that make up the Gibson aspect were too early to receive Mississippi influences, and in fact passed on to the Mississippi some of its physiognomic elements—specifically those of presumed Middle American origin—depends on the outcome of the dating controversy to which allusion has already been made. From the developmental point of view, it is interesting that these earlier phases are more explicitly Formative than the later (Fulton aspect) phases of Caddoan culture.[97] A similar change may be seen in some of the later phases of the Coles Creek–Plaquemine culture of the lower Mississippi Valley, particularly the Natchez.[98] In both cases we can infer, from ethnographic sources, not a developmental regression but an apparent change from a village type to something more like a neighborhood type of community organization.[99] This may in fact have been consequent on greater political stability and internal security.

We have already referred to the possibility of regarding the early "Plains Village" cultures as marginal Formative. The most extensive and characteristic of these, the Upper Republican,[100] is represented by innumerable small pit-house villages strung out along the stream terraces from South Dakota across Nebraska, Kansas, and eastern Colorado. The culture seems to reflect the initial adjustment of a sedentary farming economy to an environment that offered the additional resource of buffalo-hunting. The result was a mixed seasonal way of life favorable to the growth and persistence of sedentary communities. Owing perhaps to limitations of transport, the communities appear to have remained on a rather elementary Formative level until the introduction of the horse in early post–Spanish-contact times, when villages be-

96. Newell and Krieger, 1949.
97. Krieger, 1946; C. H. Webb, 1948a; Suhm and Krieger, 1954.
98. Quimby, 1942.
99. Murdock, 1949, p. 80.
100. Strong, 1935; Wedel, 1947; Kivett, 1949.

came a good deal larger. The Lower Loup phase of east-central Nebraska,[101] for example, thought to be protohistoric Pawnee, manifests a mature Formative stage of development as defined in this study.

When we look at the eastern North American Formative stage data from a broader point of view, we see two developmental peaks, one in the Hopewell culture and the other in the Mississippi culture. Hopewell developed to a remarkable intensity in a relatively restricted area (Illinois and Ohio) and radiated influences far and wide, but these in the main were not of such a nature as to lift the cultures acted upon much above the pre-existing Archaic level. Possibly this is due to Hopewell itself being a kind of florescent northern Archaic culture, or possibly to its strong orientation about a cult of the dead. Mississippi, on the other hand, has a typical Middle American configuration, most clearly expressed in the temple mound and plaza assemblages entirely lacking in Hopewell and, indeed, in the rest of North America, including the Southwest. There seems to be little doubt that this temple mound–plaza complex and the idea system behind it were diffused from Middle America, though we cannot say much about the route of that diffusion. This complex seems to have entered, in a rather small way, into the Gulf Coast, lower Mississippi Valley, and Caddoan areas some time before the Mississippi climax, but not until that climax did it develop to a point which invites comparison with late Formative and early Classic mound assemblages in Middle America. It is almost impossible not to regard this nexus of traits as closely related to, perhaps dependent on, new procedures in agriculture hitherto unknown in eastern North America. We can only assume, lacking proof, that these traits found their optimum conditions for development, not in the regions nearest their point of entry, but somewhere farther north, in the general vicinity of the confluence of the Missouri, Illinois, Ohio, and Mississippi rivers, and that the culture brought about by these innovations spread fanwise from that nuclear area, even back to-

101. Dunlevy, 1936.

ward the south, in the direction of the ultimate source of its power. Whereas Formative cultures in the Southwest are limited and confined by the small natural localities and regions that were suitable for their growth, the Formative cultures of the Mississippi Valley and the Southeast knew no such bounds. The widespread horizon style, the Southern Cult, and the attempts at large-scale geographic-political units seen in some of the protohistoric confederacies are phenomena comparable to Middle American developments on the threshold of the Classic stage.

In discussing and appraising the cultures of the southwestern and southeastern United States in accordance with the definitions of the Formative concept, we have focused our attention on the threshold or lower margins of the Formative. In turning to the regions which lie south of Middle America, to lower Central America and parts of the northern Andes, we will be more concerned with the upper limits of the Formative concept. In these regions there has been revealed, as yet, little evidence of cultures which show the beginnings of a Formative way of life.

LOWER CENTRAL AMERICA AND SOUTH AMERICA

On a Formative level the archaeological sequences of Honduras and Salvador reveal a number of close relationships with both Mexico and the Maya regions. The Playa de los Muertos, Ulua Bichrome,[102] and Cerro Zapote[103] phases are linked closely in their ceramics to the Formative phases of the Petén and Copan. Following these, the Honduran Las Flores and Santa Rita phases[104] feature a Maya-like polychrome pottery, apparently deriving its inspiration from the Tepeu[105] phase of the Classic stage of lowland Maya. A still later Naco phase in Honduras has ceramic affiliations with the Postclassic cultures of the Mexican highlands. In spite of these specific historical connections and parallels, it is questionable whether the Honduran and Salvadoran developments

102. Strong, Kidder, and Paul, 1938.   103. Lothrop, 1927.

104. Strong, Kidder, and Paul, 1938.   105. R. E. Smith, 1955.

ever go beyond what we are defining as a Formative stage. Mound-building was known in these regions as early as Yarumela III in Honduras—an archaeological phase apparently equatable in time with the Ulua Bichrome[106]—and mounds, or mounds and ball courts, were constructed at Tazumal,[107] Los Llanitos,[108] and Naco,[109] indicating the persistence or presence of these ideas in Salvador and Honduras in the late pre-Columbian periods. But aside from these architectural features (which in size and elaboration do not compare with the great mound sites of the Middle American Classic), there is little to indicate that Honduras-Salvador ever achieved the full-blown Classic stage. The Middle American contacts in themselves do not seem to have been sufficient to produce social and cultural phenomena of Classic or Postclassic rank.

Archaeological regions and phases have been suggested for Nicaragua and Costa Rica,[110] but culture sequences are lacking. In general, mound sites here are of less impressive size and layout than those of Middle America proper. Some mounds appear to have been used as bases for buildings, but, apparently, the superstructures were of perishable materials. Other tumuli may have been built solely for burials. Several types of stone statues occur, frequently in association with the mounds. Ceramics are well developed, and the Nicoya Polychrome style is linked to both Classic Maya and later Mexican styles by certain decorative motives. Such contacts would date from perhaps A.D. 800 to A.D. 1500. Nothing has yet been discovered in Costa Rica or Nicaragua that would relate, specifically, to the Formative stage phases of either Middle America or Salvador-Honduras. Yet, in spite of the fact that the chronological equations between Nicaraguan–Costa Rican archaeology and Middle America are with late Classic or Post-classic phases, the archaeological remains in this part of lower Central America suggest a level of cultural development no greater

106. Canby, 1951.
107. Boggs, 1944.
108. Longyear, 1944.
109. Strong, Kidder, and Paul, 1938.
110. Strong, 1948b.

than that of the Formative. In some traits, such as pottery and metallurgy, they reveal excellent craftsmanship, undoubtedly attributable to diffusions from both the north and the south. In other aspects, particularly architecture, site size, and site layout, they are not markedly different from southeastern North American Formative cultures.

Archaeological regions have been defined for Panama,[111] and, recently, sequence work has begun in one region.[112] Large villages and extensive cemeteries are reported. Mounds, apparently for both dwellings and burials, occur, but the constructions are very small.[113] There is also some evidence for ceremonial precincts formed by crude stone columns,[114] but non-perishable architecture is minimal. There is a fine metallurgical tradition in ornamental gold, tumbaga, and gilded copper, which clearly relates to Colombian regions such as the Quimbaya. Except for the Archaic stage Monagrillo culture of the coastal shell heaps to which we have already referred,[115] all indications are that Panamanian prehistoric cultures such as the Coclé, Veraguas, Chiriquí, and the various ceramic complexes of Darien are relatively late. The level of development, however, appears to correlate with that of the Formtive cultures in Middle America and elsewhere.

For the most part, the prehistoric remains of Colombia and Ecuador appear to be upon about the same level as those of lower Central America. That is, everywhere we have evidences, direct or inferred, of sedentary, agricultural village life with a competent, or even high, development of pottery. What are probably the earliest, and the simplest, archaeological remains in Colombia pertain to those phases of the northeastern and north-central part of the country such as Isla de los Indios,[116] Barlovento,[117] and Momíl.[118]

111. Lothrop, 1948.
112. Willey and McGimsey, 1954; Willey and Stoddard, 1954.
113. Stirling, 1949.
114. Lothrop, 1937–42.   116. Reichel-Dolmatoff, 1954.
115. Willey and McGimsey, 1954.   117. Reichel-Dolmatoff, 1955.
118. Reichel-Dolmatoff, personal communication, 1956.

The Isla de los Indios culture has a swampland habitat along the lower Magdalena River. It is distinguished by a ceramic complex featuring incised and rocker-stamped decoration. Rocker-stamped ceramic decoration, it will be recalled, is a trait of Hopewellian cultures in eastern North America, of the middle Formative levels in Mexico and Honduras, and of the early Formative in Peru.[119] Its presence in the early Isla de los Indios complex tends, thus, to imply an approximate contemporaneity with these cultures. That a comparable stage of development can be argued from this contemporaneity is, of course, less certain. The terrain of the Isla de los Indios sites would seem to be unfavorable for agriculture; however, we call this culture phase to attention at this time as a possible early Formative manifestation in Colombia. The Barlovento ceramic complex features incision, punctation, and simple vessel forms. The context is a coastal shellmound. Here, again, Formative status is questionable. For Momíl, the considerably richer ceramic inventory, including rocker-stamped pottery, suggests a stronger case for Formative status. The two phases, or subphases, of Momíl possess several ceramic traits that are reminiscent of Formative cultures in Middle America and Peru, and a full exposition of this site is awaited with interest.

The presumably later and better-known archaeological cultures in Colombia include the Quimbaya, in the Magdalena River Valley of northwestern Colombia, which is an important metallurgical center for the north Andes and for the New World.[120] Both techniques and styles of artifacts probably diffused from this region northward into Panama and other Central American countries. San Agustín, in southern Colombia, is a ceremonial and burial site of considerable size,[121] and there are vague relationships between the stone sculptures here and stone statuary in both lower Central America and the northern highlands of Peru. However, nowhere in Colombia do we find ceremonial centers with the large,

119. Willey, 1955a.
120. W. C. Bennett, 1944a, 1946a; Banco de la Republica, 1948.
121. Preuss, 1931.

impressive architecture of either Middle America or Peru, nor are there evidences of real urban development. The prehistoric Santa Marta or Tairona towns in the northeast[122] offer the nearest approach to urban centers and to large-scale public works (roads, bridges, etc.); however, the total region is rather small, and the over-all effort falls below the Middle American or Peruvian mark. Although the Chibchans, of the Bogotá Savanna, loom large in some ethnohistoric accounts[123] for their politico-military prowess, their domain was geographically small, and their population was probably not of great size.[124]

A lack of well-worked-out regional sequences in Colombian archaeology makes it difficult or impossible to appraise most of these cultures in a sequential context. It is probable, however, that there is substantial time depth to the pattern of relatively small, sedentary, agricultural villages. In northeastern Colombia, apparently later than the early and possibly Formative stage phases of Isla de los Indios, Barlovento, and Momíl, there are three sequent phases in the Río Ranchería region (La Loma, El Horno, and Portacelli) that are characterized by agricultural communities and polychrome ceramics.[125] This series was, in part, ancestral to the still later and protohistoric Santa Marta or Tairona cultures.

The archaeological sequences for the Ecuadorian highlands show a long continuity of Formative-type scattered farm or small village units.[126] In the central and southern highlands there is nothing in the way of large-scale public works or monuments until the period of the Inca invasion.

In the Ecuadorian Guayas Basin some recently reported work of Evans and Meggers[127] documents a ceramic sequence in which the earlier phases show close affinities with Middle American and

122. Mason, 1931–39; W. C. Bennett, 1946a.

123. See Restrepo, 1895.   124. Kroeber, 1946; Haury, 1953b.

125. Reichel-Dolmatoff and Reichel-Dolmatoff, 1951.

126. Collier, 1946; Collier and Murra, 1943; W. C. Bennett, 1946b.

127. Paper presented to the annual meeting of the American Anthropological Association, Boston, 1955.

Peruvian Formative cultures in such technical features as rocker-stamping, negative painting, and white-on-red painting.

On the Ecuadorian coast the settlement size and architectural achievements may imply Classic stage developments following earlier and clearly Formative cultures like the Pre-Guangala of Guayas.[128] At the site of Cerro Jaboncillo, just back of the Manabí coast, hilltop platform-mounds are associated with the remains of stone buildings which contained U-shaped zoömorphic stone chairs, bas-reliefs, and stone statues.[129] This Cerro Jaboncillo culture, probably contemporaneous with the Guangala phase of the Guayas sequence, may be coeval with the middle periods at the large Manabí coastal site of Manta. The Manta middle periods are associated with large, stone-faced, pyramidal mounds. This same Manta site, in its late pre-Columbian or Manteño period, shows extensive dwelling refuse and house-foundation remains covering several square kilometers.[130] The early ethnographic accounts of the Manabí coast support these late-period archaeological data in describing large towns whose wealth and importance were said to have been based upon maritime trade.

To sum up, no prehistoric cultural phase in lower Central America, Colombia, or highland Ecuador is outstanding for a coincidence of great ceremonial construction, monumental art, craft excellence, or urban concentrations of population. For the Ecuadorian coast the data are poorly ordered; yet we know that the Cerro Jaboncillo and Guangala phases and the presumed middle periods at Manta are characterized by specialized temple mounds, monumental stone sculpture, technically competent ceramics, a pottery figurine art of high quality, and a metallurgical industry which produced tools as well as ornaments. In the later Manteño phase, at the Manta site, there seems to have been a true urban center with extensive dwelling areas surrounding temple structures. The concurrence of all these traits argues for Classic status, but the information on these

128. Bushnell, 1951.
129. Saville, 1907–10.
130. See Jijón y Caamaño, 1930; Sanders, n.d.

coastal Ecuadorian phases is, as yet, too scant for such a classification.

In Peru a number of regional-cultural continuities are first perceived on a Formative stage of development. In each of these continuities certain themes are emphasized, such as the modeled ceramics of the north coast,[131] the multicolored pottery and textiles of the south coast,[132] or the subterranean and multistoried stone architecture of the Callejón de Huaylas.[133] Yet this regionalism is interpenetrated by common bonds of technological traits, by developmental changes within these traits, and, also, by the diffusions of specific styles. This kind of unity manifests itself during the early phases of the Formative stage and is still characteristic of native Peruvian cultures at the time of the Spanish conquest.[134] In the early Formative phases, such as the Cupisnique of Chicama,[135] the Guañape of Virú,[136] and the Early Supe and Early Ancón of the central coast,[137] villages were small and few. Maize was known, but canal irrigation probably had not commenced. Pottery and small stone carvings were of good quality. The construction of earth and stone or adobe pyramids or other ceremonial buildings seems to have started at this time, as evidenced by the structures in the Nepeña and Casma valleys.[138] An outstanding phenomenon is the widespread Chavín art style, named after the highland site of Chavín de Huantar.[139] The late Formative stage phases see the disappearance of Chavín art as an organized style, but they are linked together by a number of technical traits such as the white-on-red vessel painting of Salinar, Puerto Moorin, and Chancay or the widespread "resist-dye" or negative-painting technique on pottery.[140] Bennett[141] has noted that

131. Kroeber, 1926.
132. Gayton and Kroeber, 1927; Kroeber, 1944.
133. W. C. Bennett, 1944b.
134. W. C. Bennett, 1948.   135. Larco Hoyle, 1941.
136. Strong and Evans, 1952; Willey, 1953c.
137. Willey and Corbett, 1954.
138. Tello, 1943; Carrión Cachot, 1948; Willey, 1951b.
139. W. C. Bennett, 1944b; Willey, 1951b.
140. Willey, 1945a, 1948a.   141. Bennett and Bird, 1949.

these late Formative phases mark the advent of new food plants, and this also seems to be the time of the first canal irrigation in the coastal valleys and of significant population increases.[142] Communities remained about the same size as they were earlier, but they increased in numbers. Sizable fortifications were also constructed for the first time.

In our opinion, the line between Formative and Classic on the north coast of Peru should fall somewhere during the Gallinazo period, which succeeds the Puerto Moorin and precedes the Mochica in the Virú Valley.[143] Huge pyramid-mounds, urban living clusters, and a stylistic climax in Gallinazo pottery date from the Gallinazo III phase.[144] In the Moche and Chicama valleys, Gallinazo-related cultures may also mark the inception of the great adobe mounds; if not, the succeeding Mochica periods usher in a full-blown Classic stage. On the central coast, mound-building of this kind dates from the Florescent or Classic Maranga 3 phase.[145] On the south coast, Nazca culture has been considered Classic in the light of its magnificent textiles and painted pottery, and there is a likelihood that big adobe mounds and population centers were constructed contemporaneously.[146] In the highlands, the Recuay[147] and Classic Tiahuanaco[148] cultures are considered here as marking the beginnings of the Classic stage.

The prehistoric cultures of northern and central Chile and northwestern Argentina present the Peruvian Formative patterns in a reduced form. Many of the basic food plants, the agricultural techniques, and the domesticated animals (*Auchenia*) are the same as those of the central Andes, but the cultural achievements of the Chilean and Argentinian phases do not equal those of the north. In general, the living zones of the south Andean regions—the desert oases of northern Chile or the *quebradas* and valleys of the Argentine Andes—are small and their agricultural potential limited.

142. Willey, 1953*c*.
143. Strong and Evans, 1952.
144. W. C. Bennett, 1950.
145. Stumer, 1954.
146. Uhle, 1924*a*, 1924*b*; Strong, 1954.
147. W. C. Bennett, 1944*b*.
148. W. C. Bennett, 1934.

In Chile the Atacameñan culture of the north had some of its roots in the old Archaic stage coastal fishing cultures of the same region,[149] but, with the advent of maize agriculture, new environmental adjustments were possible and populations settled in compact oasis villages in the interior. These communities consisted of stone and mud houses, the whole surrounded by a defense wall. Public or ceremonial architecture is unreported.[150] To the south, in the vicinity of Coquimbo, are the settlements of the Diaguita tradition.[151] The environmental conditions in the Chilean Diaguita region are less severe than in Atacameño country, and there is more land suitable for agriculture. Perhaps, in consequence of this, houses are more widely scattered. Still farther south the Araucanian peoples[152] farmed the wooded central valley of Chile by clearing small, scattered plots. Settlements were small, and there are no central sites with impressive permanent architecture. Political centralization of the Araucanians seems to have been effected only in time of war. As near as can be determined from present data, maize and pottery diffused into Chile from the north or northeast at a relatively late time. There are some indications that this may have been as late as the Peru-Bolivian Derived Tiahuanaco periods, although this is by no means certain.[153] The plain pottery phases of Pichalo I and II[154] and the El Molle[155] culture of the Diaguita region may stem from earlier Peruvian stimuli. Whatever the duration of native farming villages in Chile, this stage of development was not exceeded.

The prehistoric cultures of northwestern Argentina are related to those of Chile, both in particulars and in general stage of development. Chronological evidence, both direct and inferential, though limited, makes possible some generalizations about the area.[156] The earliest phases, such as La Candelaría[157] of the central

149. Bird, 1943.
150. W. C. Bennett, 1946c.
151. Lothrop, 1946.
152. J. M. Cooper, 1946.
153. Bird, 1943.
154. *Ibid.*
155. Cornely, 1944, 1953.
156. Bennett, Bleiler, and Sommer, 1948.
157. Ryden, 1936.

region and Barreales[158] of the south, are characterized by small, scattered settlements, flimsy architecture, and relatively simple, decorated, incised, and painted pottery types. The middle and late phases of the northern, central, and southern regions see the appearance of compact villages, sometimes fortified or with forts nearby, stone or adobe architecture, small ceremonial structures within towns, the frequent use of bronze and copper, and the predominance of polychrome ceramics. Peruvian Classic and Postclassic elements are not found, however, in the same configurations that distinguish their appearance in Peru. Neither northwestern Argentina nor northern and central Chile was a center of native American urbanism comparable to Peru.

In South America east of the Andes, Formative level culture was established in prehistoric times along the major river systems and along much of the Caribbean and Atlantic coasts. We refer here to cultures of the types characterized by Steward[159] as "Tropical Forest" and "Circum-Caribbean." Steward has equated a "Circum-Caribbean" level of development with Formative stage cultures in both Middle America and the central Andes. We would also extend the Formative concept to include the lowland forest cultures maintaining stable agricultural villages, even though features such as mounds and ceremonial structures are lacking. Such an extension of our definition of Formative embraces, as we have explained, the settled, agricultural village life of the southwestern United States and the comparable communities of the south Andes.

In Venezuela there are at least two major culture subareas through which Formative stage development can be traced. In the Venezuelan Andes and the northwest region[160] such phases as the Dabajuro and Guadalupe[161] reflect influences probably related to the Río Ranchería section of northeastern Colombia. Eastward, on the middle and lower Orinoco, there is another traditional center, which is characterized by an earlier white-on-red and a later broad-line incised pottery. The white-on-red pottery idea appears

158. Debenedetti, 1931.
159. 1949*b*.
160. A. Kidder II, 1948*a*, pp. 425 ff.
161. Rouse, 1953, Fig. 2.

to diffuse out of the Venezuelan Saladero phase[162] into the West Indian phases of Cedros and Cuevas. The later incised pottery is first noted in the Early Barrancas phase of the lower Orinoco; subsequently, it spreads to the West Indies to mark the various late phases of the Taino tradition in those islands.[163] The climax developments of the Formative stage in the West Indies come in these Taino phases, especially in Puerto Rico and the Dominican Republic.[164] These developments include the dance plazas, ball courts, and specialized sculptured-stone paraphernalia associated with them.[165] The Igneri, or pre-Taino, manifestations, while reflective of an agricultural village life, do not possess these more elaborate ceremonial features.

At the mouth of the Amazon River the Marajoará phase,[166] with its deep village refuse pits, special cemetery mounds, and elaborately painted and modeled pottery,[167] almost certainly marks the Formative stage. The preceding phases on Marajó Island and in nearby regions are characterized by much smaller sites, locations which suggest hunting and fishing rather than agriculture, and much less elaborate funerary rites. The ceramics of these earlier phases are much simpler than those of Marajoará and are usually decorated with incision or brushing. They are probably closer to Archaic

162. Radiocarbon dates on Saladero range from 925 ± 130 to 615 ± 130 B.C. (Preston, Person, and Deevey, 1955, Nos. Y-42-44).

163. Recent excavations on the Ucayali River in eastern Peru, near Pucallpa, have disclosed a ceramic complex which is surely related to the Orinoco broad-line incised tradition. Although several thousand miles distant from the lower Orinoco, Pucallpa is on the upper reaches of the Amazonian river system, and, thus, by water, these two locations are not impossibly remote from each other, even by canoe transportation (D. W. Lathrap [personal communication, 1956]).

164. Rouse, 1953.

165. Rouse (1953) has emphasized the distinction between the cultural climax Taino phases of the West Indies, referring to these as "Circum-Caribbean" in type, and the earlier agricultural phases, which are designated as "Tropical Forest." This distinction has validity in the West Indian sequences, but in the present paper we are grouping both as "Formative."

166. Evans and Meggers, 1950.

167. Palmatary, 1950.

than to Formative standards. It has been noted that the Marajoará culture disappeared from the delta region and was replaced by cultures reminiscent of the pre-Marajoará periods. Evans and Meggers see in this the failure of intensive agriculture on the flooded Marajó Island flatlands and the depature of the people who brought this new subsistence pattern to the delta.[168] Such would argue for a retreat from a Formative level to something approaching the old Archaic mode.

Elsewhere on the Amazon, at Santarém,[169] Manaos,[170] and near Trinidad on the Mamoré,[171] there are evidences of settled villagers manufacturing competent pottery and, presumably, practicing agriculture. On the Atlantic Coast the Guaraní tradition may have been the first diffusion of an agricultural way of life southward, eventually reaching the Paraná Delta.[172]

168. Meggers, 1954; Evans, 1955.
169. Palmatary, 1939.
170. G. D. Howard, 1947.
171. Nordenskiöld, 1913.
172. Lothrop, 1932.

Chapter 7

Classic Stage

In our previous article[1] we observed that the criteria of the Classic stage are, to a large extent, qualitative and relative rather than quantitative and absolute. We listed such qualities as excellence in the great arts, climax in religious architecture, and general florescence in material culture. We adhere to these definitions, but we wish to add one more, which overrides them in importance. The Classic stage in New World native cultures marks the beginning of urbanism. It is the threshold of civilization in so far as "civilization" is defined as city life. Our earlier hesitancy to see the Classic as the stage of urbanism derived largely from our caution in interpreting the archaeological record of Middle America and Peru. For the succeeding stage, the Postclassic, both areas provide certain architectural evidence of large, tightly massed population concentrations. Such fitted, without cavil, the formal and physical requirements of an urban community. For the Classic the record in and on the ground is much less definite. In some instances, such as the Teotihuacán Classic in the Valley of Mexico with its numerous closely spaced apartment-like structures, or the Gallinazo III subphase of north coastal Peru with its thousands of "honeycomb" adobe-walled rooms, there is material evidence of city living. In other cases, however, of which the Classic Maya of the Petén lowlands is a prime example, urban dwelling clusters are either lacking or undiscovered. Nevertheless, for the Classic Maya,

1. Willey and Phillips, 1955.

and for other archaeological phases adjudged as Classic by our definitions, there is strong inferential evidence of an urban society. The attributes of civilization in the commonly accepted sense of the term—outstanding public architecture, great art styles, class differentiations, codified intellectual systems (preserved in writing) and some knowledge of science, formal hierarchies of deities, widespread trade in raw materials and luxury goods—are there. That such a complex achievement could have been effected without an urban basis of some sort is most unlikely.[2] Accordingly, we characterize the American Classic stage as urban.

In establishing standards for Classic stage achievement, our frame of reference has been the hemisphere. As stated in the foregoing discussions, we appreciate the historical semi-independence of the various New World cultures and concede that a "classic" stage, in the sense of a climactic point, could be defined within the limited context of any of these cultures; such a formulation would have meaning for a study of the culture growth of a particular area, subarea, or region. In an evaluation of the Western Hemisphere as a whole, however, an evaluation which considers all agricultural America as a kind of vast historic entity, only in two areas do cultures measure up to the criteria of urban civilization. From our point of view the Classic stage in the New World is limited to Middle America and the central Andes.

At the risk of some repetition we restate, then, that the American Classic stage is characterized by urbanism and by superlative performance in many lines of cultural endeavor. There is evidence not only of the mastery of technologies and arts but of their con-

2. This view emphasizes the functional, rather than the purely formal, definition of urbanism. It may well be that such attainments as those cited above were reached by the ancient Maya without the concomitant of massed, house-to-house settlement that the word "urban" connotes. The crucial factor is the number of people who could be drawn upon and organized in the interests of the society and the culture. Maya society undoubtedly drew upon and co-ordinated the energies of a great many people. This would have been possible even with primitive methods of transportation, under conditions of dispersed settlement.

junction in single cultures and societies. The various and scattered inventions and innovations of the Formative are now drawn together into rich, diverse, and yet unified patterns. The Classic is the stage of great artistic achievements in so far as greatness can be appraised not only subjectively but by the evident time, care, and emotion devoted to the artistic products. It is the stage of monumental and ambitious architecture, in the form of pyramids and special buildings which seem to have been dedicated primarily to religious purposes. Fine, specialized craft products designed as burial furniture, ceremonial appurtenances, or luxury items were turned out in profusion. In the Classic cultures of both Middle America and Peru there is evidence of strong social class distinctions and of heavy pomp and dignity surrounding the ruling classes. With the perfection of writing and astronomy, intellectual interests as well as the arts flourished in Middle America. Here, also, and to a lesser extent in Peru, there was active trade between the regional centers in ceremonial and luxury goods. In spite of this trade, however, it is noteworthy that a strong regional ethnocentrism is reflected in sharply differing art and architectural styles.

MIDDLE AMERICA

The Classic civilizations of Middle America centered in the Valley of Mexico and its environs, Oaxaca, the Guatemalan highlands, the Petén-Usumacinta-Motagua lowlands, and coastal Veracruz. The status of regions such as Michoacán, Guerrero, the Huasteca, Jalisco, Colima, and northwestern Mexico is less clear. These lie within the historical orbit of the general Middle American tradition, but their native cultures were probably below Classic standards in the arts and architecture. The chronological span of the Middle American Classic civilizations probably varies regionally, but the characteristic developments seem to have originated approximately around the beginning of the Christian Era. Gauging chronology by early dated Maya monuments (with the 11.16.0.0.0 correlation), the round figure of A.D. 300 is frequently given as a starting point for the Maya Classic of the Petén.[3] Radiocarbon dates on late Formative phases in the Valley of Mexico indicate that the Teotihuacán culture of that region had its Classic inception about contemporaneously or only a little earlier. Cross-datings with the Monte Alban sequence in Oaxaca[4] and the Kaminaljuyu sequence of the Guatemalan highlands[5] suggest that the apogee of the Zapotecan and highland Maya traditions is roughly coeval with the central Mexican highland and the Maya lowland Classic cultures. Tajín Totonac[6] of central Veracruz is, perhaps, only slightly later. The La Venta–Middle Tres Zapotes phase[7] of the Olmec regional-cultural tradition of southern Veracruz and Tabasco may be earlier than other early Classic developments; but, if so, it quite likely overlaps with them chronologically.[8] The terminal dates of the Middle American Classic cultures may coincide rather closely. The figure of A.D. 900 (11.16.0.0.0 correlation) is one postulated closing date for the Maya lowland Classic; A.D. 650 (12.9.0.0.0 correlation) is another. The apparently abbreviated and not well-defined Teotihuacán IV (Tlamimilolpa) phase of the Mexican highland Classic may have closed prior to the collapse of the great lowland Maya ceremonial centers, or it may have run contemporaneously with them.[9] A reasonable estimate for the fall of Teotihuacán is about A.D. 800. According to the best archaeological cross-referencing that can be effected, the end of the other Middle American Classic cultures is co-ordinate with these. In brief, and in gross, the Classic phases span the first millennium A.D., or most of it.

3. The 12.9.0.0.0 correlation, favored by Spinden, would place this date 260 years earlier. Recent radiocarbon dates (Kulp, Feely, and Tryon, 1951; Libby, 1954a) have favored the 12.9.0.0.0 correlation.

4. Caso, 1938.   6. García Payón, 1943.

5. Kidder, Jennings, and Shook, 1946.   7. Drucker, 1952.

8. There is considerable debate about whether Middle Tres Zapotes–La Venta is contemporaneous with, or earlier than, the Tzakol phase of lowland Maya. We are inclined to believe that it is essentially earlier. Recently announced radiocarbon dates (*New York Times*, December 29, 1956) are as early as 400–800 B.C.

9. See Armillas, 1950.

The content of the Middle American Classic civilizations is well known and needs no detailed itemization in this survey account.[10] The Classic culture of the Maya lowlands has its inception with the occurrence of the Maya corbeled vault, the initial series dates and stelae, and the ornate and unique Maya art style as this is expressed both in sculpture and in painted pottery.[11] The first appearance of this complex is in the Petén, and there is every reason to believe that it evolved, *sui generis*, in this locality or in nearby regions. During the earlier part of the Maya Classic, sometimes designated as the Tzakol phase,[12] ceremonial centers with stelae and characteristic art were first constructed in the central Petén (Uaxactún, Tikal). From here the Classic features spread to Oxkintok,[13] in Yucatán, and southeastward to Copan in Honduras. Somewhat later the great sites of Yaxchilan and Piedras Negras[14] were established on the Usumacinta drainage to the west. Certain ceramic cross-datings, utilizing the basal-flanged bowl form of Tzakol and the frescoed tripod jar of Teotihuacán II–III, indicate that during this earlier half of the Maya Classic the other major civilizations of Middle America were becoming firmly established. It was at this time that the principal monuments of Teotihuacán—the Pyramid of the Sun, and Pyramid of the Moon, and the Ciudadela—were constructed, and the distinctive pottery and moldmade-figurine styles of that culture came into being.[15] Similarly, the Monte Alban IIIa phase of Oaxaca and the Esperanza phase at Kaminaljuyu, in that order, were the first real blossomings of Classic cultures in those regions.

Aside from the few rather specific cross-finds of pottery and occasional items of architectural detail, Tzakol, Teotihuacán II–III,

10. See Thompson, 1954; Brainerd, 1954; Linné, 1934, 1942; Caso, 1938; Caso and Bernal, 1952.

11. Spinden, 1913.

12. Thompson, 1943, 1945; R. E. Smith, 1955; Proskouriakoff, 1950; Morley, 1946.

13. Thompson, 1945.   14. Maler, 1901–3; Satterthwaite, 1933.

15. Vaillant, 1941; Armillas, 1950.

Monte Alban III*a*, and Esperanza are alike only in that each expresses this first full vigor and brilliance of a regional-cultural tradition. As we have stated, the art styles are all unlike. Certain gods, or god-themes, seem to have been held in common by some of these cultures, but the particular expressions are quite different. Monte Alban shared the trait of writing with the lowland Maya, but the glyphic system is distinct and less developed. Competence in sculptural art was a feature of the Maya, and the Olmec of La Venta, but was less characteristic of the other Classic phases. The trick of the ceramic mold possessed by Teotihuacán was not shared by other Classic cultures until later.

From these facts it is evident that two fundamental forces were at work in these Classic cultures. Intercommunication existed among them and was an important factor in their growth. They profited from being a part of a larger community of ideas more than did the various cultures of the Middle American Formative. Yet this intercommunication and interchange was by no means all-embracing. Technologies, elements, goods—these were exchanged; but complete idea systems remained regionalized. How this stylistic regionalism may be interpreted in terms of sociopolitical structure is a major problem for Middle American prehistorians.

In the late Classic of the Maya lowlands (the Tepeu ceramic phase),[16] the number of active ceremonial centers increased greatly. Huge building programs were undertaken. As in the early Classic (and the late Formative), constructions were flat-topped pyramids and platforms grouped around rectangular courtyards or plazas. Temples and palaces and were elaborately carved and decorated with sculptures. In the late Classic the palace type of building—generally containing more rooms and situated upon a lower platform than a temple—became somewhat more common than in earlier times. The function of these Maya centers seems to have been largely religious and ceremonial. These were the integrating points in the network of Maya culture. It was in these centers that the peasantry of an agricultural society gathered to be in-

16. R. E. Smith, 1955; Proskouriakoff, 1950; Morley, 1946.

structed and inspired by the priest-leaders. The Maya aristocracy—regulators of agriculture, guardians of the seasons and of time—was maintained by, and in turn maintained Maya civilization with, a remarkable pact of mutual faith rather than force. When this pact dissolved, so also did the structure of Classic Maya society.[17]

The decline and abandonment of the Classic Maya centers about A.D. 900 (11.16.0.0.0 correlation) probably were preceded by the decline of the other regional Classic cultures. Teotihuacán appears to have been destroyed in the second half of the first millennium A.D.—quite possibly by invaders identified with the Tula-Toltec culture.[18] Bearers of this same Tula-Toltec culture moved into other parts of Middle America at this time or shortly thereafter.[19] The breakdown of the old regional states or confederacies of the Classic stage may, in part, be attributed to these invaders or to waves of social and political disruption and dislocation which they set in motion on the northern frontiers of the high civilizations. Other causes for these sweeping and radical changes in the cultures of Middle America at the close of the Classic have also been suggested. One of these, for which archaeologists have only partial evidence, is overpopulation or the pressures of steadily increasing population. In the Guatemalan highlands there are indications that the population around Kaminaljuyu at the close of the Formative was as great as, or greater than, the population at any time thereafter.[20] In the Valley of Mexico, at Teotihuacán, there is little doubt that population was more densely massed around that important center in the Teotihuacán IV phase than in the preceding Teotihuacán II and III phases.[21] In the Maya lowlands we know that more ceremonial centers were constructed in the latter part of the Classic than in the earlier centuries. This certainly suggests an over-all population increase for the jungle country, and recent

17. Willey, 1956a.   19. Tozzer, n.d.

18. Armillas, 1950.   20. Shook and Proskouriakoff, 1956.

21. Armillas, 1950. See also Linné, 1934; Sanders, 1956.

studies of domestic settlements in the Belize Valley of British Honduras support this suggestion.[22]

The Peruvian Classic cultures, to which we have referred in our discussion of the Formative, include the late Gallinazo-Mochica phases of the north coast, Maranga 3[23] of the central coast, Nazca of the south coast,[24] Recuay[25] and Cajamarca II and III of the northern highlands,[26] and Classic Tiahuanaco[27] and, probably, Pucara[28] of the southern highlands. Dating control is poorer here than in Middle America. Recent estimates,[29] while lengthening the Formative stage phases back in time, have still held Classic cultures, such as late Gallinazo and Mochica, to the last half of the first millennium A.D. Radiocarbon dates, however, tend to push the beginnings of the Classic phases back to the opening of the Christian Era or even earlier.[30] Terminal dates for the Peruvian Classic are based on guesswork plus historical reckoning.[31] There has been a general and provisional acceptance of A.D. 1000 as a closing date. If Classic beginnings are set back on the chronological scale, perhaps this figure should also be set back. The best we can conclude is that Peruvian Classic cultures flourished, as did those of Middle America, during the first millennium A.D. and that they were more or less contemporaneous.

The regionalistic tendencies of the Peruvian Formative crystallized in the Classic stage into distinctive civilizations and styles. On the north coast the early trends toward public building were brought to fulfilment in the massive, flat-topped, adobe pyramids and palace

22. Willey, Bullard, and Glass, 1955; Willey, 1956b.

23. Stumer, 1954.   26. Reichlen and Reichlen, 1949.

24. Gayton and Kroeber, 1927.   27. W. C. Bennett, 1934.

25. Bennett, 1944b.   28. Kidder II, 1948b.

29. Strong and Evans, 1952; Willey, 1953c.

30. See dates on Mochica and Nazca in Libby, 1952, and Broecker, Kulp, and Tucek, 1956.

31. Rowe, 1945.

complexes of the Chicama, Moche, Virú, and Santa valleys.[32] At the same time, the old north coast predisposition for three-dimensional or modeled art reached full scope in Mochica ceramics. In this same region metallurgy, which also had beginnings as early as the Chavín horizon,[33] was further developed to include casting, alloying, annealing, soldering in gold and copper, and gilding, as well as the manufacture of copper weapons and helmets.[34] The south coastal regional tradition produced a contemporaneous but separate brilliance. Multicolor painting of pottery, which began with the Formative Paracas phase,[35] reached a peak in the Nazca ceramics; and the emphasis on elaborate textiles, another Paracas trait, was also maintained in Nazca. Metallurgy, on the other hand, remained in its infancy in this south coastal section, at least until very late Nazca times.[36]

Throughout the highlands there is a strong tradition of stone architecture. The temple at Pucara is a Classic stage example, with its dressed-stone blocks and complex plan, its numerous compartments and subterranean chambers.[37] The famous Calasasaya inclosure, the monolithic gateway, and the great stairway at Tiahuanaco are even more notable examples,[38] and the carved stone statues of both Pucara and Tiahuanaco are the outstanding representations of Classic art in the southern highlands. Farther north, the stone-carving and multiple-storied stone buildings of Recuay show the continuity of an old regional tradition.[39] In this instance the earlier stone masonry and sculpture at Chavín de Huantar appears superior to the Recuay developments. As stylistic affinities indicate that Chavín de Huantar is approximately contemporaneous with the Formative coastal Chavín cultures, we may have here an example of unconformity between time-horizon and stage, at least in so far as architecture and sculpture are concerned.

32. Willey, 1953c.   33. Lothrop, 1941.

34. Root, 1949a; Larco Hoyle, 1938–39.

35. Kroeber, 1944.   36. Root, 1949b; Lothrop, 1951.

37. Kidder, 1948b; Bennett and Bird, 1949.

38. Posnansky, 1945.   39. Bennett, 1944b.

Concerning settlement and community size, it is of interest to note that large population clusters first came into being during the north coast Classic.[40] And these clusters, as was the case with Teotihuacán in central Mexico, were formed around pyramid or temple centers. An excellent example of this is the late Gallinazo period aggregation of thirty thousand adobe-walled rooms around the Gallinazo pyramid in the Virú Valley. Settlement surveys have not yet been made in many parts of Peru, but such studies as are available tend to confirm this urbanization tendency, at least for the north coast of Peru.[41] Another Classic change in north coast Peruvian sequences is the appearance of buildings composed of large rooms, courtyards, and corridors. These are usually in conjunction with, or near to, the great pyramids.[42] They have been interpreted as "palaces" or special public or governmental buildings. The comparability of this trend with a similar one in Middle America has been pointed out.[43]

Between the Peruvian and the Middle American civilizations we have designated as Classic there are many differences, both in configuration and in content. Despite these, however, some similarities in the wider configurations are evident, particularly with reference to the place and apparent significance of the Classic stage cultures in each historical setting. In the Guatemalan-Mexican regions, as well as in Peru, the Classic cultures take form out of a somewhat less differentiated Formative base. That is, in each of these two major areas there is a greater homogeneity of culture in the Formative than in the Classic stage. Also of interest, from the point of view of history and diffusion, this homogeneity is shared in the Formative between these two areas.[44] Subsequent to the Formative, differentiation rises in accordance with regional interests. Many of these Classic interests or preoccupations can be seen in certain tendencies manifested in the Formative, but they are underlined and dramatized during the Classic stage.

40. Bennett, 1950; Willey, 1953c.
41. Schaedel, 1951.
42. Willey, 1953c, p. 356.
43. Adams, 1956.
44. Willey, 1955a.

Another phenomenon may also be noted at this point. At the same time that regional differentiation moves to its Classic completeness in the various geographical localities of Peru and Middle America, there is a growing trend for each of these two great culture areas, or co-traditions, to diverge from each other. Thus, despite the parallelisms, it is also a fact that the civilizations of Middle America and Peru are more unlike each other, both in content and in pattern, during their Classic stages than at any time previously or later. In the Formative they present a cultural similarity and evenness due, presumably, to the common possession of many historically interrelated traits of a New World sedentary-agricultural way of life. In the Postclassic there is again a leveling of a more complex sort, historically distinct in the two areas and deriving, as near as we can tell, from internal social and political causes. The Classic cultures, between the Formative and the Postclassic, enjoy the greatest freedom and independence from either historical or functional causality.[45]

45. Willey, 1955b.

Chapter 8

Postclassic Stage

The Postclassic stage in Middle America and Peru is marked by the breakdown of the old regional styles of the Classic stage, by a continuing or increased emphasis upon urban living, and, inferentially, by tendencies toward militarism and secularism. Concerning the leveling of stylistic regionalism, we have observed that diffusion between regions in the Classic stage both in the central Andes and in Middle America was either the not easily detectable movement of technological ideas and isolated elements or the trade in actual objects and manufactures. In the Postclassic we see the wide, interregional transferences of total art and architectural styles. The mechanisms behind these transferences are debatable, but it is reasonable to interpret many of them as actual movements of large groups of people often accompanied by military force. These trends toward militarism and large-scale warfare are reflected in the archaeological record by late Postclassic stage increases in fortifications and fortified communities in many Middle American and Peruvian regions. The implications for a gradually increasing secularization of culture and society in the Postclassic are less direct. We would, however, argue that a decrease in the number, size, and elaboration of pyramid mounds and other kinds of religious structures is one clue to the waning of religious authority. Another is the aesthetic decline from Classic standards which characterizes much of Postclassic art in Peru and Middle America. In some regions this tendency is seen in standardization and mass production of objects. In citing such definitions, we are attempting, it must be remembered, to weigh and give classificatory value to trends. Warfare and non-religious authority were certainly not absent from either the Peruvian or the Middle American scene in the Classic or even the Formative stages; but, in so far as we can measure such things from the archaeological evidence, both militarism and secularism were in the ascendancy during the Postclassic stage.

We have discussed and defined urbanism in some of its aspects in our treatment of the Classic stage, but it is from the Postclassic level that we know most, from both archaeological and ethnohistorical sources, about the native American city. These cities were formed around politico-religious nuclei—pyramids, temples, palaces—and the urban zones contained not only the rulers, priests, and their entourages but various craftsmen and handlers of produce. In the Inca system all these city dwellers were governmental employees; under the Aztec many of them were independent artisans and merchants. In brief, the native city of the New World had large population aggregates either within residence or within reach, was the seat of politico-religious power, served as an economic and social center, and maintained complex and diverse divisions of labor among its citizens.

SOUTH AMERICA

Peruvian Postclassic cultures include all those of the Tiahuanaco horizon and of later times. Their time span is approximately from A.D. 1000 to A.D. 1532.[1] In the final years Inca sovereignty spread over all Peru and into adjacent Andean territories,[2] but just prior to this there were important regional kingdoms such as the Chimu,[3] Cuismancu, and Chincha[4] of the coast and numerous smaller states in the highlands.

We know that in ancient Peru, cities so defined came into being on the Classic stage, at least in some regions, such as the north and

1. Rowe, 1945. As observed in the discussions of the Peruvian Classic, this beginning date may have to be moved back two or three centuries.

2. Means, 1931; Rowe, 1946.   3. Rowe, 1948.   4. Rowe, 1946.

south coasts. There is an important difference, however, between the Peruvian Postclassic city and its presumed Classic stage prototype. The north coast Classic population aggregate appears to have grown by accretion, somewhat haphazardly, around a temple center, while the Postclassic city follows a planned or partially planned layout.[5] It is as though the necessity for, and idea of, city life had been accepted in Postclassic times whereas, in the earlier stage, the problem had not yet been dealt with consciously. We are not certain of the time of the first appearance of the "planned city" in Peru, but there are several indications that it may have marked the beginnings of the Postclassic on the Tiahuanaco style horizon.[6] By the latter part of the Postclassic the symmetrically arranged urban center was characteristic of north coast sites such as Chan Chan, Pacatnamu, and El Purgatorio.[7]

Coexistent with the Peruvian cities are the tendencies toward secularism and militarism mentioned above as defining the Postclassic stage. The big religious centers and shrines dominated prehistoric Peru during the Formative and, particularly, the Classic. Beginning with the *castillo* at Chavín de Huantar and the other Chavín horizon temples in the Nepeña and Casma valleys,[8] the temple pyramid reached gigantic proportions in Classic stage constructions such as the Huaca Cortada in the Chicama Valley, the Pyramid of the Sun in the Moche Valley,[9] the Gallinazo and Huancaco mounds in the Virú Valley,[10] and the Maranga pyramids in the Rimac Valley.[11] In the Postclassic, pyramids continued to be built, but these were usually placed within the inclosures of large architectural complexes.[12] Like the pyramids within the walls of Chan Chan, they tended to be smaller in absolute size than those of the Classic, and they lost still more in impressiveness by the size

5. Willey, 1953c, pp. 396–99.

6. Willey, 1953c, pp. 412 ff.; Stumer, 1954.

7. Schaedel, 1951.   8. Tello, 1943.   9. Kroeber, 1925.

10. W. C. Bennett, 1950; Willey, 1953c.

11. Jijón y Caamaño, 1949.

12. Schaedel, 1951; Willey, 1953c; Stumer, 1954.

and numbers of the palaces and city buildings which surrounded them. There are other trends which support these inferences drawn from architecture. During the Postclassic, Peruvian art, as a whole, moved away from representational or what could be interpreted as god-themes. Following the Tiahuanaco horizon, the drift was toward stultification and geometric decorative art. Also, we know from ethnohistoric sources that the Inca state was highly secularized. The Inca sun-god was imposed upon conquered peoples, but there was no concerted effort made to obliterate local religions.[13] Power was conceived of as military and bureaucratic might.

Militarism seems to have been a force in old Peruvian society from an early time. In this, as in many other of its trends and emphases, Peru differs from Middle America. Large fortifications of a refuge nature have been identified as far back as the late Formative White-on-red horizon,[14] and fortified strongholds, or *castillos*, are a common feature of north coast Classic. There seems little doubt, however, that organized warfare was stepped up at the close of the Classic and throughout the Postclassic. The Tiahuanaco stylistic horizon was probably propelled by military force,[15] and long-distance roads date from this time.[16] Essentially, the difference between Classic and Postclassic warfare in Peru was probably one of scope. Fighting was, undoubtedly, intense on an intravalley or small intervalley scale in the Classic, but wide-scale geographical strategy and maneuvers belong to the later stage. This is indicated by a change in the nature of fortifications as well as by ethnohistoric accounts of Inca activities.

MIDDLE AMERICA

The Postclassic centers of Middle America are those well known in the literature of the ethnohistoric period. Aztec Tenochtitlán in the Valley of Mexico is the most famous example.[17] Mitla in Oaxa-

13. Means, 1931; Rowe, 1946.   15. Willey, 1948a.
14. Willey, 1953c, pp. 358–59.   16. Willey, 1953c, p. 370.
17. Prescott, 1843; Vaillant, 1941; Sanders, 1956.

ca,[18] Tzintzuntzan in the Tarascan country,[19] Totonacan Cempoala in Veracruz, and Mayapan[20] in Yucatán are others. Most of these cities were seats of power in the late centuries just antedating, or coming up to, the Spanish conquest. Somewhat earlier, in the centuries between A.D. 800 and A.D. 1200, there was another set of centers such as Tula, in Hidalgo,[21] and Mexicanized Chichén Itzá.[22] The Middle American Postclassic varies regionally in total time range, as did the Classic. In the central Mexican highlands its beginnings may be considered coincident with the fall of the Teotihuacán IV culture and the concomitant rise of Tula (ca. A.D. 800). Elsewhere, it may be a century or two later. The terminus of the Postclassic is marked by the early sixteenth-century arrival of the Spanish, who found Tenochtitlán full of vigor and Mayapan abandoned.

The history of Middle American urbanism cannot be followed in the same detail as that of northern Peru, but, as we have remarked, the Teotihuacán IV phase in the Valley of Mexico was a foreshadowing of the city life seen later in sixteenth-century Tenochtitlán. The Aztec city, with an estimated population of sixty thousand persons,[23] was supported by a thick fringe of chinampa (floating garden) farmers on its margins and around the shores of Lake Texcoco. Water transportation—a mobility factor—was almost certainly of importance in the maintenance of a community of such size, and this same factor may well have been important in Teotihuacán times. Temple pyramids were dwarfed by the large and elaborate cities surrounding them in much the same fashion as in Postclassic Peru. There is not much question that religion was always a stronger force in the life of prehistoric Middle America than in Peru, but there are indications that secular and military powers were in the ascendancy during the Aztec regime. The Tenochcas rose to dominance in central Mexico during several

18. Parsons, 1936.
19. Foster, 1948.
20. Roys, 1950.
21. Acosta, 1940, 1944, 1945.
22. Morris, Charlot, and Morris, 1931; Tozzer, n.d.
23. Sanders, 1956.

centuries of bitter intercity fighting following the collapse of Teoti-huacán, and in this period the war-god rose to a commanding position in Aztec society.[24]

Militarism, secularism, and urbanism in Postclassic[25] Mexico and Central America have been discussed at length by others;[26] but, apparently, these trends do not march evenly in all quarters of the Middle American area. There are some indications that the highland basin environments were more favorable for urban growth than the lowlands;[27] thus, the urban classification seems to fit better in western Mexico, Oaxaca, and the Guatemalan highlands than on the east coast or in the Maya lowlands. Yet there are significant variations among the highland regions. In the Guatemalan highlands some of the largest site zones date from the Formative. The Miraflores phase at Kaminaljuyu offers evidence of a great occupation zone and politico-religious center outstripping in size anything that came later.[28] Guatemalan highland late Postclassic sites are well fortified, however, and attest to a period of widespread warfare and strife linked to the disruptions in central Mexico. In the Maya lowlands at Chichén Itzá, the Tula-Toltec art and the new constructions at an old Classic ceremonial center suggest that long-distance conquest was a feature of the early Postclassic in that region. Just how much of an urban center Chichén Itzá ever became is not clear. There are numerous house mounds around the center, but it is unlikely that the dwelling pattern here was comparable to that of compact Tenochtitlán. Later, however, the Yucatecan Maya attempted an urban center at the walled site of Mayapan. Within the inclosing wall some four thousand household units have been mapped over an area about two to three kilometers in extent.[29] It is the most urbanized of any known lowland Maya site, but whether the greater part of its inhabitants lived within the walls most of the year following non-farming occupations is still a matter for con-

24. Vaillant, 1941.

25. The term "Militaristic" has been used for this stage (Armillas, 1951).

26. *Ibid.*

27. Sanders, 1953.

28. Shook and Proskouriakoff, 1956.

29. Ruppert and Smith, 1952.

jecture. In any case, we can conclude that urbanization was decidedly less successful in the Maya lowlands than in the Valley of Mexico.

There is an important phenomenon connected with the Postclassic stage of development that has not been significant in earlier stages. This is, in effect, the large-scale exportation and implantation of the Postclassic features of militarism, secularism, and urbanism into and upon other cultural traditions where they had been lacking. Mayapan may have been modified by such an implantation, deriving its Postclassic patterns from central Mexico. In Peru this was certainly the case with the Inca empire. Roads, fortifications, and administrative quarters were constructed by the Inca from Ecuador to central Chile. These traits and much of the Inca system must have had profound effects upon the local inhabitants, although we do not know to what extent these conquered cultures were modified. Possibly, too, Postclassic phenomena exerted equally great, but less direct, influences in ways other than conquest and incorporation. It has been suggested that real cities may have grown up on the Ecuadorian coast in response to the rich trade with the Postclassic Chimu kingdom of the Peruvian north coast. If this is true, the process which gave rise to some of the ancient Mediterranean trading cities of the Old World would have its counterpart in the New. Such a development is an excellent example of the interlocking effects of diffusion and internal culture development.

Summary

We have postulated five major stages by which the culture-history of aboriginal America may be recounted. These stages are sequential and are derived from an inspection of archaeological sequences throughout the hemisphere. Certain criteria were selected for generalization from a detailed examination of numerous local and regional sequences. The method is comparative, and the resulting definitions are abstractions which *describe* culture change through time in native America. The stages are not formulations which *explain* culture change. Explanation, we believe, lies in the complex interplay of the multiple factors of natural environment, population densities and groupings, group and individual psychologies, and culture itself. Our culture-stage constructs are fashioned for the infinitely simpler purpose of describing types of cultures and the arrangement of these types in sequential order in the various parts of the New World.

Our earliest stage, the *Lithic*, is characterized by chipped-stone tools and weapons. These artifacts are found in environmental contexts of the late Pleistocene, under conditions indicating a climate quite different from that of the present and often with remains of extinct fauna. We have suggested the possibility of a major division within this Lithic stage, an earlier era featuring crude percussion-flaked choppers and scrapers and a later era in which stone-chipping was much more finely finished and in which lanceolate point forms were a diagnostic. As yet, however, the evidence for such a division is not conclusive. In general, it is believed that the period of the Lithic stage ranged from perhaps as early as 20000 B.C. down to about 5000 B.C., although this later limit varies considerably. Subsistence was based upon hunting and gathering, with emphasis varying according to environmental conditions. Populations were small and scattered, but by 5000 B.C., or before, man had found his way over most of the New World. The stage is best represented, however, in the High Plains and the Greater Southwest of North America.

Our next stage, the *Archaic*, sees the continuation of hunting and gathering cultures into environmental conditions approximating those of the present. There is a dependence upon smaller and perhaps more varied fauna than in the Lithic stage and, in many places, an increase in gathering. Stone implements and utensils used in the preparation of wild vegetable foods first appear in this stage. Many of these were shaped by use rather than design, although, in many Archaic stage cultures, techniques of stone-grinding and stone-polishing were known. Domesticated plants, including maize, are found in some Archaic contexts, but it should be stressed that the presence of these food plants is not evidence for agriculture in the full sense of that term. As near as the archaeologist is able to tell, the Archaic cultures in question had but slight economic dependence upon these primitive crops. In most instances where such domesticated plants do occur on the Archaic level, the prehistoric societies involved seem to have been composed of smaller populations than the other Archaic cultures, where fishing or gathering was the means of subsistence.

Many Archaic stage sites of the rivers and coasts of the eastern United States, of the California and north Pacific coasts, and of the Atlantic littoral of Brazil show large, deep refuse deposits of shell, suggesting sizable and stable populations. In addition to numerous ground- and polished-stone implements and ornaments, pottery is sometimes present, as are carved bone, shell, and horn objects. Elaborate woodworking is an associated trait in many regions. From all this it is fully evident that an Archaic-type economy provided the basis for material wealth as well as sociopolitical and religious complexity in those societies where food supplies were adequate. Thus, in a sense, certain Archaic phases, such as those of California or the Eastern Woodlands, represent a climax for the New World hunting-gathering tradition.

It is difficult to set meaningful date limits to the Archaic stage. At the earlier end of the range there is obvious overlap between cultures that we are forced to classify as Archaic and those whose technological inventory and environmental context is of a Lithic stage type. Thus, some Archaic cultures seem to antedate 5000 B.C., our very approximate and arbitrary upper limit for the Lithic stage. At the other end of the time scale, we know that many American cultures of the historic present subsist with an Archaic-type economy and technology. This does not impute to them "archaicism" or "backwardness" in non-technological aspects of culture but rather implies a great richness in the non-material fields for many of the prehistoric Archaic cultures that are known only from the meager archaeological record.

With the advent of the *Formative* stage there is, for most American areas, a fundamental economic shift from hunting-gathering to agricultural food production. This is the most profound change in our scheme of stages. The geographical focus moves from North America to Middle America and, perhaps, even farther south to the central Andes. All the gradual steps by which a sedentary, village, Formative way of life was achieved are not yet clear. It is likely that slow, steady experimentation and use of food plants by Archaic gathering peoples, such as those who occupied the Tamaulipas or New Mexican caves, eventuated in village life in which the primary dependence was upon crops like maize and beans. Agricultural villages and towns appear in Middle America, in several regions, in the earliest phases of Formative sequences and probably date back to as early as the middle of the second millennium B.C. In Peru similar agriculture-based village cultures are believed to be as old as the beginning of the first millennium B.C. Presumably, from these nuclear American centers, a knowledge of agriculture, fully developed maize, and other plants diffused, or were carried, over much of North and South America. By A.D. 1000, if not earlier, the southwestern and most of the eastern United States were within this Formative orbit; and, in the other direction, the southern Andes and much of lowland South America were following an agricultural, village or town tradition.

A stable village or town life, with its potentialities for cultural and social development may, however, be made possible by economies other than agricultural. We have noted that, in certain Archaic stage archaeological phases, the size of the sites and the general indications of stability and wealth approximate conditions which are comparable to, or even surpass, those of the agriculture-based Formative stage cultures. Hence, we have placed the emphasis of our Formative definition upon settlement size, stability, and the social and cultural implications which these carry, rather than upon an agricultural economy per se. We have defined the Formative stage for the New World "by the presence of agriculture, or any other subsistence economy of comparable effectiveness, and by the successful integration of such an economy into well-established sedentary village life." But, in so doing, we must keep in mind that the economic potential for even the richest of the hunting-gathering societies was definitely limited in such a way that further development to what we have defined as a New World Classic stage was precluded. Such a development was possible only with agriculture and only in certain natural environmental settings.

The agriculture-based Formative cultures are characterized by the abundant use of ceramics. Weaving is usually well developed. The competencies of the Lithic and Archaic stages in the chipping, grinding, and polishing of stone are carried on. Site occupation tends to be stable and of long duration. Houses and other buildings are of permanent or semipermanent quality. The Formative village is the basic sociopolitical unit, and in some regions it is of town size. Specialized politico-religious architecture and/or sites are frequently features of the Formative stage. These may take the form of pyramidal mound-based temples within, or apart from, the village or town communities, as in Middle America or the southeastern United States, or, as in the Puebloan Southwest, the special construction may be a subterranean kiva in the heart of the settlement. In many places these special buildings or sites imply a politico-religious organization and authority reaching beyond the confines of a single site or community.

The *Classic* stage marks the beginning of urban life in native America. The early New World cities were built around the temple pyramids and palace platforms of the ceremonial centers. They would, thus, appear to be the logical developments out of such centers and towns of the Formative stage. In many instances they are, indeed, the same sites, showing earlier Formative occupation and architectural levels overlaid by the later habitations and monuments of the Classic. These Classic stage cities were, most certainly, the nuclei of political and religious governments, of artistic and intellectual achievement, and of commerce and crafts. The temples, palaces, and other public buildings of the Classic are of great size and elaboration, attesting to the planning, skill, and labor organization of the builders. The Classic stage is also characterized by the appearance of great art styles, and these styles tend to be limited to well-defined regions. Craftsmanship in ceramics, weaving, stoneworking, carving of all kinds, and, in some places, metallurgy is of a high order. Craft specialization is a certainty. Differentiation in burial goods, in architecture, in the representations in art styles—all these things indicate the presence of a well-developed class stratification.

The Classic stage, as defined, is limited to southern Mexico and adjacent upper Central America (the area called Middle America) and to the Peru-Bolivian coast and highlands (the Central Andean area). These are the two centers of aboriginal American civilization, although it is possible that these Classic patterns may also be found along the Ecuadorian coast. Middle American and Peru-Bolivian Classic phases appear to be roughly contemporaneous and to occupy most of the first millennium A.D.

The *Postclassic* stage follows the Classic. It, too, is urban, perhaps more so than the Classic. It is confined to Middle America and Peru. At the onset of the Postclassic, each area sees the breakdown of the great regional art styles of the Classic. There are evidences of population shiftings and migrations, of war and troubled times. A decline in the aesthetic level of the Classic and in religious architecture suggests an increasing secularization of society. An increase in fortifications and fortified cities or towns gives a militaristic cast to many of the Postclassic cultures. The Postclassic civilizations are generally dated in the last six hundred years or so preceding the Spanish conquests of Mexico and Peru.

This completes our survey of a rather considerable sample of the data of New World prehistory solely for the purpose of testing a proposed historical-developmental classification. The difficulties of this kind of interpretation and the defects of our particular scheme have been candidly exposed and need not be repeated here. In its adherence to the broad outlines of historical reality the scheme has a certain value as a recapitulation of American archaeology, but it does not provide short and simple answers to the outstanding problems of history and process in that field. The adequacy of the data selected and the extent to which they have upheld the scheme we leave to the reader's better judgment.

Bibliography

Bibliography

ACOSTA, JORGE R.
1940 "Exploraciones en Tula, Hidalgo, 1940," *Revista mexicana de estudios antropológicos* (Mexico, D.F.), **4**, 172–94.
1944 "La tercera temporada de exploraciones arqueológicas en Tula, Hidalgo, 1942," *ibid.*, **6**, No. 3, 125–57.
1945 "La cuarta y quinta temporada de excavaciones en Tula, Hidalgo," *ibid.*, **7**, 23–64.

ADAMS, ROBERT McC.
1941 "Archaeological Investigations in Jefferson County, Missouri," *Transactions of the Academy of Science of St. Louis*, **30**, No. 5, 151–221.

ADAMS, ROBERT M.
1956 "Some Hypotheses on the Development of Early Civilizations," *American Antiquity*, **21**, 227–32.

ALEGRIA, RICARDO, NICHOLSON, H. B., and WILLEY, G. R.
1955 "The Archaic Tradition in Puerto Rico," *American Antiquity*, **21**, 113–21.

AMEGHINO, F.
1911 "Une nouvelle industrie lithique," *Anales Museo Nacional* (Buenos Aires), **20** (Ser. 3, Vol. 13), 189–204.

AMSDEN, CHARLES AVERY
1949 *Prehistoric Southwesterners from Basket Maker to Pueblo*. Los Angeles: Southwest Museum.

ARMILLAS, PEDRO
1948 "A Sequence of Cultural Development in Meso-America," in *A Reappraisal of Peruvian Archaeology*, ed. WENDELL C. BENNETT, pp. 105–11. (Society for American Archaeology Memoir No. 4.) Menasha, Wis.
1950 "Teotihuacán, Tula, y los Toltecas: Las culturas post-Arcaicas y pre-Aztecas del Centro de Mexico: Excavaciones y estudios, 1922–1950," *Runa* (Buenos Aires), **3**, 37–70.
1951 "Tecnología, formaciones socio-económicas y religión en Mesoamerica," in *The Civilizations of Ancient America*, pp. 19–30. (*Selected Papers of the XXIXth International Congress of Americanists*, ed. SOL TAX, Vol. 1.) Chicago: University of Chicago Press.

ARNOLD, J. R., and LIBBY, W. F.
1951 "Radiocarbon Dates," *Science*, **113**, No. 2927 (February 2), 111–20.

AVELEYRA ARROYO DE ANDA, LUIS
1956 "The Second Mammoth and Associated Artifacts at Santa Isabel Iztapan, Mexico," *American Antiquity*, **22**, 12–28.

AVELEYRA ARROYO DE ANDA, LUIS, and MALDONADO-KOERDELL, MANUEL
1953 "Association of Artifacts with Mammoth in the Valley of Mexico," *ibid.*, **18**, 332–40.

BAERREIS, DAVID ALBERT
1950 "Comments on South American Archaic Relations," *American Antiquity*, **16**, 165–66.
1951 *The Preceramic Horizons of Northeastern Oklahoma.* ("Museum of Anthropology, University of Michigan, Anthropological Papers," No. 6.) Ann Arbor.

BAGGERLY, CARMEN
1954 "Waterworn and Glaciated Stone Tools from the Thumb District of Michigan," *American Antiquity*, **20**, 171–73.

BANCO DE LA REPUBLICA
1948 *El Museo del Oro.* Bogotá, Colombia.

BARRETT, SAMUEL A., and HAWKES, E. W.
1919 ˙ *The Kratz Creek Mound Group.* (Bulletin of the Public Museum of the City of Milwaukee, Vol. 3, No. 1.)

BARTLETT, K.
1942 "Notes upon a Primitive Stone Industry of the Little Colorado Valley," *Plateau* (Northern Arizona Society of Science and Art; Museum of Northern Arizona, Flagstaff, Ariz.), **14**, No. 3, 37–41.
1943 "A Primitive Stone Industry of Little Colorado Valley," *American Antiquity*, **8**, 266–68.

BEALS, R. L.
1932 *The Comparative Ethnology of Northern Mexico, before 1750.* ("Ibero-Americana," No. 2.) Berkeley: University of California Press.

BEARDSLEY, RICHARD K.
1948 "Culture Sequences in Central California Archaeology," *American Antiquity*, **14**, 1–28.

BELOUS, RUSSELL E.
1953 "The Central California Chronological Sequence Re-examined," *American Antiquity*, **18**, 341–52.

BENNETT, JOHN W.

1944 "Middle American Influences on Cultures of the Southeastern United States," *Acta Americana* (Mexico, D.F.), **2**, 25–50.

1952 "The Prehistory of the Northern Mississippi Valley," in *Archeology of Eastern United States*, ed. JAMES B. GRIFFIN, pp. 108–23. Chicago: University of Chicago Press.

BENNETT, WENDELL C.

1934 *Excavations at Tiahuanaco.* ("American Museum of Natural History, Anthropological Papers," Vol. 34.) New York.

1944a *Archaeological Regions of Colombia: A Ceramic Survey.* ("Yale University Publications in Anthropology," No. 30.) New Haven.

1944b *The North Highlands of Peru: Excavations in the Callejón de Huaylas and at Chavín de Huantar.* ("American Museum of Natural History, Anthropological Papers," Vol. 39, Part 1.) New York.

1946a "The Archaeology of Columbia," in *Handbook of South American Indians*, ed. JULIAN H. STEWARD, **2**, 823–50. (Smithsonian Institution, Bureau of American Ethnology Bulletin No. 143.) Washington, D.C.

1946b *Excavations in the Cuenca Region, Ecuador* ("Yale University Publications in Anthropology," No. 35.) New Haven.

1946c "The Atacameño," in *Handbook of South American Indians*, ed. JULIAN H. STEWARD, **2**, 599–618. (Smithsonian Institution, Bureau of American Ethnology Bulletin No. 143.) Washington, D.C.

1948 "The Peruvian Co-tradition," in *A Reappraisal of Peruvian Archaeology*, ed. WENDELL C. BENNETT, pp. 1–7. (Society for American Archaeology Memoir No. 4.) Menasha, Wis.

1950 *The Gallinazo Group, Virú Valley.* ("Yale University Publications in Anthropology," No. 43.) New Haven.

BENNETT, WENDELL C., and BIRD, J. B.

1949 *Andean Culture History.* ("American Museum of Natural History, Handbook Series," No. 15.) New York.

BENNETT, W. C., BLEILER, E. F., and SOMMER, F. H.

1948 *Northwest Argentine Archaeology.* ("Yale University Publications in Anthropology," No. 38.) New Haven.

BENNYHOFF, J. A.

1950 "Californian Fish Spears and Harpoons," *Anthropological Records* (Berkeley), **9**, 295–337.

BERRY, BREWTON, and CHAPMAN, CARL

1942 "An Oneota Site in Missouri," *American Antiquity*, **7**, 290–305.

Bird, J. B.

1938 "Antiquity and Migrations of the Early Inhabitants of Patagonia," *Geographical Review*, **28**, 250–75.

1943 *Excavations in Northern Chile.* ("American Museum of Natural History, Anthropological Papers," Vol. 38, Part 4.) New York.

1948a "America's Oldest Farmers," *Natural History*, **57**, 296–303, 334.

1948b "Preceramic Cultures in Chicama and Virú," in *A Reappraisal of Peruvian Archaeology*, ed. Wendell C. Bennett, pp. 21–28. (Society for American Archaeology Memoir No. 4.) Menasha, Wis.

1951 "South American Radiocarbon Dates," in *Radiocarbon Dating*, ed. Frederick Johnson. (Society for American Archaeology Memoir No. 8.) *American Antiquity*, **17**, No. 1, Part 2, 37–49.

Black, Glenn A.

1944 *Angel Site, Vanderburgh County, Indiana.* ("Indiana Historical Society, Prehistory Research Series," Vol. 2, No. 5.) Indianapolis.

Bliss, Wesley L.

1950 "Early and Late Lithic Horizons in the Plains," *Proceedings of the 6th Plains Archaeological Conference, 1948*, pp. 108–14. ("University of Utah Anthropological Papers," No. 11.) Salt Lake City.

Boas, Franz

1913 "Archaeological Investigations in the Valley of Mexico by the International School, 1911–1912," *Proceedings, 18th International Congress of Americanists* (London), pp. 176–79.

Boggs, S. H.

1944 "Excavations in Central and Western El Salvador," Appendix C in J. M. Longyear, *Excavations in El Salvador*, pp. 53–74. ("Memoirs of the Peabody Museum," Vol. 9, No. 2.) Cambridge, Mass.

Borden, Charles E.

1950 "Preliminary Report on Archaeological Investigations in the Fraser Delta Region," *Anthropology in British Columbia*, No. 1, pp. 13–27.

1951 "Facts and Problems of Northwest Coast Prehistory," *ibid.*, No. 2, pp. 35–52.

1954 "Some Aspects of Prehistoric Coastal-Interior Relations in the Pacific Northwest," *ibid.*, No. 4, pp. 26–32.

Braidwood, Robert J.

1952 *The Near East and the Foundations for Civilization.* (London Lectures.) Eugene: Oregon State System of Higher Education.

BRAINERD, GEORGE W.

1953 "A Re-examination of the Dating Evidence for the Lake Mohave Artifact Assemblage," *American Antiquity*, **18**, 270–71.

1954 *The Maya Civilization*. Los Angeles: Southwest Museum.

BRAY, ROBERT T.

1956 "The Culture-Complexes and Sequence at the Rice Site (23SN200), Stone County, Missouri," *Missouri Archaeologist* (Columbia, Mo.), **18**, Nos. 1–2, 47–134.

BREW, JOHN OTIS

1946 *Archaeology of Alkali Ridge, Southeastern Utah*. ("Papers of the Peabody Museum," Vol. 21.) Cambridge, Mass.

BREW, JOHN OTIS, and SMITH, WATSON

1954 "Comments on 'Southwestern Cultural Interrelationships and the Question of Area Co-tradition,' by Joe Ben Wheat," *American Anthropologist*, **56**, 586–88.

BROECKER, W. S., KULP, J. L., and TUCEK, C. S.

1956 "Lamont Natural Radiocarbon Measurements III," *Science*, **124** (July 27), 154–65.

BRYAN, ALAN LYLE

1955 "An Intensive Archaeological Reconnaissance in the Northern Puget Sound Region." Unpublished Master's thesis, University of Washington, Seattle.

BRYAN, KIRK, and McCANN, FRANKLIN T.

1943 "Sand Dunes and Alluvium near Grants, New Mexico," *American Antiquity*, **8**, 281–90.

BRYAN, KIRK, and TOULOUSE, JOSEPH H., JR.

1943 "The San Jose Non-ceramic Culture and Its Relation to Puebloan Culture in New Mexico," *ibid*., pp. 269–80.

BURNETT, E. K.

1945 *The Spiro Mound Collection in the Museum*. ("Contributions from the Museum of the American Indian," Vol. 14.) New York: Heye Foundation.

BUSHNELL, G. H. S.

1951 *Archaeology of the Santa Elena Peninsula in Southwest Ecuador*. ("Cambridge University Museum on Archaeology and Ethnology, Occasional Publications," No. 1.) Cambridge, England.

BYERS, DOUGLAS S.

1954 "Bull Brook, a Fluted Point Site in Ipswich, Massachusetts," *American Antiquity*, **19**, 343–51.

1955 "Additional Information on the Bull Brook Site, Massachusetts," *ibid*., **20**, 274–76.

BYERS, DOUGLAS S.—*Continued*
1956 "Ipswich B.C.," *Essex Institute Historical Collections* (Salem, Mass.), July.

CALDWELL, JOSEPH R.
1954 "The Old Quartz Industry of Piedmont Georgia and South Carolina," *Southern Indian Studies* (Chapel Hill, N.C.), **6**, 37–39.

CALDWELL, JOSEPH, and McCANN, CATHERINE
1941 *Irene Mound Site, Chatham County, Georgia.* Athens, Ga.: University of Georgia Press.

CAMPBELL, ELIZABETH W. C., and CAMPBELL, WILLIAM H.
1935 *The Pinto Basin Site: An Ancient Aboriginal Camping Ground in the California Desert.* With geological introduction by DAVIS SCHARF and description of the artifacts by CHARLES AVERY AMSDEN. ("Southwest Museum Papers," No. 9.) Los Angeles.
1940 "A Folsom Complex in the Great Basin," *Masterkey* (Southwest Museum, Los Angeles), **14**, 7–11.

CAMPBELL, ELIZABETH W. C., *et al.*
1937 *The Archaeology of Pleistocene Lake Mohave.* A symposium by ELIZABETH W. C. CAMPBELL, WILLIAM H. CAMPBELL, ERNST ANTEVS, CHARLES AVERY AMSDEN, JOSEPH A. BARBIERI, and FRANCIS D. BODE. ("Southwest Museum Papers," No. 11.) Los Angeles.

CAMPBELL, JOHN MARTIN, and ELLIS, FLORENCE H.
1952 "The Atrisco Sites: Cochise Manifestations in the Middle Rio Grande Valley," *American Antiquity*, **17**, 211–21.

CAMPBELL, THOMAS N.
1948 "The Merrell Site: Archaeological Remains Associated with Alluvial Terrace Deposits in Central Texas," *Texas Archaeological and Paleontological Society Bulletin*, **19**, 7–35.

CANBY, JOEL S.
1951 "Possible Chronological Implications of the Long Ceramic Sequence Recovered at Yarumela, Spanish Honduras," in *The Civilizations of Ancient America*, pp. 79–85. (*Selected Papers of the XXIXth Congress of Americanists*, ed. SOL TAX, Vol. 1.) Chicago: University of Chicago Press.

CARLSON, ROY L.
1954 "Archaeological Investigations in the San Juan Islands." Unpublished Master's thesis, University of Washington, Seattle.

CARRIÓN CACHOT, REBECCA
1948 "La cultura chavín. Dos nuevas colonias: Kuntur Wasi y Ancon," *Revista del Museo Nacional de Antropología y Arqueología* (Lima, Peru), **2**, 97–172.

CARTER, G. F.

1949 "Evidence for Pleistocene Man at La Jolla, California," *Transactions of the New York Academy of Sciences*, Ser. 2, **2**, 254–57.

1950 "Evidence for Pleistocene Man in Southern California," *Geographical Review*, **40**, 84–102.

1952 "Interglacial Artifacts from the San Diego Area," *Southwestern Journal of Anthropology*, **8**, 444–56.

1954 "An Interglacial Site at San Diego, California," *Masterkey* (Southwest Museum, Los Angeles), **28**, 165–74.

CASO, ALFONSO

1938 *Exploraciones en Oaxaca, quinta y sexta temporadas, 1936–37.* (Instituto Panamericano de Geografía e Historia Publicación 34.) Mexico, D.F.

1947 *Calendario y escritura de las antiguas culturas de Monte Alban.* Mexico, D. F.: Talleres Gráficos de la Nación.

1953 "New World Culture History: Middle America," in *Anthropology Today*, ed. A. L. KROEBER, pp. 226–37. Chicago: University of Chicago Press.

CASO, ALFONSO, and BERNAL, IGNACIO

1952 *Urnas de Oaxaca.* ("Memorias del Instituto Nacional de Antropología e Historia," Vol. 2.) Mexico, D.F.

CHAMPE, JOHN L.

1946 *Ash Hollow Cave.* ("University of Nebraska Studies," N.S., No. 1.) Lincoln, Neb.

CHAPMAN, CARL H.

1948 "A Preliminary Survey of Missouri Archaeology. Part IV. Ancient Cultures and Sequence," *Missouri Archaeologist* (Columbia, Mo.), **10**, No. 4, 136–64.

1952 "Recent Excavations in Graham Cave," appendix to *Graham Cave, an Archaic Site in Montgomery County, Missouri*, by WILFRED D. LOGAN, pp. 87–101. (Missouri Archaeological Society Memoir No. 2.) Columbia, Mo.

1954 "Preliminary Salvage Archaeology in the Pomme de Terre Reservoir Area, Missouri," *Missouri Archaeologist*, Vol. 16, Nos. 3–4.

1956 "Preliminary Salvage Archaeology in the Table Rock Reservoir Area, Missouri: A Résumé of Table Rock Archaeological Investigations," *ibid.*, **18**, Nos. 1–2, 6–45.

CHAPMAN, CARL H., MAXWELL, THOMAS J., and KOZLOVICH, EUGENE

1951 "A Preliminary Archaeological Survey of the Table Rock Reservoir Area, Stone County, Missouri," *ibid.*, **13**, No. 2, 3–39.

CHILDE, V. GORDON
1946 *What Happened in History.* New York: Penguin Books, Inc.
1950 *Prehistoric Migrations in Europe.* (Institutet før Sammenlignende Kulturforskning, Ser. A. Forelesninger, Vol. 20, Part 5.) Oslo.

CLAFLIN, WILLIAM H., JR.
1931 *The Stalling's Island Mound, Columbia County, Georgia.* ("Papers of the Peabody Museum," Vol. 14, No. 1.) Cambridge, Mass.

CLARKE, J. G. D.
1936 *The Mesolithic Settlement of Northern Europe.* Cambridge: Cambridge University Press.
1952 *Prehistoric Europe: The Economic Basis.* London: Methuen.

CLEMENTS, THOMAS, and CLEMENTS, LYDIA
1951 "Evidence of Pleistocene Man in Death Valley, California" (Abstract), *Bulletin of the Geological Society of America*, **62**, No. 12, Part 2, 1498–99.

COLE, FAY-COOPER
1943 "Chronology in the Middle West," *Proceedings of the American Philosophical Society*, **86**, No. 2, 299–303.

COLE, FAY-COOPER, and DEUEL, THORNE
1937 *Rediscovering Illinois.* Chicago: University of Chicago Press.

COLE, FAY-COOPER, et al.
1951 *Kincaid, a Prehistoric Illinois Metropolis.* Chicago: University of Chicago Press.

COLLIER, DONALD
1946 "The Archaeology of Ecuador," in *Handbook of South American Indians*, ed. JULIAN H. STEWARD, **2**, 767–84. (Smithsonian Institution, Bureau of American Ethnology Bulletin No. 143.) Washington, D.C.
1955 *Cultural Chronology and Change as Reflected in the Ceramics of the Virú Valley, Peru.* ("Fieldiana: Anthropology," Vol. 43.) Chicago: Chicago Natural History Museum.

COLLIER, DONALD, and MURRA, J. V.
1943 *Survey and Excavations in Southern Ecuador.* ("Field Museum of Natural History, Anthropological Series," Vol. 35.) Chicago.

COLLINS, HENRY B.
1937 *Archaeology of St. Lawrence Island, Alaska.* ("Smithsonian Miscellaneous Collections," Vol. 96, No. 1.) Washington, D.C.
1953a "Recent Developments in the Dorset Culture Area," in *Asia and North America: Transpacific Contacts*, ed. MARIAN W. SMITH. (Society for American Archaeology Memoir No. 9.) *American Antiquity*, **18**, No. 3, Part 2, 32–39.
1953b "Radiocarbon Dating in the Arctic," *ibid.*, **18**, 197–203.

Cook, Harold J.
1927 "New Geological and Paleontological Evidence Bearing on the Antiquity of Mankind in America," *Natural History*, **27**, 240–47.
Cooper, John M.
1946 "The Araucanians," in *Handbook of South American Indians*, ed. Julian H. Steward, **2**, 687–760. (Smithsonian Institution, Bureau of American Ethnology Bulletin No. 143.) Washington, D.C.
Cooper, L. R.
1933 *The Red Cedar Variant of the Wisconsin Hopewell Culture.* (Bulletin of the Public Museum of the City of Milwaukee, Vol. 16, No. 2.)
Cornely, F. L.
1944 "Cultura de El Molle," *Revista chilena de historia natural* (Santiago, Chile), Vol. 48.
1953 *Cultura de El Molle.* (Revision of 1944 article.) Santiago, Chile: Museo de Arqueología de La Serena.
Cotter, John
1954 "Indications of a Paleo-Indian Co-tradition for North America," *American Antiquity*, **20**, 64–67.
Crane, H. R.
1955 "Antiquity of the Sandia Culture: Carbon 14 Measurements," *Science*, **122**, 689–90.
1956 "University of Michigan Radiocarbon Dates, I," *ibid.*, **124**, 664–72.
Cressman, L. S.
1951 "Western Prehistory in the Light of Carbon 14 Dating," *Southwestern Journal of Anthropology*, **7**, 289–313.
Cressman, L. S., *et al.*
1942 *Archaeological Researches in the Northern Great Basin.* (Carnegie Institution of Washington Publication 538.) Washington, D.C.
Cruxent, J. M., and Rouse, Irving
1956 "A Lithic Industry of Paleo-Indian Type in Venezuela," *American Antiquity*, **22**, 172–79.
Cummings, Byron
1933 *Cuicuilco and the Archaic Culture of Mexico.* (University of Arizona Bulletin, Vol. 4, No. 8; Social Science Bulletin, No. 4.) Tucson, Ariz.
Cunningham, Wilbur M.
1948 *A Study of the Glacial Kame Culture.* ("Museum of Anthropology, University of Michigan, Occasional Contributions," No. 12.) Ann Arbor.

CUSHING, F. H.
1897 "A Preliminary Report on the Exploration of Ancient Key-Dwellers' Remains on the Gulf Coast of Florida," *Proceedings of the American Philosophical Society*, **35**, 329–448.

DAUGHERTY, RICHARD D.
1956 *Early Man in the Columbia Intermontane Province.* ("University of Utah Anthropological Papers," No. 24.) Salt Lake City.

DAVIS, E. MOTT
1953 "Recent Data from Two Paleo-Indian Sites on Medicine Creek, Nebraska," *American Antiquity*, **18**, 380–86.

DAVIS, E. MOTT, and SCHULTZ, C. BERTRAND
1952 "The Archaeological and Paleontological Salvage Program at the Medicine Creek Reservoir, Frontier County, Nebraska," *Science*, **115**, 288–90.

DEBENEDETTI, S.
1931 *L'ancienne civilisation des Barreales.* ("Ars Americana," Vol. 2.) Paris: G. Van Oest.

DEJARNETTE, DAVID L.
1952 "Alabama Archeology: A Summary," in *Archeology of Eastern United States*, ed. JAMES B. GRIFFIN, pp. 272–84. Chicago: University of Chicago Press.

DEJARNETTE, DAVID L., and WIMBERLY, S. B.
1941 *The Bessemer Site.* (Geological Survey of Alabama, Museum Paper 17.) University, Ala.

DELLINGER, S. C.
1936 "Baby Cradles of the Ozark Bluff Dwellers," *American Antiquity*, **1**, 197–214.

DELLINGER, S. C., and DICKINSON, S. D.
1942 "Pottery from the Ozark Bluff Shelters," *ibid.*, **7**, 276–90.

DEUEL, THORNE, *et al.*
1952 *Hopewellian Communities in Illinois.* ("Illinois State Museum, Scientific Papers," Vol. 5.) Springfield.

DICK, HERBERT W.
1952 "Evidences of Early Man in Bat Cave and on the Plains of San Augustin, New Mexico," in *Indian Tribes of Aboriginal America*, pp. 158–63. (*Selected Papers of the XXIXth International Congress of Americanists*, ed. SOL TAX, Vol. 3.) Chicago: University of Chicago Press.

DIPESO, CHARLES C.
1951 *The Babocomari Village Site on the Babocomari River, Southeastern Arizona.* (The Amerind Foundation, Inc., No. 5.) Dragoon, Ariz.

1953   *The Sobaipuri Indians of the Upper San Pedro River Valley, Southeastern Arizona.* (The Amerind Foundation, Inc., No. 6.) Dragoon, Ariz.

DRUCKER, PHILIP

1943   *Ceramic Sequences at Tres Zapotes, Vera Cruz, Mexico.* (Smithsonian Institution, Bureau of American Ethnology Bulletin No. 140.) Washington, D.C.

1948   *Preliminary Notes on an Archaeological Survey of the Chiapas Coast.* ("Middle American Research Records," Vol. 1, No. 11.) New Orleans: Tulane University.

1952   *La Venta, Tabasco: A Study of Olmec Ceramics and Art.* (Smithsonian Institution, Bureau of American Ethnology Bulletin No. 153.) Washington, D.C

1955   "Sources of Northwest Coast Culture," in *New Interpretations of Aboriginal American Culture History*, pp. 59–81. (75th Anniversary Volume, Anthropological Society of Washington.) Washington, D.C.

DUFF, WILSON, and BORDEN, CHARLES E.

1954   "A Scottsbluff-Eden Point from British Columbia," *Anthropology in British Columbia*, No. 4 (1953–54), pp. 33–36.

DUNLEVY, MARION L.

1936   "A Comparison of the Cultural Manifestations of the Burkett and Gray-Wolfe Sites," *Chapters in Nebraska Archaeology* (Lincoln), Vol. 1, No. 2.

EKHOLM, GORDON F.

1944   *Excavations at Tampico and Pánuco in the Huasteca, Mexico.* ("American Museum of Natural History, Anthropological Papers," Vol. 38, Part 5.) New York.

ELDRIDGE, WILLIAM, and VACARO, JOSEPH

1952   "The Bull Brook Site, Ipswich, Massachusetts," *Bulletin of the Massachusetts Archaeological Society* (Attleboro), **13**, No. 4, 39–43.

EVANS, CLIFFORD, JR.

1950   "A Report on Recent Archaeological Investigations in the Lagoa Santa Region of Minas Gerais, Brazil," *American Antiquity*, **15**, 341–43.

1954   "Spaulding's Review of Ford: II," *American Anthropologist*, **56**, 114.

1955   "New Archaeological Interpretations in Northeastern South America," in *New Interpretations of Aboriginal American Culture History*, pp. 82–94. (75th Anniversary Volume, Anthropological Society of Washington.) Washington, D.C.

EVANS, CLIFFORD, JR., and MEGGERS, B. J.
1950 "Preliminary Results of Archaeological Investigations at the Mouth of the Amazon," *American Antiquity*, 16, 1–9.

FAIRBANKS, CHARLES H.
1942 "The Taxonomic Position of Stalling's Island, Georgia," *American Antiquity*, 7, 223–31.
1949 "A General Survey of Southeastern Prehistory," in *The Florida Indian and His Neighbors*, ed. JOHN W. GRIFFIN, pp. 55–75. (Papers delivered at an Anthropological Conference held at Rollins College, April 9–10, 1949.) Winter Park, Fla.
1952 "Creek and Pre-Creek," in *Archeology of Eastern United States*, ed. JAMES B. GRIFFIN, pp. 285–300. Chicago: University of Chicago Press.

FEWKES, JESSE WALTER
1924 *Preliminary Archaeological Explorations at Weeden Island, Florida.* ("Smithsonian Miscellaneous Collections," Vol. 76, No. 13.) Washington, D.C.

FIGGINS, J. D.
1927 "The Antiquity of Man in America," *Natural History*, 27, 229–39.
1933 "A Further Contribution to the Antiquity of Man in America," *Proceedings of the Colorado Museum of Natural History*, 12, No. 2, 4–8.

FORBIS, RICHARD G., and SPERRY, JOHN D.
1952 "An Early Man Site in Montana," *American Antiquity*, 18, 127–33.

FORD, JAMES A.
1936 *Analysis of Indian Village Site Collections from Louisiana and Mississippi.* (Department of Conservation, Louisiana Geological Survey, Anthropological Study No. 2.) New Orleans.
1951 *Greenhouse: A Troyville–Coles Creek Period Site in Avoyelles Parish, Louisiana.* ("American Museum of Natural History, Anthropological Papers," Vol. 44, Part 1.) New York.
1952 *Measurements of Some Prehistoric Design Developments in the Southeastern States.* ("American Museum of Natural History, Anthropological Papers," Vol. 44, Part 3.) New York.
1954a "Spaulding's Review of Ford: I," *American Anthropologist*, 56, 109–12.
1954b "The Type Concept Revisited," *ibid.*, pp. 42–54.
1954c "Comment on A. C. Spaulding 'Statistical Techniques for the Discovery of Artifact Types,'" *American Antiquity*, 19, 390–91.

1954d "Additional Notes on the Poverty Point Site in Northern Louisiana," *ibid.*, pp. 282–85.

FORD, JAMES A., PHILLIPS, PHILIP, and HAAG, WILLIAM G.
1955 *The Jaketown Site in West-Central Mississippi.* ("American Museum of Natural History, Anthropological Papers," Vol. 45, Part 1.) New York.

FORD, JAMES A., and QUIMBY, GEORGE I.
1945 *The Tchefuncte Culture: An Early Occupation of the Lower Mississippi Valley.* (Society for American Archaeology Memoir No. 2.) Baton Rouge: Louisiana State University Press.

FORD, JAMES A., and WEBB, CLARENCE H.
1956 *Poverty Point: A Late Archaic Site in Louisiana.* ("American Museum of Natural History, Anthropological Papers," Vol. 46, Part 1.) New York.

FORD, JAMES A., and WILLEY, GORDON R.
1940 *Crooks Site: A Marksville Period Burial Mound in La Salle Parish, Louisiana.* (Department of Conservation, Louisiana Geological Survey, Anthropological Study No. 3.) New Orleans.
1941 "An Interpretation of the Prehistory of the Eastern United States," *American Anthropologist*, 43, 325–63.
1949 *Surface Survey of the Virú Valley, Peru.* ("American Museum of Natural History, Anthropological Papers," Vol. 43, Part 1.) New York.

FOSTER, GEORGE M.
1948 *Empire's Children: The People of Tzintzuntzan.* (Smithsonian Institution, Institute of Social Anthropology Publication No. 6.) Washington, D.C.

FOWKE, GERARD
1928 "Archaeological Investigations II," *Smithsonian Institution, Bureau of American Ethnology, 44th Annual Report*, pp. 405–540. Washington, D.C.

FOWLER, MELVIN L., and WINTERS, HOWARD
1956 *Modoc Rock Shelter: Preliminary Report.* (Illinois State Museum, Report of Investigations No. 4.) Springfield.

GARCÍA PAYÓN, J.
1943 *Interpretación cultural de la zona arqueológica de El Tajín.* Mexico, D.F.: Universidad Nacional Autónoma de Mexico.

GAYTON, A. H., and KROEBER, A. L.
1927 *The Uhle Pottery Collections from Nazca.* ("University of California Publications in American Archaeology and Ethnology," Vol. 24, No. 1.) Berkeley.

GIDDINGS, J. L., JR.
1951 "The Denbigh Flint Complex," *American Antiquity*, **16**, 193–203.
1952 "Early Man in the Arctic," *Scientific American*, **190**, No. 6, 82–88.
1955 "The Denbigh Flint Complex Is Not Yet Dated," *American Antiquity*, **20**, 375–76.

GIFFORD, E. W., and SCHENCK, W. EGBERT
1926 *Archaeology of the Southern San Joaquin Valley.* ("University of California Publications in American Archaeology and Ethnology," Vol. 23, No. 1.) Berkeley.

GILMORE, MELVIN R.
1930 "Vegetal Remains of the Ozark Bluff-Dweller Culture," *Papers of the Michigan Academy of Science, Arts and Letters*, **14**, 83–102.

GJESSING, G.
1944 *The Circumpolar Stone Age.* ("Acta Arctica," fasc. 2.) Copenhagen.

GLADWIN, HAROLD S.
1928 *Excavations at Casa Grande, Arizona.* ("Southwest Museum Papers," No. 2.) Los Angeles.

GLADWIN, H. S., et al.
1937 *Excavations at Snaketown: Material Culture.* ("Medallion Papers," No. 25.) Globe, Ariz.: Gila Pueblo.

GOGGIN, JOHN M.
1949 "Culture Traditions in Florida Prehistory," in *The Florida Indian and His Neighbors*, ed. JOHN W. GRIFFIN, pp. 13–44. (Papers delivered at an Anthropological Conference held at Rollins College, April 9–10, 1949.) Winter Park, Fla.
1952 *Space and Time Perspective in Northern St. Johns Archaeology, Florida.* ("Yale University Publications in Anthropology," No. 47.) New Haven.

GONZÁLEZ, ALBERTO REX
1952 "Antiguo horizonte preceramico en las Sierras Centrales de la Argentina," *Runa* (Buenos Aires), **5**, 110–33.

GREENGO, ROBERT C.
1957 "Prehistory in the Lower Mississippi Valley: The Issaquena Phase." Unpublished Ph.D. dissertation, Harvard University. Pp. 369.

GREENMAN, EMERSON F.
1927 "Michigan Mounds, with Special Reference to Two in Missaukee County," *Papers of the Michigan Academy of Science, Arts and Letters*, **7**, 1–9.

1932　"Excavation of the Coon Mound and an Analysis of the Adena Culture," *Ohio Archaeological and Historical Quarterly*, 41, 369–523.

1938　"Hopewellian Traits in Florida," *American Antiquity*, 3, 327–32.

GRIFFIN, JAMES B.

1937　"The Archaeological Remains of the Chiwere Sioux," *American Antiquity*, 2, 180–81.

1943　*The Fort Ancient Aspect: Its Cultural and Chronological Position in Mississippi Valley Archaeology.* Ann Arbor: University of Michigan Press.

1944　"The De Luna Expedition and the 'Buzzard Cult' in the Southeast," *Journal of the Washington Academy of Science*, 34, 299–303.

1946　"Cultural Change and Continuity in Eastern United States Archaeology," in *Man in Northeastern North America*, ed. FREDERICK JOHNSON, pp. 37–95. ("Papers of the Robert S. Peabody Foundation for Archaeology," Vol. 3.) Andover, Mass.: Phillips Academy.

1949　"The Cahokia Ceramic Complexes," *Proceedings of the Fifth Plains Conference for Archeology*, pp. 44–58. (Laboratory of Anthropology, University of Nebraska, Notebook No. 1.) Lincoln.

1950　"Review: 'The George C. Davis Site, Cherokee County, Texas,' by H. Perry Newell and Alex D. Krieger," *American Anthropologist*, 52, 413–15.

1951　"Some Adena and Hopewell Radiocarbon Dates," in *Radiocarbon Dating*, ed. FREDERICK JOHNSON. (Society for American Archaeology Memoir No. 8.) *American Antiquity*, 17, No. 1, Part 2, 26–29.

1952a　"Culture Periods in Eastern United States Archeology," in *Archeology of Eastern United States*, ed. JAMES B. GRIFFIN, pp. 352–64. Chicago: University of Chicago Press.

1952b　"An Interpretation of the Place of Spiro in Southeastern Archaeology," in "The Spiro Mound," *Missouri Archaeologist* (Columbia, Mo.), 14, 89–106.

1952c　"Prehistoric Cultures of the Central Mississippi Valley," in *Archeology of Eastern United States*, ed. JAMES B. GRIFFIN, pp. 226–38. Chicago: University of Chicago Press.

GRIFFIN, JAMES B., and MORGAN, RICHARD G. (eds.)

1941　*Contributions to the Archaeology of the Illinois River Valley.* ("Transactions of the American Philosophical Society," Vol. 32, Part 1.) Philadelphia.

GROSS, H.

1951　"Mastodon, Mammoth, and Man in America," *Texas Archaeological and Paleontological Society Bulletin*, 22, 101–31.

GUERNSEY, E. Y.
1939   "Relationships among Various Clark County Sites," *Proceedings of the Indiana Academy of Science*, **48**, 27–32.
1942   "The Culture Sequence of the Ohio Falls Sites," *ibid.*, **51**, 60–67.
GUERNSEY, S. J.
1931   *Explorations in Northeastern Arizona: Report on the Archaeological Field Work of 1920–1923.* ("Papers of the Peabody Museum," Vol. 12, No. 1.) Cambridge, Mass.
HAAG, WILLIAM G.
1942   "Early Horizons in the Southeast," *American Antiquity*, **7**, 209–22.
HAAG, WILLIAM G., and WEBB, CLARENCE H.
1953   "Microblades at Poverty Point," *ibid.*, **18**, 245–48.
HARDING, M.
1951   "La Jollan Culture," *El Museo* (San Diego, Calif.), **1**, 10–11, 31–38.
HARP, ELMER
1951   "An Archaeological Survey in the Strait of Belle Isle Area," *American Antiquity*, **16**, 203–20.
1952   "The Cultural Affinities of the Newfoundland Dorset Eskimo." Unpublished Ph.D. dissertation, Harvard University. Pp. 340.
HARRINGTON, M. R.
1924   "The Ozark Bluff-Dweller," *American Anthropologist*, **26**, 1–21.
1933   *Gypsum Cave, Nevada.* ("Southwest Museum Papers," No. 8.) Los Angeles.
1934   "The Meaning of Gypsum Cave," *Texas Archaeological and Paleontological Society Bulletin*, **6**, 58–69.
1948a   "America's Oldest Dwelling," *Masterkey* (Southwest Museum, Los Angeles), **22**, 148–52.
1948b   *An Ancient Site at Borax Lake, California.* ("Southwest Museum Papers," No. 16.) Los Angeles.
1948c   "A New Pinto Site," *Masterkey*, **22**, No. 4, 116–18.
1951   "Latest from Little Lake," *ibid.*, **25**, No. 6, 188–91.
1955   "Man's Oldest Date in America," *Natural History*, **64**, 512–55.
HAURY, EMIL W.
1932   *Roosevelt: 9:6, a Hohokam Site of the Colonial Period.* ("Medallion Papers," No. 11.) Globe, Ariz.
1936   *The Mogollon Culture of Southwestern New Mexico.* ("Medallion Papers," No. 20.) Globe, Ariz.
1945   *The Excavation of Los Muertos and Neighboring Ruins of the Salt River Valley, Southern Arizona.* ("Papers of the Peabody Museum," Vol. 24, No. 1.) Cambridge, Mass.

1953a "Artifacts with Mammoth Remains, Naco, Arizona," *American Antiquity*, **19**, 1–14.

1953b "Some Thoughts on Chibcha Culture in the High Plains of Colombia," *ibid.*, pp. 76–78.

HAURY, EMIL W., *et al.*

1950 *The Stratigraphy and Archaeology of Ventana Cave.* Albuquerque: University of New Mexico Press.

1956 "An Archaeological Approach to the Study of Cultural Stability," in *Seminars in Archaeology: 1955.* (Society for American Archaeology Memoir No. 11.) Salt Lake City.

HAYNES, C. V.

1955 "Evidence of Early Man in Torrance County, New Mexico," *Texas Archaeological Society Bulletin*, **26**, 144–64.

HEIZER, ROBERT F.

1941 "The Direct-Historical Approach in California Archaeology," *American Antiquity*, **7**, 98–122.

1949 *The Archaeology of Central California I: The Early Horizon.* ("University of California Anthropological Records," Vol. 12, No. 1.) Berkeley: University of California Press.

1951a "An Assessment of Certain Nevada, California and Oregon Radiocarbon Dates," in *Radiocarbon Dating*, ed. FREDERICK JOHNSON. (Society for American Archaeology Memoir No. 8.) *American Antiquity*, **17**, No. 1, 23–25.

1951b "Preliminary Report on the Leonard Rockshelter Site, Pershing County, Nevada," *ibid.*, **17**, 89–98.

HEIZER, ROBERT F., and FENENGA, F.

1939 "Archaeological Horizons in Central California," *American Anthropologist*, **41**, 378–99.

HEIZER, ROBERT F., and LEMERT, E. M.

1947 *Observations on Archaeological Sites in Topanga Canyon, California.* ("University of California Publications in American Archaeology and Ethnology," Vol. 44, No. 2.) Berkeley.

HIBBEN, FRANK C.

1937 "Association of Man with Pleistocene Mammals in the Sandia Mountains," *American Antiquity*, **2**, 260–63.

1941 *Evidences of Early Occupation in Sandia Cave, New Mexico, and Other Sites in the Sandia-Manzano Region.* ("Smithsonian Miscellaneous Collections," Vol. 99, No. 23.) Washington, D.C.

1943 "Evidences of Early Man in Alaska," *American Antiquity*, **8**, 254–59.

1946 "The First Thirty-eight Sandia Points," *ibid.*, **11**, 257–58.

HIBBEN, FRANK C.—*Continued*
1951 "Sites of the Paleo-Indian in the Middle Rio Grande Valley," *ibid.*, **17**, 41–46.
1955 "Specimens from Sandia Cave and Their Possible Significance," *Science*, **122**, 688–89.
HILL, A. T., and KIVETT, MARVIN
1940 "Woodland-like Manifestations in Nebraska," *Nebraska History Magazine*, **21**, No. 3, 146–243.
HILL, A. T., and WEDEL, W. R.
1936 "Excavations at the Leary Indian Village and Burial Site, Richardson County, Nebraska," *ibid.*, **17**, No. 1, 1–73.
HILL, MALCOLM W.
1953 "What Was the Purpose of the Single-shouldered Yuma Blade?" *Tennessee Archaeologist*, **9**, No. 1, 22–23.
HOFFMAN, BERNARD G.
1952 "Implications of Radiocarbon Datings for the Origin of the Dorset Culture," *American Antiquity*, **18**, 15–17.
HOLDER, PRESTON, and WIKE, JOYCE
1949 "The Frontier Culture Complex, a Preliminary Report on a Prehistoric Hunters' Camp in Southwestern Nebraska," *American Antiquity*, **14**, 260–65.
HOWARD, EDGAR B., *et al.*
1935– "The Occurrence of Flints and Extinct Animals in Fluvial Deposits near Clovis, New Mexico," *Proceedings of the Academy of Natural Sciences of Philadelphia*, Vols. 87–90.
HOWARD, G. D.
1947 *Prehistoric Ceramic Styles of Lowland South America, Their Distribution and History.* ("Yale University Publications in Anthropology," No. 37.) New Haven.
HOWARD, G. D., and WILLEY, G. R.
1948 *Lowland Argentine Archaeology.* ("Yale University Publications in Anthropology," No. 39.) New Haven.
HUGHES, JACK T.
1949 "Investigations in Western South Dakota and Northeastern Wyoming," *American Antiquity*, **14**, 266–77.
HURT, WESLEY R., JR.
1942 "Folsom and Yuma Points from the Estancia Valley, New Mexico," *American Antiquity*, **7**, 400–402.
1953 "A Comparative Study of the Preceramic Occupations of North America," *ibid.*, **18**, 204–19.
IRVING, WILLIAM
1955 "Burins from Central Alaska," *American Antiquity*, **20**, 380–83.

JENNESS, DIAMOND
1925 "A New Eskimo Culture in Hudson Bay," *Geographical Review*, **15**, 428–37.

JENNINGS, JESSE D.
1953 "Danger Cave: A Progress Summary," *El Palacio* (Santa Fe, N.M.), **60**, No. 5, 179–213.

JENNINGS, JESSE D., and NORBECK, EDWARD
1955 "Great Basin Prehistory: A Review," *American Antiquity*, **21**, 1–11.

JIJÓN Y CAAMAÑO, J.
1930 "Una gran marea cultural en el noroeste de Sudamerica," *Journal de la Société des Américanistes de Paris*, **22**, 107–97.
1949 *Maranga: Contribución al conocimiento de los aborígenes del Valle del Rimac, Peru.* Quito: La Prensa Católica.

JOHNSON, FREDERICK
1946 "An Archaeological Survey along the Alaska Highway, 1944," *American Antiquity*, **11**, 183–86.
n.d. "Radiocarbon Dates and Early Man in America" (MS). R. S. Peabody Foundation, Andover, Mass.

JOHNSON, FREDERICK (ed.)
1951 *Radiocarbon Dating.* (Society for American Archaeology Memoir No. 8.) *American Antiquity*, Vol. 17, No. 1, Part 2.

JUDD, NEIL M.
1954 *The Material Culture of Pueblo Bonito.* ("Smithsonian Miscellaneous Collections," Vol. 124.) Washington, D.C.

KELLEY, J. CHARLES
1947a "The Cultural Affiliations and Chronological Position of the Clear Fork Focus," *American Antiquity*, **13**, 97–109.
1947b "The Lehmann Rock Shelter: Stratified Site of the Toyah, Uvalde, and Round Rock Foci," *Texas Archaeological and Paleontological Society Bulletin*, **18**, 115–28.
1951 "Review of 'Stratigraphy and Archaeology of Ventana Cave,' by Emil W. Haury, 1950," *American Antiquity*, **17**, 152–54.

KELLEY, J. CHARLES, CAMPBELL, T. N., and LEHMER, D. J.
1940 *The Association of Archaeological Materials with Geological Deposits in the Big Bend Region of Texas.* (West Texas Historical and Scientific Society Publication No. 10.) Alpine, Tex.

KELLY, A. R.
1933 "Some Problems of Recent Cahokia Archaeology," *Transactions of the Illinois State Academy of Science*, **25**, No. 4, 101–3.

KELLY, A. R.—*Continued*
1938 *A Preliminary Report on Archaeological Explorations at Macon, Georgia.* (Smithsonian Institution, Bureau of American Ethnology Bulletin No. 119; "Anthropological Papers," No. 1.) Washington, D.C.

KEYES, CHARLES
1942 "An Outline of Iowa Archaeology," *Minnesota Archaeologist*, **8**, No. 1, 4–7

KIDDER, A. V.
1924 *An Introduction to the Study of Southwestern Archaeology.* New Haven: Yale University Press (for Department of Archaeology, Phillips Academy, Andover, Mass.).

KIDDER, A. V., and GUERNSEY, S. J.
1919 *Archaeological Explorations in Northeastern Arizona.* (Smithsonian Institution, Bureau of American Ethnology Bulletin No. 65.) Washington, D.C.

KIDDER, A. V., JENNINGS, J. D., and SHOOK, E. M.
1946 *Excavations at Kaminaljuyu, Guatemala.* (Carnegie Institution of Washington Publication 561.) Washington, D.C.

KIDDER, A., II
1948a "The Archaeology of Venezuela," in *Handbook of South American Indians*, ed. JULIAN H. STEWARD, **4**, 413–38. (Smithsonian Institution, Bureau of American Ethnology Bulletin No. 143.) Washington, D.C.
1948b "The Position of Pucara in Titicaca Basin Archaeology," in *A Reappraisal of Peruvian Archaeology*, ed. WENDELL C. BENNETT, pp. 87–89. (Society for American Archaeology Memoir No. 4.) Menasha, Wis.

KING, ARDEN
1950 *Cattle Point: A Stratified Site in the Southern Northewst Coast Region.* (Society for American Archaeology Memoir No. 7.) Menasha, Wis.

KIRCHHOFF, PAUL
1943 "Mesoamerica," *Acta Americana* (Mexico, D.F.), **1**, 92–107. (English translation, SOL TAX *et al.*, *Heritage of Conquest*, pp. 17–30. Glencoe, Ill.: Free Press, 1952.)
1954 "Gatherers and Farmers in the Greater Southwest," *American Anthropologist*, **56**, 529–50.

KIVETT, MARVIN F.
1949 "Archaeological Investigations in Medicine Creek Reservoir," *American Antiquity*, **14**, 278–84.

1952 *Woodland Sites in Nebraska.* ("Nebraska State Historical Society, Publications in Anthropology," No. 1.) Lincoln.

KLEINE, HAROLD K.
1953 "A Remarkable Paleo-Indian Site in Alabama," *Tennessee Archaeologist*, **9**, No. 2, 31–37.

KLUCKHOHN, CLYDE, and REITER, PAUL (eds.)
1939 *Preliminary Report on the 1937 Excavations, Bc 50–51, Chaco Canyon, New Mexico.* (University of New Mexico Bulletin, Whole No. 345; "Anthropological Series," Vol. 3, No. 2.) Albuquerque.

KNEBERG, MADELINE
1952 "The Tennessee Area," in *Archeology of Eastern United States*, ed. JAMES B. GRIFFIN, pp. 190–98. Chicago: University of Chicago Press.
1954 "The Duration of the Archaic Tradition in the Lower Tennessee Valley," *Southern Indian Studies* (Chapel Hill, N.C.), **6**, 40–44.

KRIEGER, ALEX D.
1945 "An Inquiry into Supposed Mexican Influence on a Prehistoric 'Cult' in the Southern United States," *American Anthropologist*, **47**, 483–515.
1946 *Culture Complexes and Chronology in Northern Texas.* (University of Texas Publication No. 4640.) Austin.
1948 "Importance of the 'Gilmore Corridor' in Culture Contacts between Middle America and the Eastern United States," *Texas Archaeological and Paleontological Society Bulletin*, **19**, 155–78.
1951a "Early Man [Notes and News]," *American Antiquity*, **17**, 77–78.
1951b "A Radiocarbon Date on the Davis Site in East Texas," *ibid.*, pp. 144–45.
1952 "Review of 'Greenhouse: A Troyville–Coles Creek Period Site,' by James A. Ford," *ibid.*, **18**, 175–79.
1953 "New World Culture History: Anglo-America," in *Anthropology Today*, ed. A. L. KROEBER, pp. 238–64. Chicago: University of Chicago Press.

KROEBER, A. L.
1916 *Zuñi Potsherds.* ("American Museum of Natural History, Anthropological Papers," Vol. 18, Part 1.) New York.
1925 *The Uhle Pottery Collections from Moche.* ("University of California Publications in American Archaeology and Ethnology," Vol. 21.) Berkeley.
1926 *Archaeological Explorations in Peru, Part I: Ancient Pottery from Trujillo.* ("Field Museum of Natural History, Anthropological Memoirs," Vol. 2, No. 1.) Chicago.

KROEBER, A. L.—*Continued*

1939 *Cultural and Natural Areas of Native North America.* ("University of California Publications in American Archaeology and Ethnology," Vol. 38.) Berkeley.

1940 "Conclusions: The Present Status of Americanistic Problems," in *The Maya and Their Neighbors*, ed. C. L. HAY *et al.*, pp. 441–90. New York: Appleton-Century Co.

1944 *Peruvian Archaeology in 1942.* ("Viking Fund Publications in Anthropology," No. 4.) New York.

1946 "The Chibcha," in *Handbook of South American Indians*, ed. JULIAN H. STEWARD, **2**, 887–910. (Smithsonian Institution, Bureau of American Ethnology Bulletin No. 143.) Washington, D.C.

1948 "Summary and Interpretations," in *A Reappraisal of Peruvian Archaeology*, ed. WENDELL C. BENNETT, pp. 113–21. (Society for American Archaeology Memoir No. 4.) Menasha, Wis.

KROEBER, A. L. (ed.)

1953 *Anthropology Today: An Encyclopedic Inventory.* (International Symposium on Anthropology, Wenner-Gren Foundation for Anthropological Research, 1952.) Chicago: University of Chicago Press.

KULP, J. LAURENCE, FEELY, HERBERT W., and TRYON, LANSING E.

1951 "Lamont Natural Radiocarbon Measurements, I," *Science*, **114**, No. 2970 (November 30), 565–68.

LAGUNA, FREDERICA DE

1946 "The Importance of the Eskimo in Northeastern Archaeology," in *Man in Northeastern North America*, ed. FREDERICK JOHNSON, pp. 106–42. ("Papers of the Robert S. Peabody Foundation for Archaeology," Vol. 3.) Andover, Mass.: Phillips Academy.

1947 *The Prehistory of Northern North America as Seen from the Yukon.* (Society for American Archaeology Memoir No. 3.) *American Antiquity*, Vol. 12, No. 3, Part 2.

LANCASTER, JAMES A., *et al.*

1954 *Archaeological Excavations in Mesa Verde National Park, Colorado, 1950.* ("U.S. Department of the Interior, National Park Service, Archaeological Research Series," No. 2.) Washington, D.C.

LARCO HOYLE, RAFAEL

1938– *Los Mochicas.* 2 vols. Lima: Rimac, S.A.
39

1941 *Los Cupisniques.* Lima: La Cronica y Variedades, S.A.

1948 *Cronología arqueológica del Norte del Peru.* Buenos Aires: Sociedad Geográfica Americana.

LARSEN, HELGE, and RAINEY, FROELICH
1948 *Ipiutak and the Arctic Whale Hunting Culture.* ("American Museum of Natural History, Anthropological Papers," Vol. 42.) New York.

LATHRAP, DONALD W.
n.d. "Preceramic South America." (MS prepared in 1954.) Peabody Museum Library, Harvard University.

LAUGHLIN, WILLIAM S.
1951 "Notes on an Aleutian Core and Blade Industry," *American Antiquity*, **17**, 52–55.

LAUGHLIN, WILLIAM S., and MARSH, GORDON H.
1954 "The Lamellar Flake Manufacturing Site on Anangula Island," *ibid.*, **20**, 27–39.

LAUGHLIN, WILLIAM S., MARSH, G. H., and LEACH, J. W.
1952 "Supplementary Note on the Aleutian Core and Blade Industry," *ibid.*, **18**, 69–70.

LEECHMAN, DOUGLAS
1943 "Two New Cape Dorset Sites," *American Antiquity*, **8**, 363–75.

LEWIS, T. M. N.
1953 "The Paleo-Indian Problem in Tennessee," *Tennessee Archaeologist*, **9**, No. 2, 38–40.

1954a "A Suggested Basis for Paleo-Indian Chronology in Tennessee and the Eastern United States," *Southern Indian Studies* (Chapel Hill, N.C.), **6**, 11–13.

1954b "Sandia Points," *Tennessee Archaeologist*, **10**, No. 1, 26–27.

LEWIS, T. M. N., and KNEBERG, MADELINE
1941 "Prehistory of the Chickamauga Basin in Tennessee." ("Division of Anthropology, University of Tennessee, Tennessee Anthropological Papers," No. 1.) Knoxville. (Mimeographed.)

1946 *Hiwassee Island: An Archaeological Account of Four Tennessee Indian Peoples.* Knoxville: University of Tennessee Press.

1947 *The Archaic Horizon in Western Tennessee.* ("Tennessee Anthropological Papers," No. 2; "University of Tennessee Record Extension Series," Vol. 23, No. 4.) Knoxville.

1951 "Early Projectile Point Forms, and Examples from Tennessee," *Tennessee Archaeologist*, **7**, No. 1, 6–19.

LIBBY, W. F.
1951 "Radiocarbon Dates, II," *Science*, **114**, 291–96.
1952 *Radiocarbon Dating.* Chicago: University of Chicago Press.
1954a "Chicago Radiocarbon Dates, IV," *Science*, **119**, 135–40.
1954b "Chicago Radiocarbon Dates, V," *ibid.*, **120**, 733–42.

Lillard, J. B., Heizer, R. F., and Fenenga, F.
1939   *An Introduction to the Archaeology of Central California.* (Department of Anthropology, Sacramento Junior College, Bulletin No. 2.) Sacramento, Calif.

Lillard, Jeremiah B., and Purves, W. K.
1936   *The Archaeology of the Deer Creek–Cosumnes Area.* (Department of Anthropology, Sacramento Junior College, Bulletin No. 1.) Sacramento, Calif.

Lilly, Eli
1937   *Prehistoric Antiquities of Indiana: A Description of the More Notable Earthworks, Mounds, Implements and Ceremonial Objects Left in Indiana by Our Predecessors, Together with Some Information as to Their Origin and Antiquity, and the Prehistory of Indiana.* Indianapolis: Indiana Historical Society.

Linné, Sigvald
1934   *Archaeological Researches at Teotihuacán, Mexico.* ("Publications of the Ethnographical Museum of Sweden," N.S., No. 1.) Stockholm.
1942   *Mexican Highland Cultures: Archaeological Researches at Teotihuacán, Calpulalpan and Chalchicomula in 1934–1935.* ("Publications of the Ethnographical Museum of Sweden," N.S., No. 7.) Stockholm.

Logan, Wilfred D.
1952   *Graham Cave, an Archaic Site in Montgomery County, Missouri.* (Missouri Archaeological Society Memoir No. 2.) Columbia, Mo.

Longyear, J. M., III
1944   *Archaeological Investigations in El Salvador.* ("Memoirs of the Peabody Museum," Vol. 9, No. 2.) Cambridge, Mass.

Lothrop, Samuel K.
1927   *Pottery Types and Their Sequence in El Salvador.* ("Indian Notes and Monographs," Vol. 1, No. 4.) New York: Museum of the American Indian, Heye Foundation.
1932   "Indians of the Paraná Delta, Argentina," *Annals of the New York Academy of Sciences,* **33,** 77–232.
1937–   *Coclé: An Archaeological Study of Central Panama.* ("Memoirs of
42   the Peabody Museum," Vols. 7 and 8.) Cambridge, Mass.
1941   "Gold Ornaments of Chavín Style from Chongoyape, Peru," *American Antiquity,* **6,** 250–62.
1946   "The Diaguita of Chile," in *Handbook of South American Indians,* ed. Julian H. Steward, **2,** 634–35. (Smithsonian Institution, Bureau of American Ethnology Bulletin No. 143.) Washington, D.C.

1948 "The Archaeology of Panama," *ibid.*, **4**, 143–68.
1951 "Peruvian Metallurgy," in *The Civilizations of Ancient America*, pp. 219–23. (*Selected Papers of the XXIXth International Congress of Americanists*, ed. Sol Tax, Vol. 1.) Chicago: University of Chicago Press.

LOUD, L. L., and HARRINGTON, M. R.
1929 *Lovelock Cave*. ("University of California Publications in American Archaeology and Ethnology," Vol. 25, No. 1.) Berkeley.

McCARY, BEN C.
1951 "A Workshop Site of Early Man in Dinwiddie County, Virginia," *American Antiquity*, **17**, 9–17.

McGIMSEY, C. R., III
1956 "Cerro Mangote: A Preceramic Site in Panama," *American Antiquity*, **22**, 151–61.

McGREGOR, JOHN C.
1950 "Weighted Traits and Traditions," in *For the Dean*, ed. ERIK K. REED and DALE S. KING, pp. 291–98. Santa Fe, N.M.: Hohokam Museum Association and Southwestern Monuments Association.

McINTIRE, WILLIAM G.
1954 *Correlation of Prehistoric Settlements and Delta Development: Trafficability and Navigability of Delta Type Coasts: Trafficability and Navigability of Louisiana Coastal Marshes*. (Louisiana State University, Technical Report No. 5.) Baton Rouge.

McKERN, W. C.
1928 *The Neale and McClaughry Mound Groups*. (Bulletin of the Public Museum of the City of Milwaukee, Vol. 3, No. 3.)
1930 *The Kletzien and Nitschke Mound Groups*. (Bulletin of the Public Museum of the City of Milwaukee, Vol. 3, No. 4.)
1931a "Regarding the Origin of Wisconsin Effigy Mounds," *American Anthropologist*, **31**, 562–64.
1931b *A Wisconsin Variant of the Hopewell Culture*. (Bulletin of the Public Museum of the City of Milwaukee, Vol. 10, No. 2.)
1939 "The Midwestern Taxonomic Method as an Aid to Archaeological Culture Study," *American Antiquity*, **4**, 301–13.
1956 "On Willey and Phillips' 'Method and Theory in American Archaeology' [Letters to the Editor]," *American Anthropologist*, **58**, 360–61.

MacNEISH, R. S.
1947 "A Preliminary Report on Coastal Tamaulipas, Mexico," *American Antiquity*, **13**, 1–14.
1948 "The Pre-pottery Faulkner Site of Southern Illinois," *ibid.*, pp. 232–43.

MacNeish, R. S.—*Continued*

1950 "A Synopsis of the Archaeological Sequence in the Sierra de Tamaulipas," *Revista mexicana de estudios antropológicos* (Mexico, D.F.), **11**, 79–96.

1951 "An Archaeological Reconnaissance in the Northwest Territories," in *Annual Report of the National Museum of Canada, 1949–50*, pp. 24–41. (Bulletin No. 123.) Ottawa.

1952 "The Archeology of the Northeastern United States," in *Archeology of Eastern United States*, ed. James B. Griffin, pp. 46–58. Chicago: University of Chicago Press.

1953 "Archaeological Reconnaissance in the Mackenzie River Drainage," in *Annual Report of the National Museum of Canada, 1951–1952*, pp. 23–39. (Bulletin No. 128.) Ottawa.

1954a "The Pointed Mountain Site near Fort Liard, Northwest Territories, Canada," *American Antiquity*, **19**, 234–52.

1954b *An Early Archaeological Site near Panuco, Vera Cruz*. ("Transactions of the American Philosophical Society," Vol. 44, No. 5.) Philadelphia.

Mahan, E. C.

1954– "A Survey of Paleo-Indian and Other Early Flint Artifacts from 55 Sites in Northern, Western and Central Alabama," *Tennessee Archaeologist*, **10**, No. 2, 37–58; **11**, No. 1, 1–8.

Maler, Teobert

1901– *Researches in the Central Portion of the Usumatsintla Valley.* 3 ("Memoirs of the Peabody Museum," Vol. 2, Nos. 1 and 2.) Cambridge, Mass.

Mangelsdorf, Paul C., and Smith, C. Earle

1949 "New Archaeological Evidence on Evolution in Maize," *Botanical Museum of Harvard University Leaflets*, **13**, No. 8, 213–47.

Martin, Paul S.

1939 *Modified Basket Maker Sites in the Ackmen-Lowry Area, Southwestern Colorado.* ("Field Museum of Natural History, Anthropological Series," Vol. 23, No. 3.) Chicago.

Martin, Paul S., Quimby, George I., and Collier, Donald

1947 *Indians before Columbus: Twenty Thousand Years of North American History Revealed by Archeology.* Chicago: University of Chicago Press.

Martin, Paul S., and Rinaldo, John B.

1947 *The SU Site: Excavations at a Mogollon Village, Western New Mexico, Third Season, 1946.* ("Field Museum of Natural History, Anthropological Series," Vol. 32, No. 3.) Chicago: Natural History Museum.

1950a *Turkey Foot Ridge Site: A Mogollon Village, Pine Lawn Valley, Western New Mexico.* ("Fieldiana: Anthropology," Vol. 38, No. 2.) Chicago: Natural History Museum.

1950b *Sites of Reserve Phase, Pine Lawn Valley, Western New Mexico.* ("Fieldiana: Anthropology," Vol. 38, No. 3.) Chicago: Natural History Museum.

1951 "The Southwestern Co-tradition," *Southwestern Journal of Anthropology*, **7**, 215–29.

MARTIN, PAUL S., RINALDO, JOHN B., and ANTEVS, ERNST
1949 *Cochise and Mogollon Sites, Pine Lawn Valley, Western New Mexico.* ("Fieldiana: Anthropology," Vol. 38, No. 1.) Chicago: Natural History Museum.

MARTIN, PAUL S., et al.
1952 *Mogollon Cultural Continuity and Change: The Stratigraphic Analysis of Tularosa and Cordova Caves.* ("Fieldiana: Anthropology," Vol. 40.) Chicago: Natural History Museum.

1956 *Higgins Flat Pueblo, Western New Mexico.* ("Fieldiana: Anthropology," Vol. 45.) Chicago: Natural History Museum.

MARTÍNEZ DEL RIO, PABLO
1953 "La cueva mortuoria de la Candelaria, Coahuila," *Cuadernos americanos* (Mexico, D.F.), July–August.

MASON, JOHN ALDEN
1931– *Archaeology of Santa Marta, Colombia.* ("Field Museum of Natu-
39 ral History, Anthropological Series," Vol. 20, Nos. 1–3.) Chicago.

MAXWELL, MOREAU S.
1951 *The Woodland Cultures of Southern Illinois: Archaeological Excavations in the Carbondale Area.* ("Logan Museum Publications in Anthropology," Bulletin No. 7.) Beloit, Wis.

MAYER-OAKES, WILLIAM J.
1951 "Starved Rock Archaic: A Prepottery Horizon from Northern Illinois," *American Antiquity*, **16**, 313–24.

1955 *Prehistory of the Upper Ohio Valley: An Introductory Archaeological Study.* ("Annals of the Carnegie Museum, Vol. 34, Anthropological Series," No. 2.) Pittsburgh, Pa.

MEANS, PHILIP A.
1931 *Ancient Civilizations of the Andes.* New York: Charles Scribner's Sons.

MEGGERS, B. J.
1954 "Environmental Limitation on the Development of Culture," *American Anthropologist*, **56**, 801–24.

MELGAARD, JORGEN
  1952 "A Paleo-Eskimo Culture in West Greenland," *American Antiquity*, 17, 222–30.
MENGHÍN, O. F. A.
  1952a "Las pinturas rupestres de la Patagonia," *Runa* (Buenos Aires), 5, 5–22.
  1952b "Fundamentos cronológicos de la prehistoria de Patagonia," *ibid.*, pp. 23–43.
  1953– "Culturas preceramicas en Bolivia," *ibid.*, 6, 125–32.
  54
MENGHÍN, O. F. A., and BÓRMIDA, MARCELO
  1950 "Investigaciones prehistoricas en cuevas de Tandilia, Provincia de Buenos Aires," *ibid.*, Vol. 3, Parts 1–2.
MILES, SUZANNA W.
  1951 "A Revaluation of the Old Copper Industry," *American Antiquity*, 16, 240–47.
MILLER, CARL F.
  1950 "Early Cultural Horizons in the Southeastern United States," *American Antiquity*, 15, 273–88.
  1956 "Life 8000 Years Ago Uncovered in an Alabama Cave," *National Geographic Magazine*, 110, No. 4 (October), 542–58.
MILLS, WILLIAM C.
  1902 "Excavations in the Adena Mound," *Ohio Archaeological and Historical Quarterly*, 10, 452–79.
  1909 "Explorations of the Seip Mound," *ibid.*, 18, 268–321.
  1922 "Exploration of the Mound City Group," *ibid.*, 31, 423–584.
MOORE, CLARENCE B.
  1901 "Certain Aboriginal Remains of the Northwest Florida Coast, Part 1," *Journal of the Academy of Natural Sciences of Philadelphia*, Ser. 2, 11, Part 4, 419–97.
  1902 "Certain Aboriginal Remains of the Northwest Florida Coast, Part 2," *ibid.*, 12, Part 2, 125–335.
  1903 "Certain Aboriginal Mounds of the Florida Central West Coast," *ibid.*, Part 3, pp. 361–438.
  1905 "Certain Aboriginal Remains of the Black Warrior River," *ibid.*, 13, 125–244.
  1907a "Crystal River Revisited," *ibid.*, Part 3, pp. 406–25.
  1907b "Moundville Revisited," *ibid.*, pp. 337–405.
  1918 "The Northwestern Florida Coast Revisited," *ibid.*, 16, Part 4, 514–77.

MOOREHEAD, WARREN K.
1890   *Fort Ancient.* Cincinnati: Robert Clark & Co.
1922*a*   *The Hopewell Mound Group of Ohio.* ("Field Museum of Natural History, Anthropological Series," Vol. 6, No. 5.) Chicago.
1922*b*   *A Report on the Archaeology of Maine.* Andover, Mass.: Department of Archaeology, Phillips Academy.
MOOREHEAD, WARREN K., and LEIGHTON, MORRIS M.
1923   "The Cahokia Mounds," *University of Illinois Bulletin*, 21, No. 6, 1–97.
MOOREHEAD, WARREN K., *et al.*
1929   *The Cahokia Mounds.* Urbana: University of Illinois.
1932   *Etowah Papers.* New Haven: Yale University Press (for Department of Archaeology, Phillips Academy, Andover, Mass.).
MORGAN, RICHARD G.
1952   "Outline of Cultures in the Ohio Region," in *Archeology of Eastern United States*, ed. JAMES B. GRIFFIN, pp. 83–98. Chicago: University of Chicago Press.
MORLEY, SYLVANUS G.
1946   *The Ancient Maya.* Stanford, Calif.: Stanford University Press.
MORRIS, EARL H.
1939   *Archaeological Studies in the La Plata District, Southwestern Colorado and Northwestern New Mexico.* Appendix, "Technology of La Plata Pottery" by ANNA O. SHEPARD. (Carnegie Institution of Washington Publication 519.) Washington, D.C.
MORRIS, EARL H., and BURGH, ROBERT F.
1954   *Basket Maker II Sites near Durango, Colorado.* (Carnegie Institution of Washington Publication 604.) Washington, D.C.
MORRIS, EARL H., CHARLOT, J., and MORRIS, A. A.
1931   *The Temple of the Warriors at Chichén Itzá, Yucatán.* (Carnegie Institution of Washington Publication 406.) Washington, D.C.
MOSS, JOHN H., *et al.*
1951   *Early Man in the Eden Valley.* ("University Museum, University of Pennsylvania, Museum Monographs.") Philadelphia.
MULLOY, WILLIAM
1954   "The McKean Site in Northeastern Wyoming," *Southwestern Journal of Anthropology*, 10, 432–60.
MURDOCK, GEORGE P.
1949   *Social Structure.* New York: Macmillan Co.
NASH, PHILLEO
1933   *The Excavation of Ross Mound Group I.* (Bulletin of the Public Museum of the City of Milwaukee, Vol. 16, No. 1.)

NEWCOMB, WILLIAM W.
1956 "A Reappraisal of the 'Cultural Sink' of Texas," *Southwestern Journal of Anthropology*, 12, 145–53.
NEWELL, H. PERRY, and KRIEGER, ALEX D.
1949 *The George C. Davis Site, Cherokee County, Texas*. (Society for American Archaeology Memoir No. 5.) *American Antiquity*, Vol. 14, No. 4, Part 2.
NORDENSKIÖLD, ERLAND VON
1913 "Urnengraber und Mounds in bolivianischen Flachlande," *Baessler Archiv*, 3, 205–55.
ORR, KENNETH G.
1946 "The Archaeological Situation at Spiro, Oklahoma: A Preliminary Report," *American Antiquity*, 11, 228–56.
1952 "Survey of Caddoan Area Archeology," in *Archeology of Eastern United States*, ed. JAMES B. GRIFFIN, pp. 239–55. Chicago: University of Chicago Press.
ORR, PHIL C.
1943 *Archaeology of Mescalitan Island and Customs of the Canalino.* ("Santa Barbara Museum of Natural History, Occasional Papers," No. 5.) Santa Barbara, Calif.
1952 "Review of Santa Barbara Channel Archaeology," *Southwestern Journal of Anthropology*, 8, 211–26.
ORSSICH, ADAM, and ORSSICH, E. S.
1956 "Stratigraphic Excavations in the Sambaquí of Araujo II," *American Antiquity*, 21, 357–69.
OSGOOD, CORNELIUS
1942 *The Ciboney Culture of Cayo Redondo, Cuba*. ("Yale University Publications in Anthropology," No. 25.) New Haven.
PALMATARY, H. C.
1939 *Tapajó Pottery*. ("Etnologiska Studier," No. 8.) Göteborg, Sweden.
1950 *The Pottery of Marajó Island, Brazil*. ("Transactions of the American Philosophical Society," Vol. 39, Part 3.) Philadelphia.
PARSONS, ELSIE CLEWS
1936 *Mitla, Town of Souls*. Chicago: University of Chicago Press.
PHILLIPS, PHILIP
1939 "Introduction to the Archaeology of the Mississippi Valley." Unpublished Ph.D. dissertation, Harvard University. Pp. 768.
1940 "Middle American Influences on the Archaeology of the Southeastern United States," in *The Maya and Their Neighbors*, ed. C. L. HAY *et al.*, pp. 349–67. New York: Appleton-Century Co.

1955   "American Archaeology and General Anthropological Theory,"
        Southwestern Journal of Anthropology, 11, 246–50.

PHILLIPS, PHILIP, FORD, JAMES A., and GRIFFIN, JAMES B.
1951   *Archaeological Survey in the Lower Mississippi Alluvial Valley,
        1940–1947*. ("Papers of the Peabody Museum," Vol. 25.) Cam-
        bridge, Mass.

PHILLIPS, PHILIP, and WILLEY, GORDON R.
1953   "Method and Theory in American Archaeology: An Opera-
        tional Basis for Culture-historical Integration," *American An-
        thropologist*, 55, 615–33.

PORTER, M. N.
1953   *Tlatilco and the Pre-Classic Cultures of the New World*. ("Viking
        Fund Publications in Anthropology," No. 19.) New York.

POSNANSKY, ARTHUR
1945   *Tihuanacu: La cuna del hombre americano* ("Tihuancu: The
        Cradle of American Man"). English trans. by J. F. SHEARER.
        New York: J. J. Augustin.

PRESCOTT, W. H.
1843   *The Conquest of Mexico*. New York: Modern Library.

PRESTON, R. S., PERSON, E., and DEEVEY, E. S.
1955   "Yale Natural Radiocarbon Measurements, II," *Science*, 122,
        954–60.

PREUSS, K. T.
1931   *Arte monumental prehistórico*. Bogotá: Escuelas Salesianas de
        Tipografía y Fotograbado.

PROSKOURIAKOFF, TATIANA
1950   *A Study of Classic Maya Sculpture*. (Carnegie Institution of Wash-
        ington Publication 593.) Washington, D.C.

QUIMBY, GEORGE I.
1941a *The Goodall Focus: An Analysis of Ten Hopewellian Components in
        Michigan and Indiana*. ("Indiana Historical Society, Prehistory
        Research Series," Vol. 2, No. 2.) Indianapolis.
1941b "Hopewellian Pottery Types in Michigan," *Papers of the Michi-
        gan Academy of Science, Arts and Letters*, 26, 489–94.
1942   "The Natchezan Culture Type," *American Antiquity*, 7, 255–75.
1951   *The Medora Site, West Baton Rouge Parish, Louisiana*. ("Field
        Museum of Natural History, Anthropological Series," Vol. 24,
        No. 2.) Chicago.
1952   "The Archeology of the Upper Great Lakes Area," in *Arche-
        ology of Eastern United States*, ed. JAMES B. GRIFFIN, pp. 99–107.
        Chicago: University of Chicago Press.

REDFIELD, ROBERT
1953 *The Primitive World and Its Transformations.* Ithaca, N.Y.: Cornell University Press.

REICHEL-DOLMATOFF, GERARDO
1954 "A Preliminary Study of Space and Time Perspective in Northern Colombia," *American Antiquity,* 19, 352–66.
1955 "Excavaciones en los conchales de la costa de Barlovento," *Revista colombiana de antropología* (Bogotá), 4, 249–72.

REICHEL-DOLMATOFF, GERARDO, and REICHEL-DOLMATOFF, ALICIA
1951 "Investigaciones arqueológicas en el Departamento del Magdalena, Colombia, 1946–1950," *Boletín de arqueología* (Bogotá), Vol. 3, Nos. 1–6.

REICHLEN, HENRI, and REICHLEN, PAULE
1949 "Recherches archéologiques dans les Andes de Cajamarca: Premier rapport de la mission ethnologique française au Pérou septentrional," *Journal de la Société des Américanistes de Paris,* 38, 137–74.

RENAUD, E. B.
1938 *The Black's Fork Culture of Southwest Wyoming.* (The Archaeological Survey of the High Western Plains, 10th Report.) Denver, Colo.: University of Denver.
1940 *Further Research in the Black's Fork Basin, Southwest Wyoming, 1938–1939.* (The Archaeological Survey of the High Western Plains, 12th Report.) Denver, Colo.: University of Denver.

RESTREPO, V.
1895 *Los Chibchas antes de la conquista española.* Bogotá: Impronto de la Luz.

RICKETSON, O. G., JR., and RICKETSON, E. B.
1937 *Uaxactún, Guatemala: Group E—1926–1931.* (Carnegie Institution of Washington Publication 477.) Washington, D.C.

RITCHIE, WILLIAM A.
1932 "The Lamoka Lake Site," *Researches and Transactions of the New York State Archaeological Association* (Lewis H. Morgan Chapter), 7, No. 4, 79–134.
1934 *An Algonkian-Iroquois Contact Site on Castle Creek, Broome County, N.Y.* ("Rochester Municipal Museum, Research Records," No. 2.) Rochester, N.Y.
1938 *Certain Recently Explored New York Mounds and Their Probable Relation to the Hopewell Culture.* ("Rochester Museum of Arts and Sciences, Research Records," No. 4.) Rochester, N.Y.

1944   *The Pre-Iroquoian Occupations of New York State*. (Rochester Museum of Arts and Sciences, Museum Memoir No. 1.) Rochester, N.Y.

1949   *The Bell-Philhower Site, Sussex County, New Jersey*. ("Indiana Historical Society, Prehistory Research Series," Vol. 3, No. 2.) Indianapolis.

1951a   "A Current Synthesis of New York Prehistory," *American Antiquity*, **17**, 130–36.

1951b   "Ground Slates: Eskimo or Indian?" *Pennsylvania Archaeologist*, **21**, Nos. 3–4, 46–52.

1952   *The Chance Horizon: An Early Stage of Mohawk Iroquois Cultural Development*. (New York State Museum Circular 29.) Albany.

1953   "A Probable Paleo-Indian Site in Vermont," *American Antiquity*, **18**, 249–58.

1955   *Recent Discoveries Suggesting an Early Woodland Burial Cult in the Northeast*. (New York State Museum and Science Service Circular 40.) Albany.

RITCHIE, WILLIAM A., and MACNEISH, RICHARD S.

1949   "The Pre-Iroquoian Pottery of New York State," *American Antiquity*, **15**, 97–124.

RITCHIE, WILLIAM A., *et al*.

1953   *An Early Owasco Sequence in Eastern New York*. (New York State Museum Circular 32.) Albany.

RITZENTHALER, ROBERT E., and SCHOLZ, PAUL

1946   "The Osceola Site: An 'Old Copper' Site near Potosi, Wisconsin," *Wisconsin Archaeologist*, **27**, No. 3, 53–70.

RITZENTHALER, ROBERT E., and WITTRY, WARREN L.

1952   "The Oconto Site: An Old Copper Manifestation," *ibid.*, **33**, No. 4, 199–223.

ROBERTS, FRANK H. H.

1929   *Shabik'eshchee Village: A Late Basket Maker Site in the Chaco Canyon, New Mexico*. (Smithsonian Institution, Bureau of American Ethnology Bulletin No. 92.) Washington, D.C.

1931   *The Ruins at Kiatuthlanna, Eastern Arizona*. (Smithsonian Institution, Bureau of American Ethnology Bulletin No. 100.) Washington, D.C.

1935   *A Folsom Complex: Preliminary Report on Investigations at the Lindenmeier Site in Northern Colorado*. ("Smithsonian Miscellaneous Collections," Vol. 94, No. 4.) Washington, D.C.

1936a   *Additional Information on the Folsom Complex: Report on the Second Season's Investigations at the Lindenmeier Site in Northern Colorado*.

("Smithsonian Miscellaneous Collections," Vol. 95, No. 10.) Washington, D.C.

1936b "A Survey of Southwestern Archaeology," *American Anthropologist*, **37**, 1–35.

1937 "Archaeology in the Southwest," *American Antiquity*, **3**, 3–33.

1939 *Archaeological Remains in the Whitewater District, Eastern Arizona*, Part I: *House Types*. (Smithsonian Institution, Bureau of American Ethnology Bulletin No. 121.) Washington, D.C.

1940 *Archaeological Remains in the Whitewater District, Eastern Arizona*, Part II: *Artifacts and Burials*. (Smithsonian Institution, Bureau of American Ethnology Bulletin No. 126.) Washington, D.C.

1942 *Archaeological and Geological Investigations in the San Jon District, Eastern New Mexico*. ("Smithsonian Miscellaneous Collections," Vol. 103, No. 4.) Washington, D.C.

1951 "Radiocarbon Dates and Early Man," in *Radiocarbon Dating*, ed. FREDERICK JOHNSON. (Society for American Archaeology Memoir No. 8.) *American Antiquity*, **17**, No. 1, Part 2, 20–22.

ROGERS, DAVID B.
1929 *Prehistoric Man of the Santa Barbara Coast*. Santa Barbara, Calif.: Santa Barbara Museum of Natural History.

ROGERS, MALCOLM J.
1929 "The Stone Art of the San Dieguito Plateau," *American Anthropologist*, **31**, 454–67.

1939 *Early Lithic Industries of the Lower Basin of the Colorado River and Adjacent Desert Areas*. ("San Diego Museum Papers," No. 3.) San Diego, Calif.

1945 "An Outline of Yuman Prehistory," *Southwestern Journal of Anthropology*, **1**, 167–98.

ROOSA, WILLIAM B.
1956 "The Lucy Site in Central New Mexico," *American Antiquity*, **21**, 310.

ROOT, W. C.
1949a "Metallurgy," in *Handbook of South American Indians*, ed. JULIAN H. STEWARD, **5**, 205–26. (Smithsonian Institution, Bureau of American Ethnology Bulletin No. 143.) Washington, D.C.

1949b "The Metallurgy of the Southern Coast of Peru," *American Antiquity*, **15**, 10–37.

ROUSE, IRVING
1941 *Culture of the Ft. Liberté Region, Haiti*. ("Yale University Publications in Anthropology," No. 24.) New Haven.

1948   "The Ciboney," in *Handbook of South American Indians*, ed.
Julian H. Steward, **4**, 495–503. (Smithsonian Institution, Bureau of American Ethnology Bulletin No. 143.) Washington,
D.C.

1949   "The Southeast and the West Indies," in *The Florida Indian and
His Neighbors*, ed. John W. Griffin, pp. 117–38. (Papers delivered at an Anthropological Conference held at Rollins College,
April 9–10, 1949.) Winter Park, Fla.

1951*a*   "Prehistoric Caribbean Culture Contact as Seen from Venezuela," *Transactions of the New York Academy of Sciences*, Ser. 2,
13, 342–47.

1951*b*   *A Survey of Indian River Archaeology, Florida.* ("Yale University
Publications in Anthropology," No. 44.) New Haven.

1952   *Porto Rican Prehistory.* ("Scientific Survey of Porto Rico and the
Virgin Islands," Vol. 18, Parts 3 and 4.) New York: New York
Academy of Sciences.

1953   "The Circum-Caribbean Theory: An Archaeological Test,"
American Anthropologist, **55**, 188–200.

1954   "On the Use of the Concept of Area Co-tradition," *American
Antiquity*, **19**, 221–25.

1955   "On the Correlation of Phases of Culture," *American Anthropologist*, **57**, 713–22.

Rowe, John H.
1945   "Absolute Chronology in the Andean Area," *American Antiquity*, **10**, 265–84.

1946   "Inca Culture at the Time of the Spanish Conquest," in *Handbook of South American Indians*, ed. Julian H. Steward, **2**, 183–
330. (Smithsonian Institution, Bureau of American Ethnology
Bulletin No. 143.) Washington, D.C.

1948   "The Kingdom of Chimor," *Acta Americana* (Mexico, D.F.), **6**,
26–59.

Rowley, Graham
1940   "The Dorset Culture of the Eastern Arctic," *American Anthropologist*, **42**, 490–99.

Roys, R. L.
1950   "Historical Source Material for the History of Mayapan."
Washington, D.C.: Carnegie Institution of Washington. (Mimeographed.)

Ruppert, Karl, and Smith, A. L.
1952   Excavations in House Mounds at Mayapan. (Carnegie Institution of Washington, Current Report No. 4.) Washington, D.C.

RYDEN, S.
1936 *Archaeological Researches in the Department of La Candelaria.* ("Etnologiska Studier," No. 3.) Stockholm.

SANDERS, WILLIAM T.
1953 "The Anthropogeography of Central Veracruz," *Revista mexicana de estudios antropológicos* (Mexico, D.F.), **13**, Nos. 2 and 3, 27–78.
1956 "The Central Mexican Symbiotic Region: A Study in Prehistoric Settlement Patterns," in *Prehistoric Settlement Patterns in the New World*, ed. G. R. WILLEY, pp. 115–27. ("Viking Fund Publications in Anthropology," No. 23.) New York.
n.d. "The Archaeology of the North and Central Coast of Ecuador" (MS). Peabody Museum, Harvard University, files of G. R. Willey.

SATTERTHWAITE, LINTON
1933 *Description of the Site (Piedras Negras) with Short Notes on the Excavations of 1931–1932.* ("Piedras Negras Preliminary Papers," No. 1.) Philadelphia: University Museum.

SAVILLE, M. H.
1907– *The Antiquities of Manabí, Ecuador.* ("Contributions to South
10 American Archaeology," Vols. 1 and 2.) New York: Museum of the American Indian, Heye Foundation.

SAYLES, E. B., and ANTEVS, ERNST
1941 *The Cochise Culture.* ("Medallion Papers," No. 29.) Globe, Ariz.: Gila Pueblo.

SCHAEDEL, RICHARD P.
1951 "Major Ceremonial and Population Centers in Northern Peru," in *The Civilizations of Ancient America*, pp. 232–43. (*Selected Papers of the XXIXth International Congress of Americanists*, ed. SOL TAX, Vol. 1.) Chicago: University of Chicago Press.

SCHENCK, W. EGBERT
1926 *The Emeryville Shellmound: Final Report.* ("University of California Publications in American Archaeology and Ethnology," Vol. 23.) Berkeley.

SCHENCK, W. EGBERT, and DAWSON, ELMER J.
1929 *Archaeology of the Northern San Joaquin Valley.* ("University of California Publications in American Archaeology and Ethnology," Vol. 25, No. 4.) Berkeley.

SCHULTZ, C. BERTRAND, and FRANKFORTER, W. D.
1948 "Preliminary Report on the Lime Creek Sites: New Evidence of Early Man in Southwestern Nebraska," *Bulletin of the University of Nebraska State Museum*, **3**, No. 4. Part 2, 43–62.

SEARS, WILLIAM H.

1948 "What Is the Archaic?" *American Antiquity*, 14, 122–24.

1951a *Excavations at Kolomoki: Season I, 1948.* ("University of Georgia Series in Anthropology," No. 2.) Athens.

1951b *Excavations at Kolomoki: Season II, 1950.* ("University of Georgia Series in Anthropology," No. 3.) Athens.

1952 "Ceramic Development in the South Appalachian Province," *American Antiquity*, 18, 101–10.

1953 *Excavations at Kolomoki: Seasons III and IV, Mound D.* ("University of Georgia Series in Anthropology," No. 4.) Athens.

1954 "A Late Archaic Horizon on the Atlantic Coastal Plain," *Southern Indian Studies* (Chapel Hill, N.C.), 6, 28–35.

1956 *Excavations at Kolomoki: Final Report.* ("University of Georgia Series in Anthropology," No. 5.) Athens.

SELLARDS, E. H.

1941 "Stone Images from Henderson County, Texas," *American Antiquity*, 7, 29–38.

1952 *Early Man in America.* Austin, Tex.: University of Texas Press.

1955 "Fossil Bison and Associated Artifacts from Milnesand, New Mexico," *American Antiquity*, 20, 336–44.

SELLARDS, E. H., EVANS, GLEN L., and MEADE, GRAYSON E.

1947 "Fossil Bison and Associated Artifacts from Plainview, Texas" (with description of artifacts by ALEX D. KRIEGER), *Bulletin of the Geological Society of America*, 58, 927–54.

SERRANO, A.

1940a "Los Sambaquís," in *Los Sambaquís y otros ensayos de arqueología brasileña*, pp. 5–63. (Annais do III Congresso Sul-Riograndense de Historia e Geografía.) Porto Alegre, Brazil.

1940b "La cultura lítica del sur brasileño," *ibid.*, pp. 65–101.

1946 "The Sambaquís of the Brazilian Coast" in *Handbook of South American Indians*, ed. JULIAN H. STEWARD, 1, 401–7. (Smithsonian Institution, Bureau of American Ethnology Bulletin No. 143.) Washington, D.C.

SHETRONE, HENRY C.

1926 "Explorations of the Hopewell Group of Prehistoric Earthworks," *Ohio Archaeological and Historical Quarterly*, 35, 1–227.

1931 *The Mound-Builders.* New York: Appleton & Co.

SHETRONE, HENRY C., and GREENMAN, EMERSON F.

1931 "Explorations of the Seip Group of Prehistoric Earthworks," *Ohio Archaeological and Historical Quarterly*, 40, 343–509.

SHIPPEE, J. M.
1948 "Nebo Hill: A Lithic Complex in Western Missouri," *American Antiquity*, **14**, 29–32.
SHOOK, EDWIN M.
1951 "The Present Status of Research on the Pre-Classic Horizons in Guatemala," in *The Civilizations of Ancient America*, pp. 93–100. (*Selected Papers of the XXIXth International Congress of Americanists*, ed. SOL TAX, Vol. 1.) Chicago: University of Chicago Press.
SHOOK, EDWIN M., and KIDDER, A. V.
1952 *Mound E-III-3, Kaminaljuyu, Guatemala*. (Carnegie Institution of Washington Publication 596.) Washington, D.C.
SHOOK, EDWIN M., and PROSKOURIAKOFF, T.
1956 "Settlement Patterns in Meso-America and the Sequence in the Guatemalan Highlands," in *Prehistoric Settlement Patterns in the New World*, ed. G. R. WILLEY, pp. 93–100. ("Viking Fund Publications in Anthropology," No. 23.) New York.
SKINNER, ALANSON B.
1919 *Exploration of Aboriginal Sites at Throgs Neck and Clasons Point, New York City*. ("Contributions from the Museum of the American Indian, Heye Foundation," Vol. 5, No. 4.) New York.
1920 *Archaeological Investigations on Manhattan Island, New York City*. ("Indian Notes and Monographs," Vol. 2, No. 6.) New York: Museum of the American Indian, Heye Foundation.
SMITH, A. L.
1950 *Uaxactún, Guatemala: Excavations of 1931–1937*. (Carnegie Institution of Washington Publication 588.) Washington, D.C.
SMITH, BENJAMIN L.
1948 "An Analysis of the Maine Cemetery Complex," *Bulletin of the Massachusetts Archaeological Society* (Attleboro), **9**, Nos. 2–3, 21–70.
SMITH, CARLYLE S.
1949 "Archaeological Investigations in Ellsworth and Rice Counties, Kansas," *American Antiquity*, **14**, 292–300.
SMITH, ELMER R.
1941 "Archaeology of Deadman Cave," *Bulletin of the University of Utah*, Vol. 32, No. 4.
1952 *The Archaeology of Deadman Cave, Utah: A Revision*. ("University of Utah Anthropological Papers," No. 10.) Salt Lake City.
SMITH, HALE G.
1951 *The Crable Site, Fulton County, Illinois*. ("Museum of Anthropology, University of Michigan, Anthropological Papers," No. 7.) Ann Arbor.

SMITH, M. A.
1955 "The Limitations of Inference in Archaeology," *Archaeological News Letter* (London), 6, No. 1, 1–5.
SMITH, MARIAN W.
1956 "The Cultural Development of the Northwest Coast," *Southwestern Journal of Anthropology*, 12, 272–94.
SMITH, ROBERT E.
1955 *Ceramic Sequence at Uaxactún, Guatemala.* 2 vols. (Middle American Research Institute Publication No. 20.) New Orleans: Tulane University.
SODAY, FRANK J.
1954 "The Quad Site, a Paleo-Indian Village in Northern Alabama," *Tennessee Archaeologist*, 10, No. 1, 1–20.
SOLECKI, RALPH S.
1951 "Archaeology and Ecology of the Arctic Slope of Alaska," in *Smithsonian Institution, Annual Report for 1950*, pp. 469–95. Washington, D.C.
SORENSON, JOHN L.
1955 *A Chronological Ordering of the Middle American Pre-Classic.* ("Middle American Research Records," Vol. 2, No. 3.) New Orleans: Tulane University.
SPAULDING, ALBERT C.
1946 "Northeastern Archaeology and General Trends in the Northern Forest Zone," in *Man in Northeastern North America*, ed. FREDERICK JOHNSON, pp. 143–67. ("Papers of the Robert S. Peabody Foundation for Archaeology," Vol. 3.) Andover, Mass.: Phillips Academy.
1952 "The Origin of the Adena Culture of the Ohio Valley," *Southwestern Journal of Anthropology*, 8, 260–68.
1953a "Statistical Techniques for the Discovery of Artifact Types," *American Antiquity*, 18, 305–13.
1953b "Review of 'Measurements of Some Prehistoric Design Developments in the Southeastern States,' by James A. Ford," *American Anthropologist*, 55, 588–91.
1954a "Reply to 'Spaulding's Review of Ford: I,' by James A. Ford," *ibid.*, 56, 112–14.
1954b "Reply to Ford," *American Antiquity*, 19, 391–93.
1955 "Prehistoric Cultural Development in the Eastern United States," in *New Interpretations of Aboriginal American Culture History*, pp. 12–27. (75th Anniversary Volume, Anthropological Society of Washington.) Washington, D.C.

SPINDEN, H. J.
1913 *A Study of Maya Art, Its Subject Matter and Historical Develop-ment.* ("Memoirs of the Peabody Museum," Vol. 6.) Cambridge, Mass.
1928 *Ancient Civilizations of Mexico and Central America.* ("American Museum of Natural History, Handbook Series," No. 3.) New York.
1931 "Indian Symbolism," in *Introduction to American Indian Art*, Part 2. New York: The Exposition of Indian Tribal Arts, Inc.

SQUIER, E. G., and DAVIS, E. H.
1848 *Ancient Monuments of the Mississippi Valley.* ("Smithsonian Con-tributions to Knowledge," Vol. 1.) Washington, D.C.

STERNS, FRED H.
1915 "A Stratification of Cultures in Eastern Nebraska," *American Anthropologist*, **17**, 121–27.

STEWARD, JULIAN H.
1937 *Ancient Caves of the Great Salt Lake Region.* (Smithsonian Institu-tion, Bureau of American Ethnology Bulletin No. 116.) Wash-ington, D.C.
1940 "Native Cultures of the Intermontane (Great Basin) Area," in *Essays in Historical Anthropology of North America*, pp. 445–502. ("Smithsonian Miscellaneous Collections," Vol. 100.) Wash-ington, D.C.
1948 "A Functional-Developmental Classification of American High Cultures," in *A Reappraisal of Peruvian Archaeology*, ed. WEN-DELL C. BENNETT, pp. 103–4. (Society for American Archaeol-ogy Memoir No. 4.)   Menasha, Wis.
1949a "Cultural Causality and Law: A Trial of the Development of Early Civilizations," *American Anthropologist*, **51**, 1–25.
1949b "South American Cultures: An Interpretative Summary," in his *Handbook of South American Indians*, **5**, 669–772. (Smithsonian Institution, Bureau of American Ethnology Bulletin No. 143.) Washington, D.C.
1953 "Evolution and Process," in *Anthropology Today*, ed. A. L. KROEBER, pp. 313–26. Chicago: University of Chicago Press.

STEWARD, JULIAN H., *et al.*
1955 *Irrigation Civilizations: A Comparative Study. A Symposium on Method and Result in Cross-cultural Regularities.* ("Social Sci-ence Monographs," No. 1.) Washington, D.C.: Pan American Union.

STIRLING, MATTHEW W.
1949   "Exploring the Past in Panama," *National Geographic Magazine*, **95**, No. 3, 373–99.

STRONG, WILLIAM D.
1930   "A Stone Culture from Northern Labrador and Its Relation to Eskimo-like Cultures of the Northeast," *American Anthropologist*, **32**, 126–44.
1935   *An Introduction to Nebraska Archaeology*. ("Smithsonian Miscellaneous Collections," Vol. 93, No. 10.) Washington, D.C.
1948*a*   "Cultural Epochs and Refuse Stratigraphy in Peruvian Archaeology," in *A Reappraisal of Peruvian Archaeology*, ed. WENDELL C. BENNETT, pp. 93–102. (Society for American Archaeology Memoir No. 4.) Menasha, Wis.
1948*b*   "The Archaeology of Costa Rica and Nicaragua," in *Handbook of South American Indians*, ed. JULIAN H. STEWARD, **4**, 121–42. (Smithsonian Institution, Bureau of American Ethnology Bulletin No. 143.) Washington, D.C.
1954   "Recent Archaeological Discoveries in South Coastal Peru," *Transactions of the New York Academy of Sciences*, Ser. 2, **16**, No. 4, 215–18.

STRONG, W. D., and EVANS, CLIFFORD, JR.
1952   *Cultural Stratigraphy in the Virú Valley, Northern Peru*. ("Columbia Studies in Archaeology and Ethnology," Vol. 4.) New York: Columbia University Press.

STRONG, W. D., KIDDER, ALFRED, II, and PAUL, A. J. DREXEL, JR.
1938   *Preliminary Report on the Smithsonian Institution–Harvard University Archaeological Expedition to Northwestern Honduras*. ("Smithsonian Miscellaneous Collections," Vol. 97, No. 1.) Washington, D.C.

STUMER, L. M.
1954   "Population Centers of the Rimac Valley, Peru," *American Antiquity*, **20**, 130–48.

SUHM, DEE ANN
1955   "Excavations at the Collins Site, Travis County, Texas," *Texas Archaeological Society Bulletin*, **26**, 7–54.

SUHM, DEE ANN, and KRIEGER, ALEX D.
1954   "An Introductory Handbook of Texas Archaeology," *ibid.*, Vol. 25.

SULLIVAN, L. R., and HELLMAN, MILO
1925   *The Punín Calvarium*. ("American Museum of Natural History, Anthropological Papers," Vol. 23.) New York.

SWANGER, J. L., and MAYER-OAKES, W. J.
1952 "A Fluted Point from Costa Rica," *American Antiquity*, 17, 264–
65.

SWANTON, JOHN R.
1924 "Southern Contacts of the Indians North of the Gulf of Mexico," *Annaes, XX Congreso Internacional de Americanistas* (Rio de
Janeiro), pp. 53–59.

TAX, SOL (ed.)
1951– *Proceedings and Selected Papers of the XXIXth International Congress*
52 *of Americanists*. 3 vols. Vol. 1: *The Civilizations of Ancient America*; Vol. 2: *Acculturation in the Americas*; Vol. 3: *Indian Tribes of
Aboriginal America*. Chicago: University of Chicago Press.

TAX, SOL, et al. (eds.)
1953 *An Appraisal of Anthropology Today*. Supplement to *Anthropology
Today*, ed. A. L. KROEBER. Chicago: University of Chicago
Press.

TAYLOR, WALTER W.
1948 *A Study of Archaeology*. (American Anthropological Association
Memoir No. 69.) Menasha, Wis.

TELLO, J. C.
1943 "Discovery of the Chavín Culture in Peru," *American Antiquity*,
9, 135–60.

TERRA, HELMUT DE
1949 "Early Man in Mexico," in *Tepexpan Man*. ("Viking Fund Publications in Anthropology," No. 11.) New York.

THOMPSON, J. ERIC S.
1939 *Excavations at San Jose, British Honduras*. (Carnegie Institution of
Washington Publication 506.) Washington, D.C.
1940 *Late Ceramic Horizons at Benque Viejo, British Honduras*. (Carnegie
Institution of Washington Publication 528.) Washington, D.C.
1943 "A Trial Survey of the Southern Maya Area," *American Antiquity*, 9, 106–34.
1945 "A Survey of the Northern Maya Area," *ibid.*, 11, 2–24.
1954 *The Rise and Fall of Maya Civilization*. Norman, Okla.: University of Oklahoma Press.

TITTERINGTON, PAUL F.
1938 *The Cahokia Mound Group and Its Village Site Materials*. St. Louis:
Privately printed.

TOZZER, A. M.
n.d. "The Sacred Cenote of Chichen Itza and Its Toltec Relationships" (MS in press). Peabody Museum, Harvard University.

Treganza, Adan E.

1952 *Archaeological Investigations in the Farmington Reservoir Area, Stanislaus County, California.* ("Reports of the University of California Archaeological Survey," No. 14.) Berkeley.

Treganza, Adan E., and Malamud, C. G.

1950 *The Topanga Culture, First Season's Excavations of the Tank Site, 1947.* ("University of California Anthropological Records," Vol. 12, No. 4.) Berkeley: University of California Press.

Tschopik, Harry, Jr.

1946 "Some Notes on Rock Shelter Sites near Huancayo, Peru," *American Antiquity*, **12**, 73–80.

Uhle, Max

1913 "Die Ruinen von Moche," *Journal de la Société des Américanistes de Paris*, **10**, 95–117.

1924a *Explorations at Chincha.* ("University of California Publications in American Archaeology and Ethnology," Vol. 21, No. 2.) Berkeley.

1924b "Ancient Civilizations of Ica Valley," Appendix C (pp. 128–33) to *The Uhle Pottery Collections from Ica*, by A. L. Kroeber and W. D. Strong. ("University of California Publications in American Archaeology and Ethnology," Vol. 21, No. 3.) Berkeley.

1930 "Späte Mastodonten in Ecuador," *Proceedings of the 23d International Congress of Americanists*, pp. 247–58. New York.

Vaillant, George C.

1930 *Excavations at Zacatenco.* ("American Museum of Natural History, Anthropological Papers," Vol. 32, Part 1.) New York.

1932 *Some Resemblances in the Ceramics of Central and North America.* ("Medallion Papers," No. 12.) Globe, Ariz.: Gila Pueblo.

1935 *Excavations at El Arbolillo.* ("American Museum of Natural History, Anthropological Papers," Vol. 35, Part 2.) New York.

1941 *Aztecs of Mexico.* New York: Doubleday, Doran & Co.

Vignati, M. A.

1927 "Arqueología y antropología de los conchales fueginos," *Revista del Museo de La Plata* (Buenos Aires), **30**, 79–143.

Walker, Edwin F.

1951 *Five Prehistoric Archaeological Sites in Los Angeles County, California.* ("Publications of the Frederick Webb Hodge Anniversary Publication Fund," Vol. 6.) Los Angeles: Southwest Museum.

WALKER, WINSLOW M.

1936 *The Troyville Mounds, Catahoula Parish, Louisiana.* (Smithsonian Institution, Bureau of American Ethnology Bulletin No. 113.) Washington, D.C.

WALLACE, WILLIAM J.

1954 "The Little Sycamore Site and the Early Milling Stone Cultures of Southern California," *American Antiquity*, **20**, 112–23.

WALTER, H. V.

1948 *The Pre-history of the Lagoa Santa Region (Minas Gerais).* Belo Horizonte, Brazil.

WARING, A. J., JR., and HOLDER, PRESTON

1945 "A Prehistoric Ceremonial Complex in the Southeastern United States," *American Anthropologist*, **47**, 1–34.

WAUCHOPE, ROBERT

1950 *A Tentative Sequence of Pre-Classic Ceramics in Middle America.* ("Middle American Research Records," Vol. 1, No. 14.) New Orleans: Tulane University.

WEBB, CLARENCE H.

1944 "Stone Vessels from a Northeast Louisiana Site," *American Antiquity*, **9**, 386–94.

1948a "Caddoan Prehistory: The Bossier Focus," *Texas Archaeological and Paleontological Society Bulletin*, **19**, 100–147.

1948b "Evidence of Pre-pottery Cultures in Louisiana," *American Antiquity*, **13**, 227–32.

WEBB, WILLIAM S.

1938 *An Archaeological Survey of the Norris Basin in Eastern Tennessee.* (Smithsonian Institution, Bureau of American Ethnology Bulletin 118.) Washington, D.C.

1939 *An Archaeological Survey of Wheeler Basin on the Tennessee River in Northern Alabama.* (Smithsonian Institution, Bureau of American Ethnology Bulletin No. 122.) Washington, D.C.

1946 *Indian Knoll, Site Oh 2, Ohio County, Kentucky.* ("University of Kentucky Reports in Anthropology and Archaeology," Vol. 4, No. 3, Part 1.) Lexington, Ky.

1950a *The Carlson Annis Mound, Site 5, Butler County, Kentucky.* ("University of Kentucky Reports in Anthropology," Vol. 7, No. 4.) Lexington, Ky.

1950b *The Read Shell Midden, Site 10, Butler County, Kentucky.* ("University of Kentucky Reports in Anthropology," Vol. 7, No. 5.) Lexington, Ky.

1951a The Parrish Village Site. ("University of Kentucky Reports in Anthropology," Vol. 7, No. 6.) Lexington, Ky.

1951b "Radiocarbon Dating on Samples from the Southeast," in Radiocarbon Dating, ed. FREDERICK JOHNSON. (Society for American Archaeology Memoir No. 8.) American Antiquity, 17, No. 1, Part 2, 30.

WEBB, WILLIAM S., and DEJARNETTE, DAVID L.

1942 An Archaeological Survey of Pickwick Basin in the Adjacent Portions of the States of Alabama, Mississippi and Tennessee. (Smithsonian Institution, Bureau of American Ethnology Bulletin No. 129.) Washington, D.C.

1948a The Flint River Site, Ma°48. (Alabama Museum of Natural History, Museum Paper 23.) University, Ala.

1948b The Whitesburg Bridge Site, Ma°10. (Alabama Museum of Natural History, Museum Paper 24.) University, Ala.

1948c The Perry Site, Lu°25. (Alabama Museum of Natural History, Museum Paper 25.) University, Ala.

1948d Little Bear Creek Site, Ct°8, Colbert County, Alabama. (Alabama Museum of Natural History, Museum Paper 26.) University, Ala.

WEBB, WILLIAM S., and HAAG, WILLIAM G.

1939 The Chiggerville Site, Site 1, Ohio County, Kentucky. ("University of Kentucky Reports in Anthropology and Archaeology," Vol. 4, No. 1.) Lexington, Ky.

1940 Cypress Creek Villages, Sites 11 and 12, McLean County, Kentucky. ("University of Kentucky Reports in Anthropology and Archaeology," Vol. 4, No. 2.) Lexington, Ky.

1947 Archaic Sites in McLean County, Kentucky. ("University of Kentucky Reports in Anthropology," Vol. 7, No. 1.) Lexington, Ky.

WEBB, WILLIAM S., and SNOW, CHARLES E.

1945 The Adena People. ("University of Kentucky Reports in Anthropology and Archaeology," Vol. 6.) Lexington, Ky.

WEBB, WILLIAM S., and WILDER, CHARLES G.

1951 An Archaeological Survey of Guntersville Basin on the Tennessee River in Northern Alabama. Lexington, Ky.: University of Kentucky Press.

WEDEL, WALDO R.

1941 Archaeological Investigations at Buena Vista Lake, Kern County, California. (Smithsonian Institution, Bureau of American Ethnology Bulletin No. 130.) Washington, D.C.

WEDEL, WALDO R.—*Continued*

1947 "Culture Chronology in the Central Great Plains," *American Antiquity*, **12**, 148–56.

1953 "Some Aspects of Human Ecology in the Central Plains," *American Anthropologist*, **55**, 499–514.

WENDORF, FRED, and THOMAS, TULLY H.

1951 "Early Man Sites near Concho, Arizona," *American Antiquity*, **17**, 107–13.

WHEAT, JOE BEN

1954 "Southwestern Cultural Interrelationships and the Question of Area Co-tradition," *American Anthropologist*, **56**, 576–86.

1955 *Mogollon Culture Prior to A.D. 1000.* (Society for American Archaeology Memoir No. 10.) *American Antiquity*, Vol. 20, No. 4, Part 2.

WILLEY, GORDON R.

1945a "Horizon Styles and Pottery Traditions in Peruvian Archaeology," *American Antiquity*, **11**, 49–56.

1945b "The Weeden Island Culture: A Preliminary Definition," *ibid.*, **10**, 225–54.

1948a "Functional Analysis of 'Horizon Styles' in Peruvian Archaeology," in *A Reappraisal of Peruvian Archaeology*, ed. WENDELL C. BENNETT, pp. 8–15. (Society for American Archaeology Memoir No. 4.)

1948b "The Cultural Context of the Crystal River Negative-painted Style," *American Antiquity*, **13**, No. 4, Part 1, 325–28.

1949 *Archaeology of the Florida Gulf Coast.* ("Smithsonian Miscellaneous Collections," Vol. 113.) Washington, D.C.

1951a "South American–Archaic Relations: Additional Comment," *American Antiquity*, **16**, 354–55.

1951b "The Chavín Problem: A Review and Critique," *Southwestern Journal of Anthropology*, **7**, No. 2, 103–44.

1953a "Archaeological Theories and Interpretation: New World," in *Anthropology Today*, ed. A. L. KROEBER, pp. 361–85. Chicago: University of Chicago Press.

1953b "A Pattern of Diffusion-Acculturation," *Southwestern Journal of Anthropology*, **9**, 369–84.

1953c *Prehistoric Settlement Patterns in the Virú Valley, Peru.* (Smithsonian Institution, Bureau of American Ethnology Bulletin No. 155.) Washington, D.C.

1954 "Comments on Joe Ben Wheat's 'Southwestern Cultural Inter-relationships and the Question of Area Co-tradition,'" *American Anthropologist*, **56**, 589–91.

1955a "The Interrelated Rise of the Native Cultures of Middle and South America," in *New Interpretations of Aboriginal American Culture History*, pp. 28–45. (75th Anniversary Volume, Anthropological Society of Washington.) Washington, D.C.

1955b "The Prehistoric Civilizations of Nuclear America," *American Anthropologist*, **57**, No. 3, Part 1, 571–93.

1956a "The Structure of Ancient Maya Society: Evidence from the Southern Lowlands," *ibid.*, **58**, No. 5, 777–82.

1956b "Problems concerning Prehistoric Settlement Patterns in the Maya Lowlands," in *Prehistoric Settlement Patterns in the New World*, ed. G. R. WILLEY, pp. 107–14. ("Viking Fund Publications in Anthropology," No. 23.) New York.

WILLEY, GORDON R., BULLARD, W. R., JR., and GLASS, J. B.

1955 "The Maya Community of Prehistoric Times," *Archaeology*, **8**, 18–25.

WILLEY, GORDON R., and CORBETT, J. M.

1954 *Early Ancón and Early Supe Culture: Chavín Horizon Sites of the Central Peruvian Coast.* ("Columbia Studies in Archaeology and Ethnology," Vol. 3.) New York: Columbia University Press.

WILLEY, GORDON R., and McGIMSEY, C. R.

1954 *The Monagrillo Culture of Panama.* ("Papers of the Peabody Museum," Vol. 49, No. 2.) Cambridge, Mass.

WILLEY, GORDON R., and PHILLIPS, PHILIP

1944 "Negative-painted Pottery from Crystal River, Florida," *American Antiquity*, **10**, 173–85.

1955 "Method and Theory in American Archaeology. II: Historical-developmental Interpretation," *American Anthropologist*, **57**, 723–819.

WILLEY, GORDON R., and STODDARD, THEODORE

1954 "Cultural Stratigraphy in Panama: A Preliminary Report on the Girón Site," *American Antiquity*, **19**, 332–42.

WILLEY, GORDON R., and WOODBURY, R. B.

1942 "A Chronological Outline for the Northwest Florida Coast," *ibid.*, **7**, 232–54.

WILLIAMS, STEPHEN

1954 "An Archaeological Study of the Mississippian Culture in Southeast Missouri." Unpublished Ph.D. dissertation, Yale University. Pp. 327.

WILLOUGHBY, CHARLES C.

1898   *Prehistoric Burial Places in Maine.* ("Papers of the Peabody Museum," Vol. 1, No. 6.) Cambridge, Mass.

1922   *The Turner Group of Earthworks, Hamilton County, Ohio.* ("Papers of the Peabody Museum," Vol. 8, No. 3.) Cambridge, Mass.

1935   *Antiquities of the New England Indians: With Notes on the Ancient Cultures of Adjacent Territory.* Cambridge, Mass.: Peabody Museum of American Archaeology and Ethnology, Harvard University.

WITTHOFT, JOHN

1952   "A Paleo-Indian Site in Eastern Pennsylvania," *Proceedings of the American Philosophical Society,* **96,** No. 4, 464–95.

WITTRY, WARREN L.

1951   "A Preliminary Study of the Old Copper Complex," *Wisconsin Archaeologist,* **32,** No. 1, 1–18.

WITTRY, WARREN L., and RITZENTHALER, ROBERT E.

1956   "The Old Copper Complex: An Archaic Manifestation in Wisconsin," *American Antiquity,* **21,** 244–54.

WOODLAND CONFERENCE

1943   "The First Archaeological Conference on the Woodland Pattern," *American Antiquity,* **8,** 393–400.

WOODWARD, A.

1931   *The Grewe Site.* ("Los Angeles Museum of History, Science and Art, Occasional Papers," No. 1.) Los Angeles.

WORMINGTON, HANNAH M.

1949   *Ancient Man in North America.* ("Denver Museum of Natural History, Popular Series," No. 4.) Denver, Colo.

WRAY, DONALD E.

1952   "Archeology of the Illinois Valley: 1950," in *Archeology of Eastern United States,* ed. JAMES B. GRIFFIN, pp. 152–64. Chicago: University of Chicago Press.

WYMAN, JEFFRIES

1868   "An Account of the Fresh-Water Shell-Heaps of the St. Johns River, East Florida," *American Naturalist,* **2,** 393–403, 449–63.

1875   *Fresh-Water Shell Mounds of the St. Johns River.* (Peabody Academy of Science, Memoir No. 4.) Salem, Mass.

Index

Index

Fowke, Gerard, 160
Fowler, Melvin L., 113
Frankforter, W. D., 87, 122
Fraser River region, 137
Friesenhahn Cave (Tex.), 83
Fulton aspect, 168

Gallinazo period, 177, 182, 189, 191, 195
García Payón, J., 185
Gayton, A. H., 176, 189
Genetic correlation, 30–31, 33, 38, 40, 45
Georgia, 46, 115, 119, 161, 167
Gibson aspect, 168
Giddings, J. L., Jr., 98
Gifford, E. W., 134
Gila-Salt region, 18
Gilmore, Melvin R., 124
Gjessing, G., 117
Glacial Kame culture, 119
Glades Region, 19, 115, 161, 162
Gladwin, Harold S., 19, 154, 155
Glass, J. B., 189
Goggin, John M., 19, 36–37, 115, 162, 166
González, Alberto R., 102
Graham Cave site, 113, 114
Grant Mound site (Fla.), 162
Grave Creek Mound (W.Va.), 157
Great Lakes region, 162
Great Serpent Mound (Ohio), 157
Green River phase, 116
Greengo, Robert C., 160
Greenland, 138
Greenman, Emerson F., 157, 158, 159, 160
Griffin, James B., 13, 46, 65, 104–5, 118–20, 155–56, 157, 159, 164, 165, 166, 167
Gross, H., 103
Grove focus, 124
Guadalupe phase, 179
Guañape phase (Peru), 176
Guangala phases, 175
Guaraní tradition, 142, 181
Guatemala, 25–26, 29, 43, 184, 197
Guernsey, E. Y., 116
Guernsey, S. J., 131

Gypsum Cave (Nev.), 94–95, 126, 132
Gypsum types, 109, 126

Haag, William G., 96, 104, 115, 134, 156
Haiti, 143
Harding, M., 96, 133
Harp, Elmer, 138
Harrington, M. R., 83, 95, 97, 124, 129, 131, 132, 133
Haury, Emil W., 38, 86, 89, 92, 95, 129, 152, 154, 174
Hawkes, Christopher, 137
Hawkes, E. W., 162
Haynes, C. V., 92
Heizer, Robert F., 95, 96, 131, 134
Hellman, Milo, 103
Hibben, Frank C., 84, 91, 92, 99
Hidden Valley Shelter site, 113
Hill, A. T., 122, 167
Hill, Malcolm W., 92
Historical-developmental interpretation, 67; defined, 71–72, 77
Hiwassee Island phase, 165
Hoffman, Bernard G., 139
Hohokam subarea, 19, 128, 129, 151, 154–55
Holder, Preston, 104, 121, 166
Hopewell cultures, 157, 158–63, 169
Hopewellian cultures, 120, 138, 159–60
Horizon, 29–34, 37–38, 42–43; diagram, 41; in multiple-area synthesis, 62; social aspects of, 51; and tradition, 39–40
Horizon-style concept, 31–33, 166
Horner site (Wyo.), 87
House construction, 133, 139. See also Adobe houses; Pit-houses
Howard, Edgar B., 86
Howard, G. D., 142, 181
Huaca Prieta culture, 70, 140
Huanaco mounds, 195
Huasteca phase, 148, 150
Hughes, Jack T., 88
Hunters-gatherers, 68, 69, 70, 72; in Lithic stage, 80–81; in Archaic

Index

Barreales phase, 179
Barrett, Samuel A., 162
Bartlett, K., 84
Basic archaeological units, 21–28
Basket Maker culture, 124, 129, 130–31, 152–53
Basketry, 130
Bat Cave (N.M.), 128, 130, 152, 155
Baum phase, 167
Baumer phase, 119
Beals, R. L., 164
Beardsley, Richard K., 104, 134
Becerra formations, 82–83
Belize Valley (British Honduras), 189
Belous, Russell E., 134
Bennett, John W., 162, 164
Bennett, Wendell C., 26, 35, 45, 66, 103, 173, 174, 176, 177, 178, 189, 190, 191, 195
Bennyhoff, J. A., 143
Bernal, Ignacio, 186
Berry, Brewton, 167
Bessemer site (Ala.), 165
Big Bend culture, 126, 127
Bird, J. B., 26, 45, 70, 100–101, 102, 103, 140, 141, 147, 176, 178, 190
Black, Glenn A., 165
Black Rock culture, 131
Black sand phase, 119
Black's Fork culture, 84
Bleiler, E. F., 178
Bliss, Wesley L., 121
Boas, Franz, 105
Boggs, S. H., 171
Bolas stones, 101, 141, 142
Bolivia, 102, 103
Bone artifacts, 81, 110, 139, 141
Bonnevill continuum, 131
Borax Lake site, 97, 129, 133
Borden, Charles E., 97, 136, 137
Bórmida, Marcelo, 102
Braidwood, Robert J., 55, 72
Brainerd, George W., 95, 186
Bray, Robert T., 124
Brazil, 102, 142, 143
Brew, John O., 151, 153
British Columbia, 97
British Honduras, 29, 189

Bryan, Alan L., 136
Bryan, Kirk, 91, 130
Buena Vista Lake site, 133
Bullard, W. R., Jr., 189
Burgh, Robert F., 131
Burial Mound periods, 156–58, 163, 164, 165, 169, 171
Burial types, 12, 32, 110–11, 118, 133, 156, 157, 162
Burnett, E. K., 166
Bushnell, G. H. S., 175
Byers, Douglas S., 89

Cachot, Rebecca Carrión, 176
Caddoan regions, 164, 167–68
Cahokia site (Ill.), 165
Cairo Lowland phase (Mo.), 165
Cajamarca phase, 189
Calasasaya, 190
Caldwell, Joseph R., 114, 167
California cultures, 96, 131–35, 143
Campbell, E. W. C., 95, 96, 132
Campbell, John Martin, 128
Campbell, Thomas N., 126
Campbell, William H., 96, 132
Canalino sequence, 135
Canby, Joel S., 171
Candy Creek phase, 119
Carlson, Roy L., 136
Carrión Cachot, Rebecca, 176
Carter, G. F., 84
Casa Grande, 155
Casapadrense complex, 101–2
Caso, Alfonso, 66, 149, 150, 185, 186
Catlow culture, 131
Cedros phase, 180
Ceramics. *See* Pottery
Ceremonial centers, 149, 152, 173–74, 176, 185, 186, 187–88
Cerro Jaboncillo culture, 175
Cerro Mangote complex, 140
Cerro Zapote phase, 170
Chalco complex, 140
Champe, John L., 122
Chan Chan (Peru), 195
Chapman, Carl H., 113, 123, 124, 167
Charlot, J., 197
Chavín de Huantar, 190, 195

DeJarnett, David L., 104, 115, 161, 165
Dellinger, S. C., 124
Denbigh flint complex, 98, 138
Dendrochronology, 44, 45
Deptford phase, 119, 161
Descriptive correlation, 45–46
Desert cultures, 90–94, 114, 121, 126, 127–32, 140
Deuel, Thorne, 119, 159
Developmental interpretation. See Historical-developmental interpretation
Diablo phase (Mexico), 100, 139
Dick, Herbert W., 128
Dickinson, S. D., 124
Diffusion, 5, 11, 50, 137; in Formative stage, 150–51, 176
DiPeso, Charles C., 155
Distributional correlation, 30, 32–33, 44, 45
Dolmatoff, Alicia Reichel-. See Reichel-Dolmatoff, Alicia
Dolmatoff, Gerardo Reichel-. See Reichel-Dolmatoff, Gerardo
Domesticated animals, 177
Dominican Republic, 180
Dorset culture, 139
Drucker, Philip, 137, 140, 150, 185
Duff, Wilson, 97
Dunlevy, Marion L., 169

Early Ancón phase, 176
Early Lithic stage, 73, 79
Early Milling Stone culture, 96, 133
Early Supe phase, 176
Ecuador, 172–75
Eden-Scotsbluff culture, 87–90, 97, 98, 99, 122, 138
Edwards Plateau (Tex.), 125, 126
Effigy Mound culture (Wis.), 162
Ekholm, Gordon F., 148
El Arbolillo phases, 148
El Cerrillo culture, 141
El Horno phase, 174
El Molle culture, 178
El Purgatorio (Peru), 195

Eldridge, William, 89
Ellis, Florence H., 128
Enterline culture, 89
Eskimo culture, 97–98, 117, 136–39
Esperanza phase, 186
Ethnography, 4, 38, 50
Ethnology, 4, 6
Etowah phase, 161, 164, 166, 167
Eva phase, 116
Evans, Clifford, Jr., 13, 26, 88, 102, 174, 176, 177, 181, 189

Fairbanks, Charles H., 115, 119, 161, 165, 167
Farmington (Calif.), 96
Faulkner phase, 116
Fenenga, F., 134
Fewkes, Jesse Walter, 160
Field work, 4
Figgins, J. D., 86
Figurines, 148, 149, 150
Finley site (Wyo.), 87
Fishing, 110, 111, 135, 177, 180
Florescent phase, 177
Florida, 19, 29, 119, 143, 160–62
Focus, defined, 21–22
Folsom culture, 86–90
Folsum-Yuma cultures, 86, 123
Food-gathering. See Hunters-gatherers
Forbis, Richard G., 87
Ford, James A., 13, 26, 27–28, 65, 67, 96, 115, 116, 156, 160, 164, 165
Formal units 21. See also Basic archaeological units
Formative stage, 23, 25, 52–53, 74, 75, 120, 144–81; agriculture in, 144–46; in California, 134–35; in east, 155–60; in Middle America, 170–72; in Northwest, 136; in South America, 172–81; in Southeast, 160–62; Summary, 202–4
Fort Ancient site, 158, 166–67
Fort Rock caves, 131
Fort Walton (Fla.) phase, 29, 164, 167
Fortifications, 177, 179, 193, 196
Foster, George M., 197

stage, 107, 122, 123, 127, 129, 130; in California, 134, 135
Hurt, Wesley R., Jr., 92, 132

Imlay Channel (Mich.), 84
Incas, 76, 194, 196
Indian Knoll site, 116
Indian River (Fla.), 115, 161, 162
Integrative units, 29–43. *See also* Horizon; Tradition
Ipiutak phase, 139
Ipswich (Mass.), 89
Irene phase (Ga.), 167
Iroquois Confederacy, 53
Irrigation, 154, 176, 177
Irving, William, 138
Isla de los Indios phase, 172–73
Issaquena phase, 160
Iyatayet site (Alaska), 98, 138

Jenness, Diamond, 139
Jennings, Jesse D., 22, 43, 94, 126, 127, 131, 185
Jijón y Caamaño, J., 175, 195
Johnson, Frederick, 82, 91, 99, 128
Judd, Neil M., 155

Kaminaljuyu (Guatemala), 25–26, 43, 148, 185, 186, 188, 197
Kelley, J. Charles, 91, 125, 126, 130, 140
Kelly, A. R., 161, 165
Key Marco site, 162
Keyes, Charles, 167
Kidder, A. V., 22, 23, 26, 43, 131, 148, 155, 170, 171, 185, 190
Kidder, Alfred, II, 179
Kincaid phase, 165
King, Arden, 136
Kirchhoff, Paul, 20, 128, 147
Kivas, 153
Kivett, Marvin F., 122, 168
Klamath Lake, 94
Kleine, Harold K., 89, 92
Kluckhohn, Clyde, 65
Kneberg, Madeline, 89, 115, 116, 119, 165
Kolomoki site (Ga.), 46, 160
Kozlovich, Eugene, 124

Krieger, Alex D., 67, 121, 125, 126, 164, 166, 168; on percussion stage, 82–85; quoted, 68–70
Kroeber, A. L., 3, 26, 31, 45, 66, 174, 176, 189, 190, 195; quoted, 137

La Candelaría phase, 178–79
La Jolla culture, 96, 133
La Loma phase, 174
La Perra phase, 139
La Venta phase, 185
Lagoa Santa caves, 142
Laguna, Frederica de, 137, 139
Lake Mohave sites, 95, 132–33
Lamar phase, 161, 164, 167
Lamoka phase, 104, 116–17
Lancaster, James A., 153
Larco Hoyle, Rafael, 66, 103, 176, 190
Larsen, Helge, 98, 139
Las Flores phase, 170
Lathrap, Donald W., 143, 180
Laughlin, William S., 138
Laurentian formulation, 117
Leach, J. W., 138
Leechman, Douglas, 139
Lehmer, D. J., 126
Leighton, Morris M., 165
Lemert, E. M., 96
Leonard Rock Shelter culture, 131
Lerma phase, 99, 100, 139
Lewis, T. M. N., 89, 92, 113, 116, 119, 165
Lewisville site (Tex.), 87
Lillard, Jeremiah B., 134
Lilly, Eli, 159, 165
Lime Creek sites (Tex.), 121–22
Lind Coulee site (Wash.), 97
Linné, Sigvald, 186, 188
Lithic stage, 23, 52, 73–103; in Arctic, 97–99; Desert cultures, 90–94; Folsom-Yuma culture, 86–90; in Middle and South America, 99–103; mixed Lithic and Archaic stages, 112–14, 121, 125; percussion stage, 82–85; Summary, 200–201. *See also* Clovis culture; Eden-Scottsbluff cul-

Root, W. C., 190
Round Rock focus, 125
Rouse, Irving, 30–34, 35, 44–45, 67, 103, 115, 142, 143, 162, 179, 180
Rowe, John H., 189, 194, 196
Rowley, Graham, 139
Roys, R. L., 197
Ruppert, Karl, 198
Russell Cave (Ala.), 114
Ryden, S., 178

Sacramento–San Joaquin Delta culture, 134
Safety Harbor (Fla.) phase, 29
St. Johns River (Fla.), 115, 161, 162
Saladero phase, 180
Salado culture, 18, 155
Salvador, 170
Sambaquí phases, 142
San Agustín, 173
San Dieguito–Playa culture, 95
San Francisco Bay regions, 134
San Jon (N.M.), 88, 95
San José culture, 130
San Juan Anasazi region, 124, 130
San Pedro phase, 126, 128, 129
Sanders, William T., 175, 188, 196, 197, 198
Sandia culture, 84–85, 91–92, 95
Santa Marta towns, 174
Santa Rita phase, 170
Santa Rosa Island (Calif.), 83
Santa Rosa–Swift Creek (Fla.) phase, 29, 160, 161
Santa Valley (Peru), 190
Sarigua phase, 140
Satterthwaite, Linton, 186
Savannah phase, 167
Saville, M. H., 175
Sayles, E. B., 90, 91
Schaedel, Richard P., 191, 195
Schenck, W. Egbert, 134
Scholz, Paul, 117
Schultz, C. Bertrand, 87, 122
Sears, William H., 42, 46, 117, 118–19, 160, 161
Seed-gathering, 111
Seip site (Ohio), 158

Sellards, E. H., 83, 86, 88
Sequence. *See* Local sequence; Regional sequence
Serrano, A., 102, 142
Shell artifacts, 110, 141, 142
Shetrone, Henry C., 157, 158
Shippee, J. M., 123
Shook, Edwin M., 22, 26, 43, 148, 185, 188, 198
Siberian cultures, 98
Signal Butte I and II (Neb.), 121, 123
Silver Lake site, 132–33
Sioux Indians, 167
Site, defined, 18
Skinner, Alanson B., 104
Smith, A. L., 25, 198
Smith, Benjamin L., 117
Smith, C. Earle, 128
Smith, Carlyle S., 122
Smith, Elmer R., 131
Smith, Hale G., 167
Smith, M. A., 49
Smith, Marian W., 137
Smith, Robert E., 25, 148, 170, 186, 187
Smith, Watson, 151
Snow, Charles E., 157
Social aspects of archaeological units, 48–56
Society, 49–51
Soday, Frank J., 89
Solecki, Ralph S., 99
Sommer, F. H., 178
Sorenson, John L., 45
South America, 26, 31, 34–35; Lithic stage in, 100–103; Archaic stage in, 140–43; Formative stage in, 170–81; Classic stage in, 189–92; Postclassic stage in, 194–96
Southern Cult style, 33, 55, 166, 170
Spatial divisions, 18–21
Spatial-temporal relationships, 11–17, 23–24, 29, 30; difficulty in controlling, 41–42; expressed by area chronologies, 44–47; in horizon-style concepts, 32
Spaulding, Albert C., 13, 117, 157, 158; quoted, 15–16